# RAISING TEENS
## in the
# 21ST CENTURY

# RAISING TEENS

## in the

# 21ST CENTURY

## A Practical Guide to Effective Parenting

# JAMES G. WELLBORN, PhD

PRESS

Brentwood, Tennessee

Published by: 12 Mile Bayou Press
330 Franklin Road, Suite 135A-225
Brentwood, TN. 37027-3282
615.775.7822
www.12milebayoupress.com

*Publisher's Cataloging-in-Publication*

Wellborn, James G.
    Raising teens in the 21st century : a practical guide to effective parenting / James G. Wellborn. -- Brentwood, Tenn. : 12 Mile Bayou Press, c2012.
        p. ; cm.
        ISBN: 978-0-9856614-0-3 (pbk.) ; 978-0-9856614-1-0 (ebk.)
        Includes index.
        Summary: A one-stop resource with effective parenting strategies for raising happy, healthy, productive teens in the new millennium. Chapters are concise with solutions that are easy to understand and implement. Topics include everything from cell phones to spirituality, chores to curfews, grades to dating, videogames to family vacations, summer jobs to substance abuse, punishing to praising, arguing to negotiating, communicating to motivating.--Publisher.
        1. Parent and teenager. 2. Parenting. 3. Child rearing.
        4. Adolescent psychology. 5. Teenagers--Family relationships. 6. Adolescence.
        I. Title.
HQ799.15 .W45 2012        2012909995
649/.125--dc23        1208

Printed in the United States of America on acid-free paper.

    This publication is intended to educate and provide general information regarding the subject matter contained herein. It is not intended as a substitute for, or to replace, the counsel and advice of qualified mental health professionals or other qualified health care providers. The reader should consult with and seek the advice of a qualified mental health professional or other qualified health care provider with any questions he or she may have regarding a psychological, behavioral or medical condition, or a specific situation that they have experienced or are experiencing. Never disregard professional advice or delay seeking professional advice because of something read in this book.

    While the author has taken reasonable precautions in the preparation of this book and believes the facts presented herein are accurate, neither the publisher nor the author assumes responsibility for errors or omissions contained herein. The author and publisher specifically disclaim any liability resulting from the use or application of the information contained in this book. This information is not intended to serve as emotional or therapeutic advice related to individual situations.

    All anecdotes, stories and quotes are based on composites (except quotes referring to my brother Jeff; those are all true). Any resemblance to people living or dead is purely coincidental.

    The author and publisher make no warranty or guarantee concerning information products or materials provided by organizations or on web sites listed in this book. All products mentioned in this book are trademarks of their respective companies.

Book Consultant: Ellen Reid
Cover and Book Design: Patricia Bacall
Author photos: Christopher Fryer

# TABLE OF CONTENTS

## Dating, Relationships, and Sex Issues

## Discipline and Praise Issues

## Driving Issues

## Family Management Issues

This book is dedicated to
Kim—
best friend,
voice of reason,
confidant,
gentlest critic,
playmate,
and the love of my life
&
To Chelsea and Ryan—
loving, kind, generous, funny,
hardworking and principled human beings;
our pride and joy

# PREFACE

As an adolescent and family psychotherapist, most of my time is spent with teenagers who are having troubles and with families that aren't working well. One of my jobs is to help them figure out how to get things moving in a healthy direction.

Although most parents guide their kids through the adolescent years without the help of a therapist, families can always use information on effective ways to raise their kids. When a typical problem arises, it can sometimes overshadow everything else and make parents think things have gone terribly wrong. But it often turns out that simply finding a way to resolve a troublesome issue is enough to get the family back on track. Parenting books can be a great resource in these situations.

We live in an age of information overload, which is both wonderful and overwhelming. You can find a wealth of resources about raising teens in books, on internet sites, in blogs, on videos, and even through parenting workshops. But it isn't always easy to find what you are looking for when there are so many options.

Many resources on parenting teens focus on a particular problem or don't provide enough specific information. They focus on what teens are like but can be short on practical suggestions. Parents are often unable to turn to their usual source of advice, their own parents, because the challenges faced by 21st-century teens are so different from the challenges of previous generations. Some of these changes have been so recent that even parents lack personal experience with the issues faced by their own kids. And finally, many parenting resources are focused on what to do about teens with serious problems, or they concentrate on very specific topics rather than on the everyday issues all parents face in trying to raise teenagers.

This book is a distillation of the recommendations I make to parents. The information presented here is derived from my training, suggestions from experts in the field of parenting and adolescent development, research in wide-ranging areas that are relevant to parenting, lots of time spent with families refining strategies that will work with different parenting styles (and kinds of kids), ideas from creative parents and—last and least—from raising my own kids.

The suggestions provided in this book are concise, thorough, and effective. They have been refined through years of practice by families and teens. With this book, parents can turn right to a topic and get some ideas about how to address that particular issue— problem solved. They can refer to the book again later, if something else arises, or read through other sections to prepare themselves and try to head off future (predictable) problems.

However, going from cover to cover is pretty dense reading. I don't include humorous anecdotes or long discussions about the problems with teens. I don't provide a glimpse into the lives of troubled families or difficult teenagers. Unfortunately, our reality-show culture already gives us too many opportunities to peek into the private lives of others, which are rarely helpful in figuring out how to parent your own kid.

I am interested in providing help for parents who are doing everything they can to prepare their kids to be happy, healthy, and productive adults. And, as the introduction you are about to read indicates, it seems that parents are doing a pretty damned good job.

# TEENS THESE DAYS

Epidemic! Catastrophe! Violence! Drugs! Sex! Moral Corruption! Headlines are filled with upsetting incidents, dire warnings, and frightening predictions about the condition of teens these days.

Yet it turns out that, while teens have always had issues and problems that need attention from their parents, families, and communities, modern teens are a pretty healthy and impressive bunch.

When you compare today's teens to teens in other decades, they have never looked better. Take a look.*

- O Murder, violent crime, property crime, vandalism, carrying weapons, and physical fights have all decreased.[1,4]

- O While there was a gradual increase in the mid-1990s, alcohol and drug use by teens (in the ninth through twelfth grades) began to decrease and is currently down to the early 1990 levels, the lowest levels since the peak years of substance abuse in the late '70s.[3,8]

- O Fifty-four percent of teens have never had sexual intercourse, with the top three reasons being that sex is "against religion or morals," "I don't want to get pregnant," and "I haven't found the right person yet."[3,9] The rate of teen pregnancies continues to decline (down 40 percent from 1990 to 2005).[3]

---

\* The numbers following these statements refer to the resources where these facts were reported. These and other resources and references for this book can be found on the References page of the book website: www.drjameswellborn.com.

○ College enrollment (39 percent) and high school graduation rates (84 percent) are at an all-time high, while high school drop-out rates are at an all-time low (9.3 percent).[5] The number of high school students taking advanced placement (college-level) classes continues to increase.[2] The percentage of students who achieve a perfect score on the ACT has risen every year for the past ten years.[11] More kids graduate from college now than in all previous generations,[5] and intelligence test scores have been consistently increasing over the past sixty years.

Perhaps the future isn't as dismal as many people thought.

Organizations like the Josephson Institute's Center for Youth Ethics have presented some interesting statistics on teen morality:

○ Seventy-six percent of teens believe there are absolute values of right and wrong,[5] and 97 percent think it is important to be a person of good character.[10] Eighty-nine percent of teens think it is more important to be a person of good character than to be rich, and 84 percent agree that it's not worth it to lie or cheat because it hurts your character.[10]

○ Fifty-seven percent of teens frequently volunteer to help others or perform charity work, and 78 percent say they have never mistreated someone merely because they belonged in a different group.[10]

○ The highest-rated priorities for teens are being a good parent (52 percent), having a successful marriage (30 percent ), and helping others in need (21 percent).[5]

Still not impressed?

○ When asked, teens rank their family relationships (11th) higher than friendships (75th).[7] They spend an average of about eighteen hours a week with family compared to five hours a week with friends.[7]

O While teens are less often affiliated with religion than older generations were, 77 percent of them report a religious affiliation.[5] The number of teens who say they pray is comparable to that of older generations, and they are just as likely (41 percent) to report practicing daily prayer as their parents and grandparents (when they were at that same age).[5] Eighty-four percent of teens characterize themselves as religious. They participate in their parents' religious observances and report that religion is important in their lives.[6]

O While the percentage of teens who are overweight and obese is shockingly high, around 60 percent of teens participate in school athletics[12] and 62 percent report participating in club sports.[13] Many teens participate in scouting organizations, martial arts, gymnastics, skateboarding, and paintball or airsoft sports. Fifty-two percent have participated in music, art, or dance outside of school.[13]

O More teens are wearing seat belts than ever before (from 74 percent in 1990 to 90 percent in 2009).[4] (And more are wearing bicycle helmets too.[4])

Teens are doing well because of the ongoing involvement, structure, and encouragement provided by their parents. Are there areas in need of greater attention and instruction? Of course there are. Teens are still entirely too quick to respond to challenges from others with aggression and social violence (like bullying and harassment). The use of recreational drugs throws many teens off track and veering toward an unproductive adulthood (or worse). Many teens have a casual view of sex—in a culture that doesn't provide any context to make sense of it—which puts them at risk of becoming sexual too soon and confusing sex with real emotional intimacy.

Ensuring that every kid graduates from high school well-educated and prepared for this rapidly changing, highly technologically-oriented society (whether they attend college, seek technical training, or acquire a skilled trade) is a significant challenge. Teens will continue to need shepherding through the spiritual questioning years of adolescence and young adulthood to ensure they emerge with a faith that will be their anchor in times of turmoil.

Parents are also challenged with the need to promote a healthy lifestyle for teens who face a future of work and play in an environment that requires little physical exertion and supplies access to an abundance of food—both nutritious and otherwise. And, perhaps most importantly, it is essential to raise kids to be honorable, productive *citizens*, in the ancient sense of that word.

## WHAT'S THIS BOOK ABOUT?

This book is intended to help you find ideas to do what only you can do—raise your kid. It will reassure you about some of the things you are already doing. It will provide you with a range of parenting strategies so you won't be limited by your own creativity or have to rely on doing what your parents did (or didn't do).

You will find suggestions on how to address issues you may not have dealt with as a teenager yourself, either because those things weren't your style or because they didn't exist back then. This book is also a resource if you need to address issues in a healthier way than issues were addressed in your family. It can be used to help you guide your teenager away from some of the mistakes you may have made during your own formative years.

I hope you find this book helpful.

I hope you don't forget to enjoy your kid.

# HOW TO USE THIS BOOK

This is not your usual "how to raise your kid"-type of book. It is designed to be a quick and easy source of effective strategies and techniques for dealing with normal teenage issues. When you find yourself saying "What do I do about *this*?" ten minutes with this book will give you some answers (with occasional tongue-in-cheek humor thrown in since parenting shouldn't just be all stern and serious).

To start, look through the table of contents and find a topic that strikes your interest or that has become a concern. Flip to it and start reading. In a few minutes, you will have most of what you need to address the issue or resolve the problem so you can get back to enjoying the all-too-brief time you have raising your kid.

If you are looking for more detail, there are excellent books and informative web sites devoted to the individual topics in this book. However, you won't find them in the pages of this book. Specific references and some particularly good resources relevant to the issues in each chapter are on the References page of the website for this book. You can look them over online at: http://www.drjames-wellborn.com.

You should be able to find most of the answers you need to know right here to successfully resolve the issues you face raising a teen in the 21st century.

# THE ESSENTIALS
# OF PARENTING TEENS

There are seemingly endless, specific situations that require parenting strategies, as this book will attest. But where should you start when it comes to parenting teens? Are there some essential parenting practices that cut across issues and increase the likelihood of raising healthy, happy kids? Yes!

## WHAT'S A PARENT TO DO?

**Be a role model.** One of the most powerful ways to transmit your values, your beliefs and the expectations you have for how to be an adult is to show your kids by example. Look to yourself. Everything you expect of your child should be something that you have already expected of yourself. Are you accountable for your actions? Are you the kind of person you want your kid to become? If not, get to work.

**Know your kid.** What do they like? Who are their best friends? What is their favorite band? To be important to your kid, you will need to know something about them as a person. Be prepared to get to know them over and over because they will keep changing.

**5-to-1.** Years ago, a group of researchers led by John Gottman discovered they could predict successful marriages by looking at several key indicators. One of these was the ratio of positive to negative interactions. If there were five or more positive interactions for every negative one, the couple was significantly more likely to remain married. This is a good ratio to keep in mind for maintaining a healthy relationship with your kid. If you are about to criticize, yell, punish, correct or otherwise discipline your kid, you should be able to identify five positive interactions that occurred since the last time you disciplined them. A ratio of less than five to one means you need to devote more specific attention to complimenting, speaking lovingly and kindly, encouraging, hugging, helping, admiring and rewarding your kid.

**Spend time talking to them.** The more words kids hear, the more successful they become in adulthood. Talk to them. Ask their opinion. Argue with them (about ideas, not about whether they have to stop texting and go to bed). Discuss current events.

**Catch them being good.** Notice when they do the right thing. Even more importantly, focus on the specific aspect of their behavior or their responses that reflects how you want them to be instead of zeroing in on their weaknesses or how they don't measure up. Think about what you would want your kids to tell themselves. Say that. This is about creating a self-fulfilling prophecy about being the right kind of person.

**Do things together.** Your kids are influenced by the values and actions of the people they spend time with. Make sure one of those people is you. Have weekly family activities. Vacation together. Go for walks. Stargaze. Play board games. Watch movies. Together. In the same room.

**Use positive discipline.** While punitive discipline can be fun (because who doesn't like to ground their kids or take things away to make them suffer?), discipline that is designed to build skills, correct behavior, and focus on what they did right is more useful in the long run. Consider punishing them by increasing supervision (which most teens find annoying) and give direct instructions about appropriate behavior. Then guide them through the steps so that they have to "do it right this time." Be specific about what they have done right, performed well, or pursued passionately. Encourage, admire, validate. Lots of "that's right" and "exactly" and "now you've got it."

**Be hopeful.** Kids don't have the perspective to see past hurdles and catastrophes. They will need someone to carry the promise that things can turn out well and difficulties can be overcome. This doesn't mean being unrealistic; just be optimistic. Hold out the promise of a desirable future. Anticipate their success and happiness in life. Help them recognize the wonders that surround them, for hope resides therein.

**Say yes.** Kids need to pursue their own interests. They need practice taking chances and risking failure. Look for opportunities to say "yes" to some of your kid's hare-brained ideas. Encourage them to try something that could be an awesome success or a spectacular failure. Following your dreams begins with "yes."

**Say no.** Set limits. Guide and instruct. Most parents don't need a lot of practice with this, but a surprising number can't seem to say it or stick with it. The list of things kids learn from being told "no" is long and is related to most positive, desirable life outcomes.

**Have a family creed.** Your kids should be able to quote a phrase that represents one of the core values of your family. "Do unto others..." "Well begun is half done." "Let no one ever come to you without leaving better and happier" (Mother Theresa). Have them develop a personal motto as well. The search for it is invaluable. The effect of it can color their entire life. Make it visible. Paint it on the wall. Engrave it on jewelry. Refer to it often.

**Have regular family meals.** There is something about the family sharing a meal on a regular basis that leads to kids becoming well-adjusted, productive adults. Make sure your family eats together (without TV, cell phones, or other distractions) several times a week. If you have to rearrange your schedule, do it. If your kids need to miss out on time with friends, tough.

**Give them responsibilities.** Kids should have chores. One is enough, although there is nothing wrong with them having more. They should be responsible for contributing to the upkeep of the house. They need to pick up after themselves. They should help out when asked. They need to pitch in to pull their weight. This is the obligation people have to those with whom they share a space (and those with whom they share life and community).

**Be part of a faith community.** Religion matters. Religious people have morals. They care about other people. They expect you to live a life of integrity. They support you in times of need and they hold you accountable when you stray. Faith beliefs help your kids know there is something beyond this crass, commercial world that's worth setting their sights on. Attending services won't be enough; your family will need to get involved. Go every week. When terrible things happen, faith—and the community you belong to—will get you through it. Make sure the community is already part of your life.

**Volunteer.** Have your family adopt a charitable organization. Money is fine, but donating time is more important. Kids need to see that other people struggle. They need to realize that they have something to offer others in need, even if—especially if—they have also been in need. This will help them discover how satisfying it is to give to others. It is the best way to truly feel good about yourself.

**Develop (and keep) family traditions.** Creating rituals and ceremonies for your family helps structure and define important events like holidays, birthdays, losses, and accomplishments. It defines you as a family. Through expected developments, like growing up and leaving home, as well as unexpected changes like divorce or family crises, traditions will link your kids to the heart of the family. Food, religious practices, a special place to visit, and shared activities are just some of the ways to create and continue family rituals. The traditions your kids carry into adulthood will connect them across time, distance, and death to those who love them. They are a tangible legacy you will leave to your children and your children's children.

These essential parenting practices show up across the ages. They are powerful ways to influence your child's sense of connection to family and community to competently and confidently make their way in the world and will prepare them to overcome tragedy and weather life's difficulties, as well as contributing to something greater than themselves.

# ALCOHOL AND DRUG ISSUES

# ALCOHOL AND DRUGS

## Part 1:
### Talking to Teens about Alcohol and Drugs

Alcohol and drug use have turned into a rite of passage for teens. Yet there are few other activities that have the same threatening potential for throwing them completely off their developmental track.

This chapter addresses talking with your teen about:

- Risk factors for substance abuse and addiction

- General strategies for discouraging substance use

- Promoting alcohol and drug-free lifestyle choices

Similar to discussions about sex, morals, and dating, don't wait to talk to your kid about alcohol and drugs until after they face the decision whether or not to use. Your kid needs to know why using alcohol or drugs is a problem. They need to know what you expect of them when it comes to substance abuse—someone who isn't pandering to them (like advertisers and performers) or morally indifferent (also like advertisers and performers). Your kid needs someone they respect and will listen to who discourages them from using and encourages them to use their talents for more productive endeavors. Show your teen that you take this issue seriously. They need to have already thought through what they believe and what they are going to decide about alcohol or drug use before temptation presents itself.

1

## WHAT'S A PARENT TO DO?

**Risk factors.** It can be helpful to know the major risk factors of alcohol and drug abuse as you prepare to talk with your kid and establish an alcohol and drug use policy. Two of the more obvious risk factors are addiction or substance abuse by family or friends. (Substance abuse in siblings is especially influential.) A family history of substance abuse or addiction increases the possibility that your kid could have some of the heritable risk factors (i.e., high tolerance or more sensitive to the pleasure of using). Keep in mind that substance abuse is highly correlated with the amount of stress a kid is experiencing. If your kid has easy access to alcohol or drugs, if your kid is insecure or socially oriented, or if your kid is a risk taker or adrenaline junkie, they are also more at risk for substance abuse and addiction. Kids who lack clear goals or aspirations, or who are not actively involved in a faith community, are more likely to abuse alcohol or drugs.

If you checked off risk factors while reading this section, you need to pay close attention to the signs of possible alcohol or drug use in your kid. If there isn't much on this list, you have a little more breathing space. You aren't getting off the hook completely, though. Alcohol and drugs are relatively easy to find access to, more and more friends will be using as your kid grows older, and stress is a fact of life for most teenagers. Make a conscious effort to look for changes in behavior that might signal substance abuse.

**Educate yourself.** If you are going to talk to your kid about the dangers of alcohol and drug use, you need to know what you are talking about. You will find references to a couple of informative books and an excellent website located in the Reference section located on this book's website. You also need to know the signs of potential alcohol or drug use.

**Model it.** If you don't want your kids using alcohol or drugs, don't use them yourself. If you abuse alcohol or drugs, one of the best things you can do for your kid is to stop. (There are lots of resources where you can get help for this, beginning with a mental health professional as a guide.) If you use alcohol recreationally, keep it recreational. Don't be drunk around your kid, even if it is on rare occasion. When it comes to kids, you can't use drugs recreationally without promoting drug use (and yes, that includes marijuana). If you feel compelled to launch into an elaborate defense of the benefits of marijuana while reading this (regardless of the fact that you may be at least partially accurate), you have missed an important element of parenting; you don't understand the message you convey to your kid as you promote the use of an illegal substance (and it ain't about personal freedom, fighting oppression of the masses, or the struggle for human rights).

**Comment on it.** Take every opportunity to point out the negative consequences of alcohol or drug use. This ranges from foolishness to life-altering effects, such as thoughtless unprotected sex, DUI deaths, and lifelong addiction. Not to mention the suffering of everyone associated with a drunk or addict.

**Cautionary tales.** Relate the effects of substance abuse as close to home and family as possible. Talk about how it has complicated or destroyed the lives of people you both love or care about. Being able to provide your own personal experience can help, though it can be tricky sharing this without condoning it. (Refer to the Talking About Your Past chapter.)

**Praise sobriety.** Tell your kid regularly how proud you are of them for their decision not to use alcohol or drugs. Comment to relatives and friends in the presence of your kid about how nice it is that at least you don't have to worry about THAT. Talk about the depth of shame and grief you would experience should they use. Express how embarrassing it would be for your family to have a kid who was an alcoholic or drug user. Remind your child how family members admire them for deciding to not use. Have Grandma or Grandpa frequently comment on how bad drugs are and how it would probably kill them if they found out their favorite grandson or granddaughter was using. (For added effect, have Grandma clutch her chest and look like she's experiencing a sharp pain while saying it.) Talk about how much younger siblings, kids of family friends, and younger kids in the community watch what they do and say—how your child's poor choice could be the reason a young kid becomes an addict. Talk about the responsibility your kid has to give other kids a reason not to use—they aren't alone. Drive the nail of guilt, responsibility, and potential shame deep into their psyche.

**Family dinners.** Eat together as a family. Multiple times a week. At the table. No distractions but the joy of each other's company. Do it. It works. (Research proves it.)

**Goals and aspirations.** Since the absence of goals for their future is a significant risk factor for substance abuse, work on helping your kid set and work toward personal goals. If they resist, it's OK to set some for them (and being a video game master is not considered a goal for these purposes).

**Meaningful activities.** Bored teens are twice as likely to smoke, drink, and use drugs. Require them to be involved in something that matters to them (as well as to the community at large). There are lots of things for bored teens to do to stay active. Getting consistently bored teenagers to become more engaged in their lives may require more specific strategies. You can find some suggestions in the chapters on School Breaks, Apathy, and Lack of Motivation. Sometimes, kids don't remember how to PLAY (or they don't give themselves permission to play). You can find ideas for that in Play chapter. Above all else, do things as a family on a regular basis.

**Faith community.** One of the things you should be doing as a family is be actively involved in a faith community. Alcohol and drug abuse is difficult for kids to maintain when they are spending time with faithful people. Communities of faith support moral behavior, are a source of support in times of trouble, and provide a perspective on the suffering in this world. (And it may save your kid's soul for all eternity.) You will find ideas about fostering faith beliefs in teens in the Religion and Spirituality chapter.

**Public commitment.** Use social pressure to your advantage. Have your kid make a formal, verbal commitment to you about not using alcohol and drugs. Require them to list the reasons substance abuse is bad and the mistaken beliefs people have about it being "no big deal." Make them tell their grandparents, aunts, uncles, and cousins. Emphasize the importance of giving and keeping your word. Check every year or so to see whether they are still committed to their decisions about alcohol and drug use.

**Refusal skills.** Your kid will need to already know how to turn down offers to use drugs or alcohol before those offers are made. Spend time together coming up with ways to deal with being around other kids who use drugs and alcohol. Brainstorm ways that will actually work. Struggling to find the right ways to refuse an offer is actually a good thing because, as turns out, coming up with comfortable excuses isn't so easy. Come up with both personal reasons ("No, dude. I'm good." "Not my deal, man.") as well as "monster parent" reasons ("My mom is like a human (alcohol/drug) test." "If I get caught, I'll never be able to leave the house again!"). Have family refusal skills night (kind of like karaoke). Conduct ninja drug offers—suddenly, out of the blue, pretend to be someone offering them some alcohol or drugs. Be sure to address the fact that the most difficult thing about refusing is feeling left out. Problem-solve about ways they can still enjoy themselves while being sober.

**Stress management skills.** Chronically stressed kids will be looking for a way to just chill and not feel so burdened. Unfortunately, alcohol and drugs are ideally suited for this. The Stress Management section provides suggestions for helping your kid handle situational stress and for dealing with chronic stress. (See suggestions in the Stress Management chapters.)

**Limit spending money.** Keep track of your kid's spending. Knowing how they handle money is useful anyway as a way of helping them develop responsible money management skills. See the Allowance and Money chapter for ideas. While teens can be very generous to their friends in sharing alcohol or drugs, it is a good idea to make it difficult for your kid to easily afford their own stash.

**Don't talk about the statistics.** You might think that going over the statistics of alcohol or drug use would be useful. There is a complex effect of informing kids about typical teenage behavior. If they are using, statistics can help show they are out of the norm for their age. But, here's the twist. If your kid isn't using, yet a large number of kids their age *are* using, it increases the likelihood they will experiment (e.g., "I want to be a normal teen; It's not as rare as I thought; If I use now and again, I'm still not that bad."). To be safe, use stats for your own information and use other methods to influence your kid's attitudes toward alcohol and drug use. Talk instead about right and wrong and what could happen "if."

**Alcohol and drug policy.** It's most important to develop a family policy on alcohol and drug use. They need to know what will happen if they decide to stray from the path of righteousness. (See Alcohol and Drug Policy chapter.)

**Severe and swift punishment.** You want your kid to have additional reasons for not using, other than their own personal objection to alcohol or drug use. Punishment is great for that. And here's the kicker: Recent research indicates that having a "reasonable" attitude toward underage alcohol or drug use increases the likelihood of substance abuse later on. Be clear, absolute, and stern about what will happen if you discover they are using.

**Bi-annual (every two years) reviews.** So, when do you start talking about alcohol and drug use? Make the first formal effort during fifth grade. Keep it simple and general. The goal is to influence their beliefs before they actually start thinking for themselves. The next important point is seventh grade, which is right before the first significant (though small) jump in statistics for alcohol and drug use, which is eighth grade. Then, at the beginning of the summer before ninth grade (where statistics show another leap forward in the frequency of alcohol and drug use), renew the formal conversation. Ask your kid, "What are you thinking these days about using alcohol or drugs?" Alcohol and drug use rises precipitously during the summer months. Have another formal discussion at the beginning of summer before eleventh grade. Before they leave for college, there are a number of conversations you'll want to initiate. Include one about their plans regarding alcohol and drug use.

There are no guarantees to ensure that your kid will remain clean and sober. As with most aspects of parenting, the best you can do is work toward increasing the odds that they will become loving, productive and responsible adults. Most kids do, despite what is reported in the news.

# ALCOHOL AND DRUGS

## Part 2:
### Signs and Symptoms

To take action about your teen's potential alcohol or drug problem, you have to be able to recognize if there is a problem.

This chapter describes:

- Telltale signs of alcohol and drug use

- Three levels of seriousness

Remember when you were suddenly aware that something had changed in the aura of the household and you knew it was time to check on the kids? When parent intuition works, it is a beautiful thing. Unfortunately, it isn't always reliable when it comes to detecting alcohol or drug use by your kids.

## WHAT'S A PARENT TO DO?

It can help to know some of the signs and symptoms of substance use to augment your parent radar. These warning signs can be divided into three categories: worrisome, at risk, and serious.

**Worrisome signs.** Worrisome signs are those related to substance use, but they may also be aspects of normal adolescent behavior. The more signs you check off, the more you should be concerned.

Worrisome signs include:

O Questionable friends—and by "questionable," I mean kids who are low-achieving, involved with juvenile court, non-church-going (because all organized religions discourage or outright forbid substance use), and kids who have neglectful or overly permissive parents

O Keeping friends away from the family (because your kids know what you will think of their questionable friends)

O Avoiding you when they come home after being out with friends, especially at the end of the night (so you can't detect that they are under the influence)

O Being more surly than usual the day after extended time hanging out with friends (because they are coming down off the "high")

O Being overly sensitive to questions about where they have been, who they have been with, and what they were doing

O Isolating themselves from the family (unless your family is *really* annoying; then it is understandable)

O No clear aspirations or long-term goals (because using drugs or alcohol would interfere with achieving these goals)

O Being very social (because they are more susceptible to going along with the group)

When your kid is exhibiting worrisome signs, it is time to have a talk about substance use and sobriety. Don't approach them as though they are guilty, but rather let them know you want to review your expectations. It might also be worth requiring your kid to address any worrisome signs by doing the opposite of each. For example, you might require them to have some "good" friends, bring friends around to the house, spend time talking when they come home from being out, not be a jerk after they are out with their friends, keep you informed, spend time with the family, and set some goals they have to work toward.

**At risk.** Some behaviors put your kid directly at risk for substance use. The odds are very high that any personal or social constraints against using drugs and alcohol will break down under these circumstances. Again, the more signs you check off, the more you should be concerned. Signs of being at risk include:

O  Social group or siblings who use (and who might provide influence and access to substances)

O  A drop in grades or increase in school-related trouble (tardies, detentions, etc.)

O  Depression (because it sucks to be depressed and kids will naturally look for something to make them feel better)

O  Emotionally volatile moods, especially with angry outbursts and destructiveness (because drugs and alcohol leave you edgy and off-balance when you sober up)

O  Changes in friendships for the worse (because they will have less and less in common with sober friends)

O  Drug culture references and preferences (If they support and glorify illegal substances or substance abuse, substance use is just a matter of time.)

If your kid is showing signs of being at risk, it is time to have a talk about expectations and to surprise them with a drug screen that tests for marijuana, opiates, benzodiazepines, and cocaine. Better safe than sorry. Also, you have, in naval terms, fired a shot across the bow to warn them of your concerns and your heightened alertness. When they become indignant that you don't trust them, this will be a good time to have a talk about the limits of trust when you are worried about their safety and judgment. Finally, it will be useful to make sure they know what will happen if you find out they are using alcohol or drugs by elaborating an Alcohol and Drug Policy.

**Serious signs.** When you see serious signs, it means your kid is involved in an alcohol or drug culture. He or she is using, so be prepared to act. Serious signs include:

○ Catching them using

○ Telltale signs (Visine, lighters, obvious and frequent drug references, dilated or pinpoint pupils, and other physical signs)

○ Justification for legalization of recreational substances (because the number of teenagers who advocate legalization without using is so small it is not worth worrying about)

○ Unexplained lack of money or unaccounted-for money (so keep an eye on the flow of funds)

○ Drug-using close friends (enough said)

○ Presence of substances or paraphernalia (actual substances, rolling papers, small cigars or blunts, or homemade or manufactured devices like pipes, empty beer cans, or liquor bottles)

Sit down with your kid and discuss the strength of your concerns and inform them of a new policy of random drug screens approximately every two weeks for three months. Then establish an Alcohol and Drug Policy (see Alcohol and Drug Policy chapter for ideas) to clarify what they will be risking if they get caught.

Since an Alcohol and Drug Policy is integral to addressing substance use by your teen, talking about what to include in this kind of policy will be discussed in the next chapter. If you want to educate yourself about alcohol and drugs of abuse, a couple of good sites are provided in the References section of this book's website.

# ALCOHOL AND DRUGS

## Part 3:
### Alcohol and Drug Policy

I t is important for teens to have a clear understanding about what happens if they use drugs or alcohol.

> This chapter addresses talking with your teen about:
>
> • How to formulate a drug policy for your family
>
> • Consequences for initial and subsequent offenses

The percentage of teens who have ever smoked weed jumps from 5 percent in eighth grade to 35 percent by the time they are seniors (with the biggest increases from eighth to ninth grade and then again from eleventh to twelfth grade). For alcohol, use goes from 19 percent in eighth grade to 67 percent in twelfth grade, increasing steadily year to year. It's coming.

Like the topics of sex and dating, it helps to have the alcohol and drug talk before it drops into your lap. Part of that discussion should include what will happen if you catch them experimenting.

### WHAT'S A PARENT TO DO?

The previous chapter presented some of the signs that your kid may have begun to dabble in recreational substance use. This chapter provides an outline for establishing consequences for alcohol or drug use when you have a zero tolerance policy. They are divided into first and second offense categories. (If there is a third offense, their alcohol or drug use is beyond "casual" or experimental, and it's time to consult with a therapist.)

The first offense would follow the first time your kid is caught red-handed, has a positive drug screen (or refuses to take a drug screen), or you find alcohol or drugs or paraphernalia associated with their use. (If your kid is caught with anything other than alcohol or marijuana, this is another time to consult a therapist. The statistics for use of these "other drugs" are strongly against this being experimental or casual.)

So, first offense consequences would include:

○ **A clean sweep.** Tell your kid to remove all alcohol or drugs and paraphernalia from their room, the car, everywhere. This will be the one free pass, since they have already been caught. If you find anything in the future—even if it is from a time before this incident—it counts as a second offense and they are responsible. No excuses.

○ **Full grounding** until at least two weeks of clean alcohol and drug screens. This will provide lots of family time to allow for long discussions about the evils of substance abuse and to review family values. It also allows time for the drug to be out of their system while taking them out of the game for a while, to let things settle down.

○ **Two more weeks (at least) of supervised grounding**. This means time-limited outings with peers and friends as well as "long leash" family events where you are present but watching from afar (at school sporting events, etc.). They don't move off this level until they suffer the indignity of you actually being off in the distance keeping an eye on them during a couple of activities. (They really hate this one.) This "modified" grounding will enable your kid to begin to venture out into the "teen world" again while helping you confirm that they are again trustworthy, with some trade-mark suffering thrown in.

○ **Random searches**. The cost of violating trust is that people can't take you at your word. Trust has to be re-established with verification. Random searches help build the foundation for this. You don't have to wonder. Before a search, ask your kid if you will find anything. Then search with them present; it is, after all, their room (or backpack, etc.). When you don't find anything, let them know how much it means to you and that they are rebuilding trust.

○ **Include friends who were involved with your kid** in the discussion of consequences. Sit your kid down with his or her closest friends for a talk about what will happen if they become a bad influence on each other—namely, they won't be hanging out together anymore. Let your kid's friends know that, if you don't tell their parents this time, then any other instances of alcohol or drug use will result in a call to their parents.

○ **Random drug screens**. The ease and affordability of drug screens make them ideal for monitoring alcohol or drug use. I recommend weekly tests for at least four weeks followed by bi-weekly tests through the first three months. Continue randomly testing every two to four weeks until six months has passed. (A very large percentage of addicts will stay sober if they can make it for six months.) Nothing says "serious" like six months of random drug tests.

○ A **second offense** occurs if your kid uses again within twelve months or if it is the first instance of using drugs other than alcohol or marijuana (cocaine, heroin, prescription medication, etc.). If this occurs, you have a potentially serious problem, especially after going to such great lengths to make them miserable following the first offense. This is a sign they are determined to use. It is time for an alcohol and drug assessment to seek out one of three levels of therapeutic interventions. These include weekly outpatient alcohol and drug treatment with an individual therapist who specializes in addictions; involvement in an intensive outpatient treatment program (perhaps four days a week, four hours a day after school for five weeks); or enrollment in a residential alcohol and drug treatment facility. If your kid knows that this awaits them if they get busted again, it serves as a powerful incentive for them to leave that stuff alone and figure out a sober way to have fun.

# CHARACTER ISSUES

# ATTITUDE

Having an "attitude" is one way teens attempt to assert their independence. However, they often have trouble recognizing the line between attitude and disrespect.

This chapter goes over:

- Signs of adolescent attitude

- When to let it go

- How to respond

Adolescents are faced with a terrible dilemma. They have to listen to their parents go on and on about chores and homework and responsibility. They can't let you assume they agree with you—but they also can't tell you what they really think. What's a teen to do? Defiance? Too blatant. Arguing? Too tiring. Disrespect? Too direct. Attitude? The perfect solution.

With the right tone of voice, posture, eye contact, eye movement, tilt of the head, and variations of huffing and snorting, your kid can express disdain, disregard, condescension, superiority, sarcasm, disgust, disagreement, anger, and frustration, and it can all be expressed with plausible deniability. ("What? I didn't do anything!" "So now I don't breathe the way you want?" "I can't help it if you are seeing things.")

At best, attitude can be a precursor to self-confidence and assertiveness. At worst, it is the early sign of entitlement, argumentativeness, disrespect, and defiance.

## WHAT'S A PARENT TO DO?

**Let it go.** Attitude is common during the initial transition period into adolescence. This is the time kids begin to realize they can actually have an opinion (and that your opinions are wrong). As long as the attitude isn't blatant (i.e., they make an effort to hide it) or happening all the time, let them have their little rebelliousness without comment.

**Call them on it.** ("Wait. Didn't I just read that I'm supposed to let it go?" Yes. You obviously have not embraced the contradiction that is parenting teens.) If they are giving you an attitude *all* the time, that's too much. If they are presenting it to your face, that's crossing a line. If it doesn't peak and then drop away across six to nine months it isn't a phase.

For some kids, having an attitude can start to dig in and become a permanent style, growing into things like defiance, arguing, and disrespect. Worse, there are an increasing number of role models (like divas, guidos, thugs, yuppies, reality show participants, and every single celebutante) who glorify attitude that's all grown up (e.g., arrogance, entitlement, ignorance, callousness, superficiality, and nastiness). It won't help for you to address this by launching into a loud lecture. Calmly identify the problem. Let them know it isn't acceptable. Say "That's not OK" or "Wait, wait, wait. Get back here. That's not going to work."

**Immediate do-over.** A kid giving you attitude is a good place to use the parental do-over. "OK, come back here and let's try that again—only this time, without the attitude." If they don't give you any grief and respond appropriately that time, you're done. If they still want to mess with you, it may be time for a refresher course in manners.

**Manners matter.** There is a polite way to interact with people, even those you despise. Your kid's attitude may be the sign that your lessons in manners didn't take. (See the chapter on Manners.) Consider scheduling a mini-refresher course. Set aside thirty minutes and go over the whole range of mannerly behavior you expect to see in your kid, emphasizing how to respond to people without attitude. "OK, today we are going to practice responding appropriately to idiotic statements from other people. I am going to say something really obvious or annoying, and you are going to respond with the kind of manners we expect of members of this family."

**Encourage direct communication.** Kids with attitude are not good at expressing their feelings and thoughts in a straightforward way. Communicating with someone while angry, frustrated, or disgusted is a skill most of us have to learn. Help them practice disagreeing without arguing, having an attitude, or walking away. Invite them to respond but in an open but appropriate way rather than with attitude.

"Hold on. What is with that attitude?" (This is to try to help them actually identify what they are feeling.)

"Take a minute and then tell me what you're thinking." (This will help them learn how to actually talk about their feelings and opinions in the moment.)

Situations that result in attitude can provide you with the opportunity to help them express themselves in more direct ways. Note: don't be surprised if they get heated and start to step out of bounds when you initially practice this with them. That is why they were having attitude rather than saying something in the first place. Correct with understanding and have them try it again. You might also want to take a break and then come back to the topic.

**Model it.** Kids are not the only people who can have an attitude. Sarcasm; laughing when your kid says something sincere but ridiculous; talking to them in a condescending tone; rolling your eyes; and not letting them finish their point are examples of parental attitude. Remember that when you talk to a younger teen, you are modeling how mature adults should interact. Consideration for others and manners are key, even when you have all the power. So practice what you preach.

Having an attitude is a sign that your teenager is trying on their independence. As a parent, you can help shape that into the ability to appropriately stand up for themselves when they disagree with authority. This is the same skill they will need to follow their own values when faced with other forms of social pressure (like drugs, sex, and rock and roll). They will need all the preparation they can get.

# CHEATING

**B**elieve cheating delivers benefits with little risk. Unfortunately, the effects are subtle and negative.

This chapter examines:

- Why kids cheat

- Ways to discourage cheating

- What to do if you catch them

Cheating is fundamentally about fairness (or rather, unfairness). Cheaters break rules to gain personal advantage. Lots of things tempt teens to cheat: increasingly competitive college entrance requirements, the fading of cultural values, the expanding workload in school, an everyone-for-yourself mentality, insecurity, a growing emphasis on immediate gratification, and the apparent successes of notable cheaters.

According to the Josephson Institute's Center for Youth Ethics:

- 64 percent of surveyed teens cheated on a test during the previous year.

- 38 percent cheated two or more times.

- 36 percent of the teens reported using the internet to plagiarize written assignments.

- Unlike lying and stealing, girls are as likely as boys to cheat.

- Like other ethical shortcuts (such as lying and stealing), cheating can only succeed at the expense of long-term personal or communal relationships. When cheating is revealed—and it will be revealed—the damage is deep and destructive to relationships and reputation.

Cheating is selfish, wrong, and downright un-American!

## WHAT'S A PARENT TO DO?

**Model it.** Be careful about those small liberties you may be taking that fit within the category of cheating. There is a quiet power in the message you send to your kid by refusing to cheat when the opportunity presents itself. (And how profound a problem you can create by crowing about getting away with cheating!) Like so many aspects of parenting, you are accountable for your own actions in order to avoid hypocrisy and the resultant damage to your credibility.

**Expect it.** Make sure you clarify your stand on the rightness or wrongness of cheating. State unequivocally that you expect them to be honest and to avoid cheating at all costs.

**Praise it.** Praise is more effective than criticism or punishment. The problem is catching your kid when they resist the urge to cheat. Some signs to watch for include situations where your kid works harder (rather than looking for a shortcut) when pressed for time, even if it means personal sacrifices (like sleep), earns a lower grade honestly (by studying hard, even if they still score less than perfectly), loses gracefully, is a good sport, stays true to principles in difficult circumstances (e.g., not cheating in a waning dating relationship), or plays by the rules—especially if others are obviously cheating. Just a casual mention of your admiration of their taking the higher, principled road will help a lot.

**Discuss it.** Here's the problem. It doesn't feel good to compete honestly and still lose. It is even worse if your victorious opponent cheated. These feelings can fester and begin to turn to cynicism. ("If you can't beat 'em, join 'em.") Talk about the difficulty and importance of integrity, especially if they are a victim of cheating themselves. Talk about how integrity and fairness bring a return of trust and reputation that carries beyond the specific situation.

Talk about the long-term consequences of cheating as a way of dealing with difficulty. Don't have all the answers right at first. Let them talk through what they are thinking. Ask questions as a way of raising important points. Check in later to see if they have thought more about it.

**Teach it.** The most important thing you can do might be to look for the opportunity to teach your kid how to avoid temptation in the areas where cheating is likely to rear its ugly head.

What kinds of cheating affect your teens? Examples include:

O **Infidelity.** When your kid is in an exclusive dating relationship with someone, they have made a commitment to not hook up with other people. On the other hand, they aren't married. It will be important for your kid to learn how to manage desires, frustrations, and dissatisfaction while maintaining personal integrity. They can use help learning how to make the hard choices (either to stay in a relationship despite frustration or to go through all the trouble of breaking up with someone rather than cheating to split the difference). Hold your kid accountable if you uncover this kind of cheating.

O **Cheating at games.** Cheating at family games or neighborhood sports can be a form of playful ribbing of one's opponent or a sign of a deeper problem. If your kid is playful about their cheating and doesn't take the subsequent success seriously, then it is more likely to just be another way to pick at a friend. If on the other hand, your kid tries to hide and deny their cheating or if winning is everything, it is likely that the situation is in need of attention. Discussing your concerns will be important. Consider having a "ref" present who requires fidelity to the rules. This can give your kid the chance to learn how to play with integrity and to accept legitimate defeat with grace (though that may take some coaching).

○ **Video games.** There is a place in your home where cheating is actually being encouraged and rewarded. Every video game has built in "cheat codes" that allow the player to circumvent all kinds of limits to the game. It is so common no one thinks much about it. If you have concerns about your video game playing kid cheating in other areas, limiting their video game playing to non cheat code mode would be an interesting exercise in uncontaminated, honest game playing.

○ **Sports.** Playing by the rules is one part of being a good sport. Cheating at sports can take many forms including performance enhancing drugs, enhanced equipment, and purposefully violating the rules of play. Coaches can be a helpful ally in addressing cheating in the sports arena. If, on the other hand, it is the coach who is promoting this behavior, you have quite a dilemma. Talk to the coach, not talk to the coach? Make sure you include your kid on this decision. Regardless, clarify the moral behavior you expect your kid to exhibit if they want to continue participating in the sport; coach or no coach you can still bench them.

○ **Cheating in school.** School is a high risk domain for cheating. So much rides on grades: parental approval (and the lack of punishment), social status, self-concept, college admissions. Added to this is the ever growing amount of information our kids are required to retain and recall. Taking short cuts on homework, tests, projects, and papers is an inevitable and significant temptation. Keep an eye on how your kid is handling these demands. They are likely to need help staying focused on the real reason for school; that is, learning (rather than grades and other numbers). Granted, it is easier said than done.

Remind your child that cheating means cheating yourself. Cheating makes you feel like a fraud. You are always on edge, wondering when you will get caught. Then you have to try to find ways to explain it away so that you don't feel badly about yourself.

For beginners, cheating bypasses the skill acquisition process. For already highly skilled kids, it risks having all of the accomplishments derived from that skill erased upon the discovery of the cheating. The higher the stakes, the more likely the cheating will be revealed.

Ask your kid if the benefits from cheating are enough to make the destruction of his reputation and any accomplishments worthwhile. Ask, "What other moral compromises will you make to cover your cheating? How much self-deception will it take to keep from seeing the eyes of a fraud looking back at you in the mirror?"

If you catch them cheating:

O **Hear them out**. Have them explain what led to the decision to cheat. It is likely to include strong, conflicting emotions with an ethical dilemma. Keep pushing them until they get to the struggle between doing it fairly and failing versus cheating and coming out ahead (in the short run).

O **Be sympathetic**. The temptation to take a short cut is very strong. Everyone has done it, and some have done it repeatedly. Honesty and integrity are ideals toward which to strive. Help your kid realize that they will disappoint themselves at various times in their lives. Learn from it and move on.

O **Induce empathy**. "What's the big deal about cheating? It's not like anyone got hurt." Sometimes you have to help your kid understand things from other people's perspectives. The classic "How would you feel if someone did that to you?" is useful here. A story (ideally, a personal story) of someone working hard to reach a goal—only to have a cheater get ahead—can do the trick. If your kid responds by thinking the person who didn't cheat was a sucker, it may be time to consult—unless you have one of those bull-headed kids who will disagree to save face and then change their behavior anyway.

O **Generate some guilt**. Guilt gets a bad rap sometimes, in part because it can be way overused. But guilt can be a valuable mechanism for generating a sense of disappointment in yourself for falling short of your moral code. It is not an end in itself, though. Guilt is the signal to redouble your efforts to follow your own moral code. A good source of guilt is the disappointment of someone they love and whose opinion matters. Hopefully, that is you. Don't be afraid to be disappointed in them.

○ **Review the family values**. Time to go back over the moral code you expect your kid to use in making decisions and guiding actions. Don't stop with honesty, trustworthiness, and integrity. This is probably a good time to review the whole list. Make sure you require your kid to recommit to the values they intend to live by. Generate some examples of moral conflicts and help them think through what it will take to be an ethical person in the future.

○ **Consider restitution**. Depending on the size and scope of the cheating, making things right should be part of the plan. This might require them to return the ill-gotten gains, confess the infidelity, or talk to the teacher and ask to redo the assignment—fair and square.

Living a moral life is difficult. Kids need guidance and encouragement to make the hard choices required to be a good person. They are going to fall short sometimes. Everyone does. Standing with them, encouraging them, and helping them face and correct mistakes are among the greatest gifts parents can provide their children.

# GRATITUDE

G ratitude is an oft-neglected character trait in adolescents. Yet gratitude rests at the heart of successful relationships and a contented life.

This chapter considers:

- The benefits of an attitude of gratitude

- Ways to encourage gratitude in teens

Around 2001, a group of researchers began to make the study of gratitude their particular focus. Robert Emmons, Michael McCullough and their colleagues revealed a remarkable range of benefits derived from an attitude of gratitude. People who practiced gratitude were found to reported gratitude have fewer physical complaints. They felt better about their lives as a whole and were more optimistic about the upcoming week.

Gratitude also was found to be associated with greater progress toward important personal goals and higher states of alertness, enthusiasm, determination, attentiveness, and energy. People who practiced gratitude were more likely to have helped someone with a personal problem and offered emotional support to others. They were more likely to feel loved. Finally, kids who practiced gratitude were found to have more positive attitudes toward school and their families (for which their parents were also grateful).

Despite all of its benefits, gratitude is not exactly on the top of a teenager's list of priorities. Adolescence is a time of distinguishing yourself as an individual from your family and your peers. The idealism (and naïveté) of teens contributes to inflated aspirations of success and ambitions to accomplish great things. At the same time, they seem to remain keenly aware of how much their lives *suck* and of the unfairness of the world.

## WHAT'S A PARENT TO DO?

How do we foster in teens an appreciation for the blessings in their lives without holding them back from wanting more and better?

**Teach it.** Gratitude is more than just saying "thanks." Gratitude is a way of thinking about the world that reflects an awareness of the blessings present in the lives of even the most unfortunate—like your poor, mistreated child. (Sarcasm, by the way, is not a good method to use for teaching gratitude, however tempting it may be.)

To ensure your teen grasps the importance of this way of thinking, gratitude needs to be taught. Teens can be blinded to the many blessings that fill their lives. Personal relationships, possessions, wealth, the generosity of others, and their own personal qualities, skills, and talents are some of the more obvious blessings.

We are also blessed by the sacrifices made on our behalf as well as the ways we benefit from the efforts and accomplishments of others who contribute to our comfort and success. And let's not forget the wonders of life and of the natural world that surrounds us.

Gratitude shouldn't be reserved for the obvious, straightforward positive things that happen to you. If we experience gratitude only when we are rewarded or validated, then it becomes simply celebration. Gratitude also allows us to reach into the depths of pain, disappointment, and suffering to find value in the experience and lessons for the future. Recognizing the "silver lining" can help soothe the pain and provides a perspective for making your way forward in the face of difficulty.

When it is a straightforward blessing, identifying it as such and taking a moment to appreciate the event, circumstance, action, or moment is an important way to teach your kid about gratitude. If it is finding the silver lining, it will be important to first acknowledge the pain or disappointment before you jump right in and start having them "get over it." Then, gently, help them find ways to look at what they benefited from this situation.

**Model it.** Parents shape the beliefs and values of their children by example. Fostering a greater appreciation in our children for the blessings in their lives can be accomplished by your own appreciation of the little things. This means that you will have to be good at noticing things worthy of appreciation. Make a point of talking in terms of gratitude so your kids can hear and know it is worthy of attention.

**Expect it.** To develop a habit of gratitude in our kids, it is important to expect them to demonstrate it. This includes requiring them to say "thank you" for something as minor as passing the salt as well as for something as major as saving a life. Counting your blessings contributes to a richer understanding of the many areas of life worthy of gratitude. Research suggests that we can benefit from something as simple as identifying five things for which we are grateful on a daily basis. Try setting aside a moment near the end of the day (which some people already do in the form of prayer) to reflect on how you are blessed. At the very least, helping your kid stop and reflect on the many things worthy of gratitude introduces a whole new dimension to our usual parental focus, which is reviewing everything our kids have yet to accomplish (like cleaning that damned room!).

**Repeat it.** As with most important life lessons, being grateful for the blessings in life bears repeating, over and over. Look for every opportunity to point out others who exemplify an appreciation for what life has to offer. Continue to ask about what they may have to be grateful for. Have the word come up over and over: "You know what I'm grateful for?" "What can you take from that disaster that might be of use in the future?" "What did you learn about yourself?"

Recognizing the many blessings each of us enjoy is a deep and complicated process, for adults as well as teens. Gratitude requires keeping a perspective on the real value of things. It is based on an acceptance that things are what they are; we can be resentful and angry, or we can put our energy into discerning the true meaning and value of experiences, both good and bad.

Gratitude begins with a simple word: thanks.

# LYING

Every kid lies, sooner or later. It's important that teens quickly learn what lying costs them.

> This chapter discusses:
>
> - Why kids lie
> - How to discourage it
> - How to stop it
> - How kids can fix it

Your kid will lie to you about something eventually. The most obvious reason for lying is to avoid some kind of negative consequence like punishment, disappointment, incarceration, etc. Kids also lie for personal gain, to keep something private, or to avoid embarrassment. Finally, kids will lie out of loyalty, concern about hurting someone's feelings, or to build themselves up in others' eyes (or in their own mind).

Whatever the reason, lying is a short-term solution that will always catch up to them, unless they move frequently and have no lasting relationships. But lying is very tempting. The trick is to catch them at it before it goes too far.

## WHAT'S A PARENT TO DO?

**Lay the groundwork.** It is better to address the issue of lying before it comes up. Discussions about lying should be included in your ongoing discussions about morals and character, right and wrong. Stories (i.e., personal, fictional, historical, etc.) and fables of the effects of lying and truth-telling can also be important teaching tools (for example, The Boy Who Cried Wolf).

As always, model the kind of behavior you expect from your kids. Remember, teens say a parent is their hero more frequently than any other category of person. What you do matters.

Expect (and require) honesty and trustworthiness. Above all, be careful about putting yourself in the position of being considered (or possibly called) a hypocrite. Lead by example.

**Confront them.** Call them on the lie and provide the information to expose the lie. Don't let them interrupt or try to counter each of your points. If they come clean, that's a start. If they stick to the lie, explain how things will be worse if they both lie and demonstrate a lack of integrity by sticking with the lie.

**Don't call them a liar.** Avoid labeling them as a liar, no matter how many times you have caught them in a lie. Calling your kid names is generally a bad idea, in part because being labeled by someone whose opinion matters has a funny way of digging in and becoming part of a kid's identity. If you are a Liar (versus someone who has lied), there is no redemption—so why even try? Limit name-calling to the names you *want* them to become.

This doesn't mean that you should sugarcoat lying. Call it what it is (rather than what your kid is): "That is a lie. You lied to me. You haven't told me the truth. You are not being honest. That is dishonest. That's not true. I hate being lied to. Don't lie to me. Be honest with me."

**Review the problems with lying.** Make sure they understand why lying is a problem. One of the foundations of trust is honesty. When you lie, people question every other area that requires trust—even things that are completely unrelated. Kids are often surprised by this. ("But, I wouldn't lie to you about THAT!")

People dislike you when you lie to them. They feel used, vulnerable, and angry. They feel like a fool and think that the person who lied to them doesn't respect them. Lying damages trust between people. Without trust, everything you say is questioned and doubted, including the positive things like "I love you" or "I wouldn't do that to you, you're my friend."

Lying also puts a distance between you and people you care about, since you can't always respond genuinely (or the lie might come to light). Lying also makes you feel bad about yourself. When you know something you did is wrong, it eats at you. And then, sometimes, you may even come up with reasons to justify your lies ("They lie to me all the time, too" or "They're too sensitive.") so as not to feel so bad about yourself.

Finally, the whole fabric of our society would come unraveled without a minimum amount of honesty among its citizens. OK, the socio-cultural reference to the role of trust in social contracts might go over their heads—but it's worth a shot.

**Review your family creed.** The phrase "In this family, we ... " is followed by statements about the moral foundation of your family. ("Lying is not part of who we are.") Review the values system that forms the basis of your family and your relationships. Go overboard on the importance of morals. Link morals and values to your religious beliefs. Use guilt, if possible.

**Have a two-tiered punishment system.** It is one thing for your kid to mess up or do something that you don't approve of. It is another thing if they do that *and* lie about it. Give them an incentive to come clean. Whatever punishment you would impose for the misbehavior should be doubled if they also lie about it.

**Have them think before answering.** "I'm going to ask you something and I want you to think carefully before answering." Give them a moment to pause and reflect. Draw their attention to the importance of honesty as separate from the problem situation. If they have begun to answer and you know they are lying, stop them and give them a do-over. "OK, wait. I want you to stop for a minute and think about what you are about to tell me. Remember that sneaking out of the house last night was one thing—but *lying* about sneaking out of the house will be another thing added on top."

The Dirty Harry routine seems so perfect for this situation: "You've got to ask yourself one question. Do you feel lucky? Well, do you, punk?" (Leave out the .357 Magnum hand gun, though.)

**Help them resolve ethical dilemmas.** Kids can run into difficult ethical dilemmas where being honest may conflict with another important value. In these situations, your kid might need help figuring out non-lying solutions.

This doesn't mean helping them find a way to weasel their way out of acting with integrity. They can respectfully refuse to answer (rather than lie) if by answering they will violate another important ethical principle (like loyalty). Refusing to answer may be an admirable solution to a difficult situation. Unfortunately, staying true to their honesty ethic, however admirable, won't get them out of being punished for the actual transgression—but it does show that they have taken the responsible and mature route of accepting punishment, which is a stance worthy of praise.

**Make them repair the damage.** Here are some components of a formal solution to addressing a lie. (It doesn't hurt to have your kid write out their responses. You can put it in their scrapbook!)

- List the morals you live by (all of them).
- Describe what you lied about and why.
- Identify how it was your decision (rather than blaming others).
- Explain why it was wrong (including what morals it violated).
- Apologize for lying.
- Identify what you will do differently next time.
- Describe what you will have to do to re-establish trust.
- Describe what will happen if you lie again.

**Verify, then trust.** When someone is caught in a lie, you can't take their word for anything. They can't go anywhere that can't be verified ahead of time. Every report by your kid must have external validation. Tell them that you would like to trust them but that earning back trust will require a period of time with no instances of lies. ("No, I'm afraid that I will have to call Sue's mom to verify that you have actually been invited over." "You know, I really hate this, but I can't trust that you will tell me if plans change, since last time you lied about where y'all were going. You'll have to just hang around the house today.")

After two weeks of having to prove the truth of everything—and that means *everything*—your kid should be feeling the weight of their little foray into the exciting world of prevarication and deceit.

**Catch them telling the truth.** Try to catch each time they answer truthfully and accurately. Express your appreciation when they are honest. Let them know you notice when they do the right thing to keep them focused on the behavior you want to see from them.

**What if it happens again?** If it is sooner than six months, it may be time to consult. Your kid might have trouble making the connections or might have a disposition that predisposes them to take the easy way out, despite the long-term costs.

**What about tall tales?** Some kids have a knack for embellishing tales of their or other's exploits. If they don't identify the exaggerated parts of the story, tale-telling is a form of lying. Sometimes this might happen when they get caught up in spinning a good yarn. Other times, it might be an attempt to build themselves up. Tall tales can also be an indication that your kid has a self image they can't live up to.

While people may enjoy the stories, telling tall tales will end up undermining trust if tales are presented as though they really happened. The first thing to do is require your kid to identify which parts of the story really happened and which are being exaggerated. (e.g., "OK, wait. First tell me the good story and then tell me what really happened.") It may also be time to arrange some exciting adventures for your kid so they have an actual exciting story to tell. If they continue distorting events and experiences and insist they really happened, it is time to consult.

Getting caught in a lie is part of growing up. It is a valuable opportunity for parents to drive home an important moral lesson. Don't ignore it, but don't dwell too much on it—because there is always the next issue to address, right over the horizon.

# RESPECT

Being respectful is one of the core qualities of effective family functioning. It is also a basic element in civilized society.

> This chapter discusses:
>
> - The differences between respecting and respectful
> - The many forms of respect
> - The importance of respectful disagreement
> - Responding to adolescent disrespect

When kids are not required to demonstrate respect toward their parents, things go badly within the family. Courtesy and manners are characteristics that are important for smooth family functioning and healthy development. Showing respect is at the very heart of citizenship in a civil society.

Respect may be the cornerstone of freedom and liberty, but it has to be taught.

## WHAT'S A PARENT TO DO?

To begin, it will be useful to clarify what respect looks like and to review your expectations with your kid. Here is a brief list of things to include in your discussion of respect toward you (and anyone else, for that matter).

**Respectful behavior.** How your kid acts toward another person is fundamental to showing respect. Making eye contact, facing them, actively listening, and putting other things aside during the interaction show they are paying attention. Kids don't necessarily understand the importance of these non-verbal behaviors. With all of the distractions and technology available, they are increasingly likely to multitask; they may scan the computer and take and send texts while they listen to your rant about not cleaning their room. It is likely you will need to be clear about the relationship between attending to one's social partner and the demonstration of respect.

**Respectful communication.** What they say and how they respond to you is another component of respect. Tone of voice (e.g., sincere rather than sarcastic, lower- rather than higher-pitched) and how loud they talk (whether they use their inside voice or scream at you) as well as waiting their turn (rather than interrupting you after every point, sentence, or pause for breath) are signs of respect.

Teens might need help building a vocabulary of respectful words. They might need to learn to express how they feel using neutral (wrong, mistaken, rigid, over-involved) rather than inflammatory words (lying, narrow-minded, fascist, insane). They might need encouragement from you to accept your invitations to talk rather than ignoring you on the way to their room and then slamming the door behind them.

**Respectful disagreement.** Many teens have difficulty demon-strating respect when the other person (again, that's you) is obviously wrong, to the point of possible insanity. They often need help in learning how to disagree in a civil, respectful manner.

One component of respectful disagreement involves hearing the other person out. Teens often have trouble allowing the discussion to continue when the speaker is, at least in their mind, being irrational and irrelevant. You can help by teaching them to shut up until you are finished. They also might benefit from instruction about when it is a good time to take a break to keep things civil.

Teens can have trouble understanding when others are not convinced simply by listening to their arguments. After all, it is perfectly obvious they are right! You may need to help them accept that sometimes they will have to just agree to disagree (and then do what you say). (See the Negotiation chapter for additional suggestions.)

**Civil disobedience.** But what if your kid strongly disagrees with you (or the limits you impose on them)? If it is really important to them, then it will be worth suffering the consequences for disobeying you. Being responsible for your actions means you accept the cost of your decisions and subsequent actions. It really is a sign of maturity when kids accept responsibility for their actions. Be sure to express your admiration for their standing on principle and making decisions for themselves—and then nail their butts to the wall for disobeying you. It is never too soon to learn that revolutionaries are often martyred.

**Respect the sacrifices made by others.** Teens are so close to childhood that they haven't recognized their obligations to the people who provide the support and resources that make their life easier or even possible. Begin talking with your teen about respecting the debt owed to people on whom you depend—your parents, family and even your country. (Where do they think those schools, streets, and sewage systems come from? Who is defending our liberty and protecting our freedom? What obligation do you have to those who have sacrificed so that you can enjoy the life you currently have?) This will probably require helping them see that respecting obligations is not the same as blind devotion (or submission to The Man).

**Respect for experience.** There isn't a lot of this in our youth- and change-oriented society. There is much to be gained by living and learning. Perspectives change. Previously important things often pale in comparison to the discovery of fundamental truth. The significance of some things will be proven, despite the shifting sands of time. Your teen won't really get it, but it's worth throwing in so they can realize how smart you were after you're dead.

**Respect the rock of parental love and concern.** Teens aren't the only people who fail to recognize the power and importance of being loved and cared about, but they have the most trouble with this concept. Attribute this to their developmental struggle to break free of the ties that bind in pursuit of a feeling of individuality and independence. Part of the problem is that this safety net becomes obvious only when things go wrong. It won't be friends who spend the rest of their life caring for a child's paralyzed body or damaged mind (and this applies to a child of any age). That kind of devotion requires a love that transcends common interests or shared experiences, and it is found in the love of a mother or father or, if they are lucky, a spouse or committed partner.

**Respectful versus respect.** A final issue teens struggle with is the difference between respectful and respect. Most teens feel like being respectful means the other person may think they actually respect them. They just can't take having someone mistake respectful for respect. You are requiring them to be respectful regardless of whether they respect the person (sometimes, that would be you). Respectful is a quality of character. It's part of the Golden Rule. ("Do unto others … ) Being respectful doesn't depend on the other person.

**Model respect.** Teens are keenly aware of hypocrisy. If you want them to respect you—and not just be respectful—you will need to behave respectfully toward them. The nice thing about having power is that you don't have to flaunt it. You just exercise it. Practice what you preach, even though it would be a lot easier if they just did what you said when you said it how you said to do it (with a smile on their face and an attitude of gratitude).

On the other end of the scale is disrespect. What if they end up being disrespectful, despite all your hard work and training? You can expect it to happen. Here are some ways to deal with disrespect.

**Breathe.** Your first instinct might be to kill them, but the push for independence and individuality makes at least a brief period of disrespect inevitable. Stay calm and guide them through this.

**Death stare.** It is important to signal that they have crossed a line. An effective technique is silent, sustained eye contact. A close equivalent is the "Have you lost your mind?" expression; to do this, draw your eyebrows together, tense your jaw, and tilt your head slightly while looking intently into their eyes.

**Make sure they meant to do it.** "Excuse me?" Teens will pop off at the mouth, particularly during the early teen years. They don't have enough experience dealing with the strong feelings of self-righteousness and arrogance to stifle a quick, disrespectful response. A good technique to consider is giving them a do-over. "You need to say that another way." "Do you really want to go there?"

If they take it back, say it in a more respectful way, or behave more appropriately, let it go. If they don't, it is like they are begging you to punish them so that they have a reason to feel misunderstood and mistreated. Oblige them.

**Don't set them up.** You shouldn't be surprised if your kid responds disrespectfully when you rush them out of bed the morning of semester finals the day after a reckless driver ran over their new puppy. You can help them succeed by not pushing things too far until they get the hang of this respectful thing. Don't assume you need to address everything at once. Consider making time later to sit and discuss the issue.

**Give them an out.** Help them recognize when they are likely to become disrespectful. "Maybe we should take a break and talk about this in thirty minutes." While some things need to be addressed immediately, allowing time for your kid to get themselves together and start thinking again can help them respond appropriately.

**Address it in private.** Avoid making a scene, even if they don't always show you the same courtesy. "I need to speak to you in private, *now!*" That statement communicates respect for their dignity, although everyone who hears it will know what's going to happen. Two birds with one stone.

**Respect your authority.** "As long as you live in my house ... " I don't recommend that you actually say this, because it might be too provocative for teens—but it is the reality. Make it clear that one of the requirements of being a member of your family is to treat others with respect. They don't get a choice about that.

**Mutual respect.** Make sure everyone is being respectful of everyone else, including you. Asking your kid if they are being treated respectfully by everyone else can open up a valuable discussion. You (or another member of the family) may be inadvertently (or advertently) disrespectful to your kid. It might be time for a family meeting.

**Intolerables.** There are some things that will tear the family apart if not addressed. If your kid continues to be disrespectful despite your attempts to discourage it (using strategies like those recommended above), you may need to have a mental health professional help you find other, more effective ways to resolve the problem. You definitely need to consult if your kid pays no attention to your rules; uses profanity, vulgarities or cursing (especially when you don't allow that); calls you bad names; threatens or intimidates; puts their hands on you in anger or becomes physically aggressive or assaultive; refuses to let you move freely (for example, blocks the doorway so that you can't leave); throws, breaks or destroys things; or is outright defiant. These are signs that things are bad. Get some help so you get this taken care of. Now.

Happily, most teens prefer to be respectful. They just may need a little reminding now and again.

# STEALING

Lots of kids–good kids–indulge in minor stealing.

This chapter discusses:

- The importance of morals

- How to tell if it is serious problem

- Suggested strategies for different forms of stealing

Here are a few stats from a 2008 survey of teens by the Josephson Institute. Thirty-five percent of boys and 26 percent of girls admitted to stealing from a store within the previous year. That included honors students (21 percent), student leaders (24 percent), and students involved in youth activities and service clubs (27 percent). Twenty-three percent reported having stolen something from a parent or other relative, and 20 percent stole something from a friend. Unfortunately, 26 percent of the respondents reported that they lied on this questionnaire.

The good news (?) is that 93 percent of the kids taking this survey said they were satisfied with their personal ethics and character, and 77 percent reported that they are better at doing what's right than most people they know.

## WHAT'S A PARENT TO DO?

**Closing the barn door (you know, before the horse has bolted).** Before reviewing what to do when your child has stolen something, here's a word or two about the importance of helping your kid establish a moral foundation. It is crucial to address moral issues *before* there is a transgression. The short version about how to do this is model it, expect it, teach it, praise it in your kid and in the world, discuss it, tell stories about it and repeat it. You can get ahead of the game if you have already employed these strategies before your kid steals.

**Quick assessment.** There are a couple of questions about the theft that can help give you an idea how serious things are and how to craft a response. Shoplifting some gum from a convenience store when they are with friends calls for a different response than breaking into a neighbor's house and stealing their television and video game systems. The greater the accumulation of troubling answers to these questions is, the more serious the problem is.

These questions are meant as a general guide. They are not meant to minimize the actual theft nor are they definitive. Stealing is stealing.

- **Who did they steal from?** It makes a difference whether they picked up something from a store versus taking something from a close friend. In general, the closer the relationship is, the more troubling the theft should be.

- **How much planning did it take?** The more planning a crime took, the more serious the problem is. An opportunistic "right place at the right time" theft is the typical stealing event that almost all kids go through. If the theft required short-term planning, some time will need to be devoted to reviewing the importance of morals and the costs of stealing. Theft that requires long-term, intricate planning, on the other hand, suggests the absence of a deeper moral structure regarding the property of others. More intensive and elaborate retraining of your kid will be required.

- **What did they steal?** When people steal necessities, it is less of a moral issue and more of an economic one. Theft that involves internet music or video file sharing, pirated software, very-low-cost retail items (such as candy), very small amounts of money, or items off limits to minors (like alcohol and cigarettes) are cause for the least amount of concern, especially if your kid wouldn't dream of stealing from actual people (as opposed to corporations that make plenty of money or The Man). Stealing larger denominations of money and luxury items (mp3 devices, cell phones, fashionable clothing, etc.) reveals a more serious problem that will be likely to infiltrate other areas of your kid's life. Finally, stealing big ticket items like televisions or vehicles, or demanding money directly from people, are pretty clear indicators that your child has crossed over into the moral mind set of a criminal. You've got a long road ahead of you.

- **What is the kid's response to being caught?** Your kid's response to the theft and being caught can give you a rough gauge of their openness to growth and acceptance of personal responsibility. Embarrassment and shame are good signs. Fear and being upset about getting caught are better than nothing. Anger and rationalization make it hard for them to accept responsibility and use morals as a guide in the future. Indifference can be a sign that there isn't a strong moral code in place. Joking about the theft suggests a kind of hardened heart that will be hard to reach.

- **Has it happened before?** If this is more than the first time (unless you didn't really address it thoroughly the first time), you have a problem on your hands.

- **Were they alone?** While it is still a moral issue, being in the company of others when misbehaving is a mitigating factor. When a group of teenagers puts their idiotic heads together and egg each other on, they can end up going further than they otherwise would.

**Parental responses for different categories of stealing.** Ultimately, you will need to determine the seriousness of the stealing problem in order turn things around. One framework for judging what level of intervention to employ would be to think of the theft as a moral lapse, a misdemeanor, a repeat offense, or a felony.

**Moral lapse.** A moral lapse represents theft by a kid who clearly demonstrates they have morals but has violated their own personal ethics. Moral lapses result in things like taking a small amount of money that is just "lying around," taking the belongings of family members for personal use, shoplifting low-priced items (like candy), downloading pirated copies of internet products, or playing a prank on someone by taking their belongings. Moral lapses are part of their growth as a human and provide the opportunity to reassess priorities. Here is a formula for addressing this category of stealing. By the time you are done, they should be completely worn down.

Sit them down and have a long, serious, and preferably stern talk about the seriousness of stealing and how disappointed you are in their lack of following their own moral code. Be sure to remind them of their own good moral qualities while you are talking about this lapse.

O Do a morals checkup. Have them identify all of the morals they use to guide their actions.

O Your kid should be able to identify why stealing is wrong. Most lists would include:

- Violates their personal moral code for right and wrong

- Others will think of them as a thief or a bad person

- Sliding in one moral area leads to the crumbling of morals in other areas

- Damages the trust of people who are close to you

- Victims of theft feel violated and unsafe long after the possessions are returned

- If everyone just takes what they want, civilization topples into anarchy

O They should accept responsibility for their actions by acknowledging that what they did was wrong. Any attempt to make excuses indicates the need for more discussion and reeducation about morals and personal responsibility.

○ Require them to apologize to the people who were affected by their actions (i.e., victims of the theft, you and your family—because people judge a family by its members—and the community, if appropriate). Be sure to respect the dignity of your child during this process. Don't broadcast their transgression to relatives. Arrange for private apologies. Avoid using shame in dealing with their transgression.

○ Return the purloined objects or make restitution or both.

○ Have them identify their plan for avoiding a future lapse in moral judgment and to re-establish trust.

**Misdemeanor.** A misdemeanor is represented by theft that requires at least some planning with the intent of taking someone's property for their own use. This includes significant amounts of money, shoplifting large or pricey items (just about any portable electronic device), and anything taken from an unlocked vehicle or an unsecured area of someone's property (like a garage or back yard). This category of stealing indicates a lack of moral oversight requiring more intensive parental responses than with a moral lapse.

○ Take your kid through the Moral Lapse formula above.

○ If there are any friends associated with the theft, ban contact until your kid has demonstrated clear instances of morally guided behavior and the ability to stand on principle rather than go with the crowd (which should take at least a month).

○ They have obviously become too enamored of the good life, leading them down the road to ruin. It may be time to simplify by limiting access to luxuries until your kid has demonstrated an appreciation for the important things in life: quality time with the family, the simple joys of reading a good book (that has a moral about stealing), family sing-a-longs (in lieu of electronic music), helping out around the house. When they can demonstrate the ability to live a simple yet fulfilling life with a positive attitude ("Whistle while you work, la-la-la-la-la-la-la!") you can gradually re-introduce the temptations of demon technology and bad company!

○ Rebuilding trust requires consistent evidence of right behavior until it can be taken for granted again. All money must be accounted for or it is confiscated. All possessions must have a proof of purchase or they are donated.

**Repeat offender.** If stealing shows up again after employing one of the interventions above, things are more complicated than you thought. Your kid might have such a significant impulse control problem that more intensive attention needs to be devoted to developing greater self-control. Your kid's moral convictions may be significantly less well-developed than you had estimated. There may be a serious alcohol or drug problem. It would be worth your while to consult with a mental health professional to get their thoughts on what may be going on.

**Felony.** There are some acts of theft that represent a very serious problem. These include stealing a vehicle, theft that requires breaking into someone's house or vehicle, or confronting someone in order to rob them. This is a sign that your kid is seriously off track. Consult with a professional and expect to have to devote some intensive (and probably expensive) attention to trying to get your kid back on track.

# COMMUNICATION ISSUES

# ARGUMENTATIVE TEENS

Arguing is not always something to be avoided. In fact, arguing can have some very positive aspects—when it's done appropriately.

This chapter looks at:

- The up side of arguing

- What's normal

- Strategies for dealing with argumentative teens

- Shutting down an argument

All teenagers spend part of adolescence being argumentative. If your teen doesn't argue at least some of the time, you should worry. Being argumentative is often a kid's initial, awkward attempt to assert themselves and to disagree. With all the role models from reality shows, music and musicians, and (in some cases) politicians, kids can come to believe that arguments involve drama, screaming, aggression, put-downs, hurling personal insults, making wild accusations, ignoring the other person's views, and stomping off if you don't get your way.

The developmental task facing teens is to move from being argumentative to being able to argue. They need to learn how to discuss, disagree, and then argue their point. Arguing helps kids hone their opinions and discover flaws in their thinking. They learn to not let their frustration throw off their reasoning.

Arguing, as a form of dissent, can reveal flaws in the reasoning or decisions of others. It can also be a source of new ideas. While we would rather our kids just obediently absorb the wisdom we have to impart, arguing is a skill they will need that can only be acquired through practice. Want to guess who plays the role of the practice dummy? (Once again, it's you.)

Initially, normal argumentativeness is marked by yelling (without cussing); mild insults (using terms like crazy, stupid, gay, ridiculous, etc.); expressions of strong frustration ("I *hate* you, this family, my life, etc."); implying either verbally or non-verbally that the other person must be an idiot or mentally challenged for not seeing the rightness of their view; and stomping off before the other person has finished responding, when it is clear the other person isn't going to change their mind.

Teens will interrupt, contradict, and correct your mistaken views, and they might persist even after it is clear the decision has been made. There is often at least one (but, usually, not repeated) incident of serious name-calling or profanity. The parenting goal is to get them to the place where they are able to argue (not be argumentative), discuss and negotiate.

## WHAT'S A PARENT TO DO?

Here are some things you can do to help them along on the road to civil disagreements and rational debate.

**Keep your cool.** One of the hardest things to do with teens is to stay calm. They are adept at finding just the right way to say something that makes you feel like hollering at them. If you increase the intensity, they will be likely to match it. In addition, teens have a weird way of becoming smug and feeling justified in their assessment of parents as unreasonable when they can get them to lose their cool.

**Demand respect.** There is a right (acceptable) way and a wrong (unacceptable) way for kids to talk to their parents. The right way is one part civility and the other part acknowledgment of their authority. Kids need to learn how to be furious and still behave in a reasonable, civilized way. Address disrespect immediately. Everything comes to a halt until they get themselves under control. ("It is not OK for you to talk to me like that. Do you need some time to calm down?" Or, "Just who do you think you are? Don't you EVER talk to me like that again! You need to get a hold of yourself!") Regardless, require them to restate their remark in an acceptable way. Do not continue until they fix this. If they cuss you, nail their butts to the wall big time. Make it clear that cussing is a deal-breaker. You need to nip that in the bud.

**Don't allow interrupting.** Do not let them interrupt you before you are finished, and don't interrupt them before they are finished. If your kid is in the habit of interrupting, you may frequently find yourself saying, "You cut me off. I'm not finished." Be as brief as you can. Teens have trouble waiting, and parents frequently go on and on.

**Be respectful.** Teens are trying to become their own person, think their own thoughts, and make up their own mind. Talk to them respectfully so that you don't inadvertently provoke them into reacting and, thus, requiring you to punish them. Be especially careful about being sarcastic, making jokes, or laughing when they say absurd or naïve things if they are serious. Being sarcastic sends a certain percentage of teens ballistic! You'll already know if you have one. Sarcasm in a serious situation demeans all teens.

**Actually consider their opinion.** Stop and listen to what they have to say. Most of the time, the argument is trivial. However, if arguments are happening frequently, there may be something important that needs attending to. It is important for your kid to feel like you actually listened to them, even if you still don't change your mind.

**Model rational decision-making.** This is another situation where you teach your kid by example. It may seem like providing the reasoning for a decision or view you hold just gives your kid more ammunition for arguments. That can be addressed. (See Enough is enough, below.) Let them see that decisions should be based on morals, reasons, and goals like healthy teenage mental and physical development, the smooth functioning of the house, etc. At the same time ...

**Give yourself an out.** Most of us have not spent long nights elaborating the rationale for each and every expectation and require-ment we have for our kids. If you haven't got an answer you like or if you are considering changing your view, tell your kid you will need to give some thought to their point and get back with them. ("You know, a lot of parenting is by instinct or things that you just know are important. But, I'm going to have to think about that.") It helps for your kid to see that you are open to reviewing decisions or opinions.

**Don't repeat yourself over and over.** Your reasons are your reasons. Argumentative kids have a knack for getting you to go round and round. After you have said it twice, there isn't any more to say. "All I can do is tell you my reason/opinion/belief. There isn't any more to say."

**Stay on topic.** Argumentative kids often pile everything they are unhappy about into the same conversation. You can begin to argue about one thing and find yourself sliding into one or more additional issues. This has the effect of putting you on the defensive. You might find yourself trying to defend yourself, to a stupid *kid*, no less! If your kid brings up another issue ("You never listen to me anyway!"), acknowledge their additional area of unhappiness. You might say, "I am listening to you now about this. 'Never listening to you' is a whole different issue. We can talk about that but not right now." Set a time to discuss the other topic or topics. ("How about tomorrow at 7:30? But not now.") Be sure you keep the appointment.

**Let them convince you about something.** They need to win sometimes, especially if they have argued effectively and appropri-ately. Be swayed by their argument when it is something they care about. Be sure to tell them how they convinced you, and include how they argued and what evidence or reasoning swayed you. That's how they know what to do next time.

**Reinforce appropriate arguing.** Make sure you point out the good arguing techniques they use, but don't overdo it. Say this: "Now that is a good point!" "You are making it hard for me to say no when you put it like that. Let me think about it a minute." Don't say this: "You are *such* a good arguer! But, no."

**Teach them to know when to quit.** Teens can get caught up in the emotion of the argument and lose sight of their long-term objectives (like not being grounded for life). Help them learn to recognize when their cause is lost. You can do this by asking leading questions: "Do you think continuing to argue with me about this will change my mind?" "You might want to stop for a minute and consider whether continuing to argue will make things worse." "Why don't you regroup and come at this another time? If you continue to push it, I'm going to be less likely to change my mind."

**Disagreements vs. understanding.** Teens often get these two concepts confused. If you don't agree with them, they accuse you of not understanding. You will probably need to help them get the difference. Say, "No, I understand, son (and then summarize what they just said). I just don't agree with you."

**Enough is enough.** When you are done, make it clear that you are at the end of the discussion/argument. Tell them it's over ("That's it. Discussion over. I've made my decision.").

**Not only/but also.** Argumentative kids (by definition) aren't good at stopping when you indicate that the discussion is over. Help clarify for them just what they are risking by continuing to push the issue. "If you continue to argue with me about this, not only will I not change my mind, but you will also lose the use of your cell phone for the rest of the evening." Have the consequence sting just enough but not devastate.

**When to consult.** Is your kid argumentative regardless of your attempts to shape their behavior (when you do the kind of things suggested above)? Do they cuss you more than once? Do they constantly interrupt you at every point or sentence, despite your directing them to allow you to finish? Does their arguing always involve yelling? Do they regularly use name-calling as a response? Do they intentionally try to hurt the feelings of the person with whom they are arguing? These are signs that you may need to consult with a mental health professional for more intense intervention to turn their argumentativeness around.

Knowing how to (and when not to) argue effectively will serve your kid in every relationship. Most of us get no training in it. This will be your chance to give your kid a head start on refining this important social skill.

# KNOW YOUR KID

n order to really be able to stay connected to your teen, you need to know–really know–who they are and what matters to them. This chapter will help you to objectively evaluate how well you know your kid.

This chapter presents:

- A test for you to determine how well you know your kid

So, you think you know your kid? Yeah, right. You probably have one of those kids who comes in at night, sits at the end of your bed, and recounts to you all the things they did that day. Then your kid shares many of their deeply held, personal views and inner turmoil. If you are like the rest of us, however, perusing the following list of questions will make it glaringly obvious that there are whole areas of your kid's life that you know nothing about.

Also remember, as soon as you learn something about your kid, it's likely to change. It really is hard to track a moving target.

## WHAT'S A PARENT TO DO?

People keep coming up with lists of important things you should know about your kid. It is almost like some kind of ongoing mission to make parents feel inadequate, no matter how much they are doing for their kids. Here is a list of questions that will reveal just how little you really know about your kid. Scoring below 72 percent is failing.

(Or, on second thought, just forget about this list. It is probably just an exercise in futility. Ignorance really might be bliss.)

## SOCIAL

Who is your kid's best friend?

Does your kid feel liked by their peers?

Does your kid have a nickname?

What are the names, addresses, and cell phone numbers of your kid's closest friends?

Where do your kid and their friends like to hang out?

What is the information your kid posts on their social networking site (such as Facebook)?

## RELATIONSHIPS

Has your kid had their first crush? Who was it?

Has your kid been in love?

If your kid is dating someone, how serious is the relationship?

Has your kid had their first serious argument with a dating partner?

## PERSONAL

What is their most embarrassing moment?

What is your kid's biggest fear?

What would your kid pick if they could have anything in the world?

What really makes your kid angry?

What makes your kid really happy?

What does your kid worry most about?

What is your kid's most prized possession?

What kind of pet would your child prefer?

If your kid had three wishes, what would they wish for?

What would your kid say was their best talent?

Does your kid keep a diary? A blog?

## ACADEMIC AND INTELLECTUAL

When does your child prefer to do homework?

Who is your child's favorite teacher?

What is your kid's favorite subject in school?

What is the main source for your kid to find out what is happening in the world?

What would your kid say was the most important current political issue?

What does your kid think it will take for them to get into college?

## VALUES

What does your kid value most in other people?

What are your kid's core moral principles?

What is the biggest sacrifice your kid has made for someone else?

What would your kid say was the most important thing in their life?

What would your kid want to be remembered for as they look back on their life?

## FAMILY

What is your kid's biggest complaint about the family?

What embarrasses your kid most about you?

What gift from you does your kid cherish most?

What is your kid's most disliked chore?

What is your kid's favorite family occasion (Thanksgiving, annual vacation)?

What family obligation does your kid dislike the most (visiting relatives, dinner together)?

## ROLE MODELS

What person outside the family has most influenced your kid's life?

What public figure does your kid admire and why?

Who does your kid look up to among the people they know?

Who would your kid most like to be like at an adult?

## PHYSICAL ABILITIES

What is your kid's favorite physical activity?

What sport does your kid most enjoy?

Does your kid feel too small or too big for his age?

What does your kid like most about their body? Least?

## SEX

Has your kid kissed someone besides Great Aunt Bessie?

Has your kid ever made out (tongue and all)?

Has your kid ever viewed pornography?

Has your kid been involved in oral sex?

Has your kid had sex?

What are the conditions your kid thinks are necessary before having sex (first chance they get, wait 'til marriage, etc.)?

Is your kid committed to using contraception if they decide to have sex?

## ALCOHOL AND DRUGS

Does your kid plan on using alcohol or drugs?

Have they every used alcohol? Drugs?

Have they ever been drunk?

What drugs does your kid consider off limits?

## MUSIC AND ENTERTAINMENT

What is your kid's favorite kind of music?

Who is your kid's favorite musical artist?

What is your kid's favorite television show?

What movie would your kid watch over and over again?

What video game does your kid like the most?

## LEISURE

What would your kid consider a great vacation?

What is your kid's favorite way to chill?

What does your kid do for fun?

What non-school book has your child read most recently?

## ASPIRATIONS AND ACCOMPLISHMENTS

What are your kid's favorite and least favorite school subjects?

What is your kid's proudest accomplishment?

What has been the biggest disappointment in your kid's life this year?

What does your kid want to be when they grow up?

What does your kid think it takes to be successful?

## FOOD

What's your kid's favorite food?

What is your kid's favorite snack? Drink? Meal?

What foods does your kid hate?

(Parts of this list were adapted from *Families* magazine.)

# COMMUNICATION TECHNIQUES

## Part 1:
### Listening

I t may come as a surprise to learn that getting your teen to talk to you starts with listening—*you* listening. If you listen intently, there's a better chance your kid will keep talking.

This chapter describes:

- Important listening techniques
- How to ask follow up questions

Why do parents even try to talk to their teenagers? Kids think they know everything and look at you like they think you're stupid. They never take your advice. Their priorities are all wrong. Yet you can't just let them go through life with all that ignorance and naïveté.

So how do you get them to talk to you?

Theoretically, most parents really want to know their kids. Unfortunately, to really know them, you have to actually listen to what they are saying—unless, of course, you are a highly trained mental health professional with the ability to "know" a kid without having to waste all that time actually listening to them drone on and on.

Listening to your kid lays the groundwork for a closer relationship. It helps kids gain a clearer sense of their own worth. ("Someone actually cares what I think!") It also might help them learn to think for themselves instead of having others think for them and find their own voice.

## WHAT'S A PARENT TO DO?

Listening turns out to be really important, and it's more difficult than it seems. Here are some things to keep in mind.

**Be alert.** If you are going to listen, you have to recognize the signs that your kid is interested in talking. What are the signs? Do they ask you something that doesn't involve money or permission to leave the house? Have they actually spoken in your general direction? Are they in the same room with you? These should all be considered signs that your teen wants to engage in a long, detailed description of their current life circumstances. Jump on it!

**Be quiet.** To listen, you have to first shut up. Parents are constantly in the action mode: correcting, putting out fires, anticipating fires, guiding and punishing. Talking to your kid in this mode can stomp a conversation into the dust.

Listening requires you to be still and calm. You can't seem as though you are waiting to move on to the next thing, especially when listening to teenage boys. It takes them longer for their brain to move from one thought to the next; just when you think they have become paralyzed, they start up again. Be patient. Wait for at least three full minutes before you assume they have nothing more to add.

**Don't interrupt.** This would seem to be fairly obvious, but for most parents, it is easier said than done. You have all these interesting thoughts to share and all these relevant and amusing personal anecdotes you could recount. There are all these things your kid is wrong about that scream out to be corrected. Let it go. Let it go.

**Appear interested.** Listening requires you to indicate an interest in what your kid says. It helps if you are actually interested. But if you're not, you will need to be able to fake it. Here are some ways to give the appearance that you are actually interested in what your kid has to say.

- Eye contact is a sure sign of interest. It is a bit tricky with teens, though, because if you look right at them, they freak out ("What? You're *staring* at me again!"). So, you will need to practice the "glance and avert" technique. While they are talking, occasionally look at their face (preferably their nose and not directly into their eyes) and then glance upward and away, squinting your eyes ever so slightly as though you are contemplating what they are saying. Occasionally, you can also add a pursing of the lips. Repeat.

- Kids can read a great deal from your posture. For example, throwing your head back and letting it roll it from side to side as if you're suffering does not communicate interest. Leaning in, sitting forward, and cocking your head sideways are all subtle but universally recognized signs of interest.

- How your body is oriented also communicates your interest in the person speaking. Are you turned toward them? Do you visually track them as they move? Do you follow as they begin to travel? All these can be ways to show you are interested in what they are talking about.

- When you are interested in someone, you will naturally give them your full attention. This means not engaging in anything else that requires your attention. Watching TV, surfing the internet, or reading can give the impression that you aren't that interested in what your kid has to say. On the other hand, doing something that is rote and uncomplicated (like loading the dish washer, driving, walking, putting on makeup, raking leaves, etc.) can actually help by providing a moment for sharing while avoiding making it a big deal.

- Affirmations and sub-vocalizations can also indicate interest. Nodding, interested facial expressions (smiling as opposed to scowling), and responses like "Uh huh," "Really?" and

"Right" can communicate your interest in what your teen is saying. Responses like "Did you say something?" "OMG," "That is FAScinating!"—not so much.

- Finally, don't overdo the interest thing. It is important to show your kid you are interested in what they have to say, but being too interested isn't cool. It can make the kid overly self-conscious (which, during early adolescence, doesn't take much). Being self-conscious can make a teen shut down. Be interested, but not *too* interested. (Nobody said this was going to be easy.)

**Ask questions.** Surprisingly, asking questions is an effective technique for making it seem like you are listening. But remember, these are not the interrogation questions that are a parent's stock in trade. ("Where were you last night?" "Where did you get this?")

Listening questions take a couple of forms.

- **Detail**. Questions that ask for more detail are a clear indication that you are actually listening (how else would you know what details to ask for?) and, therefore that you are actually interested in what your kid is saying.

- **Elaboration**. Asking your kid to expand on what they were talking about, as though you want to know even more about it, gives them the impression that the topic is of interest to you.

- **Comment**. "Is that even possible?" "How did you manage to figure that out?" Questions can also communicate admiration and amazement. They can even be compliments.

- **Understanding**. You can also use questions to show that you actually understand what your kid is talking about. ("Do you mean … ?")

**Empathize and validate.** Demonstrating empathy for what your kid is feeling and validating their opinions or observations is another way to make your kid feel like they are being heard. This can be really hard to pull off when your kid is talking about something boring, naïve, inane, or completely obvious. Techniques to use include statements like "That's really/confusing/tough/illegal/etc.) or "Anyone would feel that way/be mad/have tried to hide from the police/etc. in that situation."

The art of listening requires you to treat someone as though they are a person you are actually interested in knowing. It can take a while to transition into this view of your teen, so start early. Once you have the listening thing down, it is time to move on to the art of actual conversations.

# COMMUNICATION TECHNIQUES

## Part 2:
### When There Isn't Any Communication

Improving communication between you and your teen depends on the *quality* (not the quantity) of your conversations.

This chapter provides:

- Suggestions for improving your communication with a teen who doesn't really talk to you

- Ideas about communicating without talking

What if interactions with your teen are mildly negative, relatively neutral, or even positive—but with an almost complete absence of conversation about anything that isn't practical or instrumental (such as "Can I borrow the car, can I have some money, can you take me to Sarah's house, can I buy this shirt, what are we having for supper, yes, no, etc.)?

## WHAT'S A PARENT TO DO?

**Keep your goal in mind.** The goal is to get your teenager to actually talk about meaningful (or just interesting) things. That means the challenge is to improve your relationship, have them share something of themselves, and allow you to know more about them—in other words, to get them to *talk* to you. Commenting, observing, asking, complimenting, and encouraging will help with this. Lecturing, educating, investigating, criticizing, correcting, and interrogating are directly opposed to this goal. Never try to talk to them and correct them at the same time.

**Know your kid.** If you are going to have a conversation with your kid, you need details. Begin to gather information from direct observation, from your brief conversations, or from other members of the family. Personal information enables you to ask relevant questions. Who are their closest friends? ("Is anything going on with Scott lately?") What level have they reached on their current video game? ("Show me where you are on *Call of Duty*.") Who is their favorite musician? ("I heard that STS9 song again. I think it's starting to grow on me.") Knowing what's important to your kid will help enable you to initiate conversations with the chance of it going somewhere.

**Time it right.** Look for a convenient and casual time to initiate a conversation. Certain moments are windows of opportunity: when you're in a good mood, during dinner, after they have had a success, when they can't escape (like in the car), when they want something, and bedtime. The worst times are when you or they are tired, furious, or busy; when they are emotional; as they are leaving the house; and when their friends are around.

**Set the stage.** Look for situations that are well-suited for talking. For example, girls may be more open to talking while curling up on the couch, lounging on the bed, or putting on makeup. Boys, on the other hand, can feel trapped if they are still. Consider engaging teens in conversation when they are riding in the car, looking for something to eat in the kitchen, or while listening to music (*their* music. OK! OK! How important is communication to you? You will have to make some sacrifices). What's the perfect time? Dinner. If you don't have dinner on a regular basis (two or more times a week) where everyone has to sit down together, it's time to reevaluate your family's eating habits. Finally, remember to avert your gaze. Talking face-to-face with teens is the conversational equivalent of staring at the sun, so position yourself side-by-side or at an angle.

**Keep it short and sweet.** Expect to have a series of brief exchanges with your kid at this phase. You want to jump in and then get out relatively quickly. The goal is to let your attempts at conversation build and expand over time. When you don't have a history of conversation with your kid, a formal sit-down to discuss America's geopolitical position in the world probably won't work—unless your kid starts the conversation. And if that happens, it means that you may not be smart enough to have conversations with a kid like this.

**Don't push.** Allow the conversation to have its natural length. You've got time. Let it work to your advantage. Small, individual conversations will accumulate. If you and your kid usually don't talk, your kid will notice when you start trying to have conversations with them. Unless they are absolutely, ragefully mad at you, they will begin to feel a little guilty about ignoring your attempts to connect with them—especially if you kind of sigh and walk away slump-shouldered but without saying anything. Quiet guilt induction is a time-honored parenting technique. Don't be afraid to use it when appropriate.

**Be specific.** "How was your day?" doesn't work. It is too general, and it reflects no real knowledge about what might be going on in your kid's life. In fact, it's such a generic question that it can sound like you aren't really interested. (The sad thing is that, most of the time, we ask our kids this question when we actually *are* interested.) When you make comments or ask questions, make them specific: "How was math today?" "How are things going with John and Stephanie?" "I saw that *As I Lay Dying* is coming to town." This is why you need to know your kid (see Know Your Kid chapter).

**Share.** If you want them to talk to you about their life, talk to them about your life. This doesn't mean launching into a detailed description of some specific aspect of your boring, irrelevant career. "You know what happened today at work? Accounting got my payroll corrections all screwed up and I had to ..." (Can you hear the snoring?) Unless you have some kind of really cool job like being a band promoter or a firefighter, you should talk about personal things, topics of interest, or even ... emotions. "I got really frustrated today at my boss ..." "I read about this new ..." "You wouldn't believe ..." 'Have you ever heard about ...?"

Interest breeds interest.

**Talk by not talking.** Don't underestimate the power of just spending time with your kid. It says something that you want to just hang out in the same space with them. This is particularly useful for boys. Watch TV or a movie with them. Sit in and observe during a video game (but don't look at them; keep your eyes on the screen). Read or surf the net in the vicinity of your kid while they do their homework. Take them (and their friends) to activities. This gets them used to you being in physical proximity (a technique wranglers use to tame wild mustangs). It is only a matter of time before someone actually says something (see Set the stage, above). Just remember that wild animals can lash out at first, so start slowly and give them plenty of room.

**Be patient and persistent.** There are many things your kid needs to learn on the road to adulthood. It would be great if they learned some of it from you. Dedicate yourself to systematically improving the length and quality of your conversations with your kid. Take your time and don't give up. The change in your kid may be subtle at first. Look for them to spontaneously talk to you about something in their life or answer your question or comment with something other than a grunt. Build on that. Once you start consistently having brief, pleasant, and meaningful exchanges, you may selfishly want more.

# COMMUNICATION TECHNIQUES

## Part 3:
### When There Isn't Enough Communication

Y ou recognize the importance of listening and you're pretty clear on how to get conversations going when communication is non-exis-tent. So now your kid will talk to you but still doesn't share more deeply personal experiences, feelings, or thoughts—and you want more.

This section provides:

- Suggestions for improving the quality of conversations you already have with your kid

- Knowing your limits

## WHAT'S A PARENT TO DO?

**Raise topics of interest to them.** Everyone likes to talk about things they are interested in. You need to be able to talk about things that interest your kids, which is something you have already mastered after following the suggestions in the previous chapters on communication. Bring topics up. Ask about them. Comment on them.

**Have deep conversations.** It is more difficult for teens to avoid talking about important issues or situations. Ask your kid what they think about things that matter, such as relationships, emotions, ideas, issues, and events. Offer your opinion about important issues. Don't shy away from controversial topics. Just remember that your goal is to engage them in conversation not to "win" an argument so ...

**Talk, don't lecture, inform, educate, correct, criticize, or drone on and on.** Keep parenting communications separate from conversations with your child. If you mix them, communication can come to a halt. This does not mean you should stop being a parent or begin treating your child like your peer. Just address parenting issues at another time.

**Questions before answers.** A common mistake we make as parents is thinking that our kids actually want to know what we think. They *need* to know what you think; it's just they aren't necessarily interested. On the other hand, they often want you to know what they think. Be sure to ask your kid what they think before you provide the definitive answer to whatever topic is under discussion. A simple "What do you think?" can go a long way toward continuing and deepening a conversation.

**Don't always know the answer.** The companion strategy to asking questions before you answer is to not always have the answer—even if you know the answer. Nobody likes a know-it-all, even if you know quite a lot. Make opportunities for your teen to know the answer. Express some uncertainty in your opinions ("I'm not sure but ..." "It could be ..."). A strategically placed "I hadn't really thought of that!" or "I think you're right" can be a powerful inducement for your kid to share the deep insights and profound wisdom they have been keeping to themselves.

**Validate before you respond.** Your kid is looking for your approval, even while getting ticked off that they want it. Make sure they get it. Compliment them on their ideas. Admire their courage. Confirm the quality of their reasoning. Empathize with their dilemmas. Sympathize with their distress. Be supportive.

**Listen.** Don't interrupt. Show interest. Give your undivided attention. (See Listening chapter for help.) Really listen to them. Do they want you to help them solve a problem? Do they want you to just be with them while they think something through? Do they want to share some of themselves with you? You have to listen to find out.

**Notice changes.** Are they happier than usual? Are they quieter than usual? Are they more surly than usual? Changes indicate the occurrence of a noteworthy event or experience. Comment on these changes to indicate you are paying attention and are available to talk ("You look kind of down today. Everything OK?" "You sure are bouncy. Something good must have happened.").

**Ask questions.** Questions can be very useful in furthering a conversation. They can elicit information ("What did y'all do last night?"). They can indicate actual interest ("But why does that part go there?"). They can express admiration ("How did you pull that off?"). They can lead and guide ("Do you think ... ?" "Is it possible ... ?" "Is there a way you could ... ?"). They can hide a suggestion or request ("I was wondering if you might ... "). They can even masquerade as a statement ("If it were me, I'd be upset!" followed by the "Don't you think?" raising of the eyebrows).

**Admit mistakes.** Acknowledging your own imperfections and screw-ups can make you appear more human and approachable. It is also a wonderful teaching moment about dealing with problems. Personal conversations often involve concerns about problems or difficulties. Admitting mistakes shows your kid that you can understand and have some compassion for what is happening to them.

**Give advice and problem-solve.** Make suggestions. Otherwise, what good are you? Help them generate solutions when they need them. Give your opinion and explain why you think it. That's what being a parent is about. That is part of the value of conversations about problems or ideas. If your kid isn't taking your suggestions so well, try changing your approach. You might try asking for an invitation to share your thoughts ("Would you like to know what I think?"), instructing through story-telling ("I did the same thing once, so I can tell you what won't work ... "), personalizing it ("It seems to me you might be able to ... "), or softening the presentation ("Have you thought about trying ... ?").

**Keep confidences.** If your kid shares private information, keep it private. Yes, it may be a funny, embarrassing adolescent incident that friends and relatives would enjoy. Yes, if you were that other kid's parents, you would want them to tell you. Don't do it. Your kid needs to know that you can keep things between the two of you. If you can't keep something confidential (because you need to keep the other parent informed, because it involves danger to the child or someone else, because it's about abuse or neglect, etc.), let your kid know you will need to share the information. "I don't feel right keeping this from your father—but I'll make sure that he doesn't freak out."

**Don't freak out.** If you are going to have your kid talk to you about important things, you have to be able to handle it. Screaming and wailing "No! No! No!" or fainting and chewing on your arm won't encourage your child to share again in the future. Keep your cool until it is safe to lose it (when you're by yourself or with people who support you or in your therapy session).

**Reward communication.** "I really enjoyed talking." "This was really nice." "It means a lot that you talked this over with me." "It's nice that you're getting old enough for us to be able to talk like this." "You know I love you, don't you?" "There's twenty dollars in it for you every time we have one of these conversations." (Not!) Find ways to let your kid know how much you value these interactions.

**Leave them wanting more.** Don't overstay your welcome. If they show signs of distraction such as the trapped eye dart (frequent glances toward the exits), bring the conversation to a close, get up, and wander off. Be sure to have an exit comment. "Well, hopefully this helped." "You've probably need to get going." "Let me know what happens." "I love you." When you are the one who stops the conversation, it shows your kid they won't be trapped in the endless torment of communication hell if they start a conversation with you.

**Follow up.** If your conversation was about some upcoming event or some situation that occurred, find out what happened. Assume they will want to talk about how things have progressed. Each conversation provides more information about your kid and their interests. Use it.

**Recognize your limits.** There are some parents who can't stop themselves from lecturing. There are some kids who just won't talk about things, even to their friends. Don't give up. Take the long view. It can take time and persistence to make things better.

Sometimes, even when you do everything right, your kid still won't open up to you. The best you can do is to keep trying. Show that you are interested and hope they find a reasonable adult they will open up to.

# COMMUNICATION TECHNIQUES

## Part 4:
### When All You Do Is Argue

I t can be really difficult to have a conversation with someone who is always yelling at you (or who you are always yelling at). Sometimes, the relationship with your teen can evolve into a series of screaming matches interspersed with periods of sullen, monosyllabic responses.

This section introduces:

- Strategies you can use to deal specifically with continual conflict with your kid

- Ways to defuse potential arguments

"Suppertime, sweetheart!"

"I'M COMING! WHY ARE YOU ALWAYS YELLING AT ME ABOUT SOMETHING?!"

"How was school today?"

"Fine."

"How was the test in math?"

"Fine."

(Sigh) "How did English go?"

"FINE! FINE! FINE! DO YOU HAVE TO KNOW WHAT HAPPENED EVERY MINUTE OF MY DAY?!"


"It's time to do your homework."

"I've DONE my homework!"

"Don't take that tone with me! Get down here right now!"

"I HATE THIS FAMILY! I'M MOVING OUT AS SOON AS I'M EIGHTEEN!"

"THAT'S FINE BY ME! I'LL HELP YOU PACK!"

## WHAT'S A PARENT TO DO?

Begin by doing some things to improve the general quality of the interactions between you and your kid.

**Take a meeting.** Before you try to address the unsatisfactory nature of communication between you and your kid, sit down with them and talk about it. Schedule a time convenient for both of you and give them a heads-up about the topic. Don't try to do this when you are in the middle of a conflict, or when they already have something planned, or when you only have fifteen minutes between activities.

Take some time to identify what you want to work on with them. How would you like your relationship to be? What would they like your relationship to be like? What needs to happen to reduce the conflict? Be sure to talk about what you need to change about yourself in addition to the long list of things they need to change.

Prepare yourself for the possibility that your kid will come up with something idiotic ("I'm sixteen years old! I should be able to come and go as I please."). Get the conversation started and you can correct the irrational expectations later. It may take more than one discussion, so just take it as far as it goes or until it starts to get too tense. Always end by having something specific you are each going to try to do differently. Schedule a follow-up after a specified period of time to see how it is going.

**5-to-1.** Research on marital relationships has shown that if the ratio of positive to negative interactions falls below five to one, the marriage is likely to disintegrate. This five-to-one rule is also a good formula to use if you are having a lot of conflict with your kid. Commit yourself to having pleasant, agreeable interactions with your kid, no matter how difficult they try to make it. This does not mean being all nicey-nicey. It means making sure that your kid has some positive experiences with you in between all the parental directing, correcting and punishing.

**Silent quality time.** Arrange times with your teen where you are just together in the same space. Watch TV. Sit with them as they do their homework while you work on your own stuff. Make time to drive them to their events or activities, even to school. Regular, ongoing time spent in close proximity can serve to diffuse bubbling tension. But at these moments, *don't talk to them.* If you want to talk to them, do it some other time. Don't act all uncomfortable either. Your job is to change the emotional tone of your time together. You have to be impervious to their natural ability to set you off about something by being surly, huffy, or non-responsive.

**Peace offerings.** Ask if they want a soda. Bring something for them when you go to get a snack for yourself. Pick up a little something for them when you are out running errands. Small, inexpensive gifts can carry a powerful message: I'm thinking about you and trying to reach out. If they are a jerk about it, look them directly in the eye for about three seconds with a mildly hurt expression on your face. Then turn and walk away without comment. Guilt them, baby! If you react badly, you just give them a way to justify their jerkiness to themselves.

There are also some specific strategies that can interrupt the negativity in your interactions, as well as to set some limits on your kid.

**Time-outs.** When emotions get heated, communication turns into argument and conflict. There are plenty of times when taking a break to chill out is all that is needed to get the discussion back on track. Time-outs work great, as long as you make sure you include a couple of key components.

- First, anyone can call a time-out, but they have to call it on themselves ("I need a time-out."). If you call it on someone else ("You need a time-out, buster!"), then you will start to argue about whether or not they need a time-out.

- Second, everyone has to honor the time-out. This means you. If your kid tries to continue, make it costly ("If you don't honor this time-out, you will be grounded from everything for a week!").

- Third, everyone has to separate and go to their respective corners. Separate rooms, different areas of the same room, bathroom break—whatever works.

- Fourth, a specific time has to be designated when everyone will reconvene and continue the argument ("I need fifteen minutes!" "We will have to get back together at six."). Be specific. Get everyone's agreement on when to get back together.

- Finally, restart at the agreed-upon time. One of the biggest problems with honoring time-outs is the expectation that, once you stop, the issue will be ignored. Nothing overrides continuing the argument at the agreed upon time.

- Go over these steps before you use the time-out (maybe during one of those meetings to talk about trying to improve communication). It is most likely to work when everyone knows how it works.

**Do-overs.** Give your kid the chance to try it again. Let them know ahead of time that both of you are going to try to fix the problem of their inappropriate responses, together. They will get one chance to do it over. If not, the ax will fall. Have an agreed-upon phrase you will use to let them know this is their chance for a do-over: "You might want to say that another way." "Why don't you try that again? Because things are about to go really badly for you." If they change their tune, act as though the other response didn't happen. If they just repeat the inappropriate or provocative response, nail their butts to the wall! ("Alright! I guess it's worth it to you to lose ... ") Then, try again the next time. (If things have not improved within two weeks, it's time to consult with a mental health professional.)

**Conversation before privileges.** For some nonverbal kids, you may have to tie things they want to having conversations with you. If they want to go out and do something with their friends, if they want to play video games, if they want to have access to their cell phone, they have to communicate with you. This can jump-start conversations, as long as you don't require an extended interaction. Try using something like the following.

**3Q/3A.** Sometimes, teens won't answer with more than single words because they're afraid that, if they give any details, it will open the flood gate of parental questions. So, try making a deal with them that you will keep your questions to a total of three in any one interaction (with one follow-up allowed per question). They, on the other hand, must provide answers composed of at least three complete sentences (with nouns, verbs, prepositional phrases, and all that grammar stuff). Once they provide answers to the three questions, you agree to stop (no matter how curious you are about other aspects of their lives). You will have to wait until the next opportunity (which should be no sooner than three hours—or better yet, the next day). Knowing there is a limit to the number of questions a parent will ask is often worth the trade-off of having to actually answer questions. Don't be too much of a stickler for the length of the three-sentence answers, as long as they aren't "yes," "no," "fine," etc.

**Be realistic.** If your kid doesn't really have to deal with you because they live with their other parent, you are severely limited. If your kid is seventeen years old and there have been five years of unending conflict between the two of you, turning things around is not likely to occur quickly or easily (and by the way, consult with a mental health professional on this one). Recognize the real challenges to repairing your relationship. Know your personal challenges. Know your kid's limitations. You may have to change your time line (but not your goals).

**Don't give up.** You can give up and be bitter and self-righteous, or you can take up the challenge, knowing it will take longer and might not even work. If it isn't worth it to you, so be it. If it is, suck it up and get back in there!

# TALKING ABOUT YOUR PAST

## Part 1:
### How to Decide

A t some point, it is likely your kid will either have heard something about your past from a family member or will just want to know about what you were like when you were younger, out of simple curiosity.

This chapter:

- Presents important issues to consider

- Identifies how your personal information can affect your teen

"Hey, Mom, did you ever smoke pot?"

"Dad, did you and Mom have sex before you were married?"

"Uncle Jeff says you got arrested once. Is that true?" (Answers to these questions are at the end of the chapter.)

Eventually, your kids will realize that you are a human being—that you were even a teenager once. Wait! If you were a teenager, you could actually have made poor choices or gotten into serious trouble! (Thanks to grandparents, uncles, and aunts, some of your exploits may already have been revealed.)

# WHAT'S A PARENT TO DO?

**Honesty.** It is important to establish and maintain an honest relationship with your child (with everyone, actually). Being honest doesn't mean that you tell them everything they want to know. It means that you don't mischaracterize, mislead, or lie to them. If you don't want to answer the question, try something like, "There are lots of things I have done in my life I may talk to you about one day when you're older. I'm not ready to talk about that with you right now."

**Truth.** Truth is one of those tricky concepts within a family. Secrets and lies can do profound damage to the fabric of the family. If you deny truth, you may set in motion a chain of events that can tear your family apart. Kids have a way of ferreting out secrets. They can often tell that something is going on—they just may not know what it is. This leads them to speculate about it themselves, and that rarely ends well. Stick to the truth. If the truth is so devastating that you are concerned it may tear the family apart, it is time to consult with a professional to consider the best course of action.

**Personal comfort.** Talking about honesty and truth brings up the issue of whether or not you are comfortable even talking about a topic. Don't back yourself into a corner by starting something you aren't ready for. It is very important to make sense of your own actions before you try to talk to your kids about them. Consider talking through some of your more upsetting experiences with someone you trust. Therapy might help. Remember, one lesson to teach your kids is that everyone is allowed to determine their personal boundaries, including what personal information they will or will not share.

**Moral development.** The value of being older and more experienced is supposed to be that you have learned a few things about life. Ask yourself if talking to your kids about your past furthers their moral development and personal growth, or helps them through a rough part of their own lives.

**Learning from others' mistakes.** Can your kids learn from your mistake? Talking about difficulties you have encountered and troubles you have experienced provides an opportunity to share a cautionary tale ("This is what can happen to you if you make poor choices."). It also personalizes and opens up a conversation between you and your adolescent that sets the stage for more mature interactions. These conversations can be a way to have an intimate discussion rather than a lecture. Maybe you can keep your kid from having to learn the hard way.

**TMI (Too Much Information).** Consider your child's developmental level when deciding to answer. You can actually freak your kid out if you provide more information than they really want. If a kid asks whether you have ever smoked pot, they are not necessarily asking about when you were a seventeen-year-old Dead Head or spent a summer of free love as you followed Phish on their cross-country tour. You might want to start slowly and build up to that. A good initial response would be, "Why do you ask?" Remember that talking to your kid about issues that would normally be discussed between two adults helps foster trust and pride in being seen as mature enough to handle the discussion. But be sure your kid can keep private matters private.

**Cost/benefit analysis.** What kind of damage could the information do to your kid? There are some hard life truths that kids may not be able to bear. Consider whether your child has experienced enough to be capable of putting the information into perspective.

**Bombshells.** What will happen if your transgressions or past life mistakes suddenly come to light? Is what you're about to share so different from the ways you present yourself now that the discovery will seriously damage your relationship with your child? Think about the tragic circumstances of public figures whose fall from grace for a transgression is more about the contrast between their pronouncements and the sin committed, rather than the sin itself. It may be time to begin shaving some height off that pedestal you're on—but be aware that it might change your relationship with your child.

**Open secrets.** Consider asking yourself, "Will some big mouth in the family tell them anyway?" It is helpful for you to use information about your past as an opportunity to teach, deepen your relationship, or model how to overcome past moral lapses and balance risk-taking with a consideration of long-term consequences. It is better if you can put the information into perspective for your kid rather than having them form their own conclusions when they hear about it through family gossip.

Answers to the questions at the beginning of this chapter: a) "You're grounded! Go to your room," b) "How could you think such a thing about your sainted mother?" and c) "Your Uncle Jeff is jealous of me and will lie right to you face! You're not allowed to ever speak to him again!" (Ways to answer these questions seriously can be found in the next chapter.)

# TALKING ABOUT
# YOUR PAST

## Part 2:
### What to Say (and Not Say)

If you decide to share stories of your youth (and youthful indiscretions) with your teen, it's important to have some limits.

This chapter discusses:

- What to discuss and what to avoid in a conversation about your past

- The best ways to reveal (and not reveal) personal information

## WHAT'S A PARENT TO DO?

**Topics.** Sharing information about your colorful past with your teens will be more or less complicated, depending on how wild (or difficult) your past has been. Less complicated issues to address would be alcohol or drug use, dating experiences, and your academic record. More thought needs to go into discussions about sexual history, serious alcohol and drug use, or other past experiences that significantly impacted your life. A quick consultation with a mental health professional (or a good reference book) might help you shape your message about more complicated topics.

**The Question First rule.** When your kid asks a question that is suspicious or uncomfortable, try using the time honored Question First rule: answer the question with a question. "Why would you like to know?" "What's going on?" This will give you time to think and gather information about what underlies the question so you can determine what level of answer is appropriate.

**I don't wanna!** OK, what if you decide not to share personal information. Four classic techniques are refusal, distraction, misdirection and changing the topic.

- **Outright refusal.** The most straightforward way to communicate that you are not willing to discuss a topic with your kid is to refuse to discuss it. Be careful, though. If the question comes from a genuine desire to know more about you or to put their own experiences in perspective, refusal can be experienced as rejecting and harsh, however gently done. You may also lose an important moment of candor from your kid. If you decide to refuse, it helps to provide some information about why you won't discuss it. "That's really personal and I'm not sure I'm ready to share that with you yet." Notice the use of the word "yet." That suggests there may be a time in the future when you consider them mature enough to discuss the issue. Another version of this is to tell them directly that they will need to be a little older before you are comfortable sharing this part of your life with them. If you follow this with a "Tell me what you have been thinking about this issue," it will reduce the sting of your refusal and might keep the conversation going.

- **Distraction.** Making your teen forget the question can be very effective ("I have cancer." "Here's a hundred bucks, now scram.").

- **Misdirection.** You can give the impression of answering, but without giving any information. Misdirection has a long, time-honored place in parent responses. This would involve immediately launching into a long-winded, irrelevant story about an extremely boring period of your childhood.

- **Topic change**. Finally, you can involve them in a relevant conversation about another subject. ("Have you cleaned your room yet?")

Once you have decided to answer your teen's question, it is useful to consider what level of detail you want to provide.

- **Short and sweet.** Sometimes the best answer is the briefest answer. ("Yes," "No," or "Go ask your mother.") You will be surprised sometimes how little your kid actually wants to know; make them work for it.

- **Minimal detail.** The next level up is to provide some detail with your direct answer—but as little as possible. "Yes, but it was a different time back then." "No, a good friend died from an overdose so I *hate* drugs, because it's like murder!"

- **Teachable moment.** Then, there is the best and most difficult answer; using their question as an opportunity to influence their beliefs and future decision-making by answering their question. Using a teachable moment can help your teen view you as someone to go to with big questions and decisions.

**Acknowledge hesitancy.** It is useful to precede your discussion by admitting to any hesitancy you have about sharing personal information with them. This signals them that they will need to take this seriously and be sensitive to your feelings. It also provides the context for teaching them how to talk with someone about very personal information—in other words, how to have intimate conversations.

**Define the purpose.** Tell them *why* you're telling them. This is where you mention things like having them learn from your mistakes, showing you know something of difficulties and temptations, etc.

**Require privacy.** Be clear with your kid about what aspects of your conversation should be considered private (meaning they cannot share the information with siblings, neighbors, friends, etc.). This is a great opportunity to address this crucial element of intimate conversations and relationships. Your kid must learn to honor the wishes of intimate social partners in keeping private things private.

**Expect maturity.** One sign of a mature, intimate relationship is that you don't use personal information shared in confidence to manipulate someone. ("You smoked weed when you were a teenager! You're such a hypocrite!") Let your kid know that it will go badly for them if they try to use personal information against you later. An excellent way for your kid to learn what happens when you violate a confidence in this way is to make them suffer. It's better for them to learn this lesson now, before it poisons a future relationship.

**Less is more.** Start with less detail and let your teen lead you into greater depth with questions. Once they realize you are willing to talk about your personal life, questions will often surface sporadically; it's kind of like having a single conversation in pieces across a week. You can signal your willingness to share with them by asking if they have any other questions. Pay attention to what your kids are asking. Their choice of questions may be an indication that they are experiencing pressure (either internally or externally) to do something they are uncomfortable with or that they are venturing into risky territory. Above all, let the reason you are sharing guide how much detail you provide. Unfiltered stories about your past are for your adult children, not for teenagers.

**Don't glamorize.** When you are sharing information, be careful not to get so caught up in reliving your glory days that you glamorize them. The benefit of age is being able to put things into perspective. Providing perspective on your own teenage experiences can help keep your kid from having to learn everything by experience. (OK, you can dream, can't you?)

**It wasn't all misery.** It's also important to actually acknowledge the fun of doing things that adults might not approve of. Don't make it all gloom and doom. Part of the lesson to be imparted is how to strike a balance between risk-taking and personal responsibility.

**Lessons learned.** What did you learn from those long ago experiences? What do you want your teen to learn from the stories you tell about yourself? This is a teachable moment; take advantage of it.

**Keeping secrets.** Privacy is one thing; secrecy is another. Teens should not be burdened with family secrets. A secret creates a bond between you, but it is a twisted chain that is bound to snap. If your teen is the first person to whom you reveal deeply personal information, or if you are sharing personal information with them that you haven't shared with a spouse or adult friend, you have gone too far. Similarly, if you share deeply personal information about others without their permission, you have gone too far.

The information needs to be helpful to *them*, not to you. If your teen has uncovered a potentially devastating or disturbing secret, it's time to consult with a mental health professional. You will need some guidance on how to help them negotiate this complicated situation.

Remember, the only time you *have* to say exactly the right thing is if you only have one shot at it. Keep those lines of communication open.

# DATING, RELATIONSHIPS, AND SEX ISSUES

# PRE-DATING
# RELATIONSHIP RULES

When should teens be allowed to date? What's normal? It is important to clarify your views about this before it becomes an issue.

This chapter looks at:

• The stages leading up to one-on-one dating

• Rules for pre-dating

As they are in so many areas of life, teens are certain that they are perfectly capable of handling relationships on their own if you will just get out of their way, thank you very much. Adolescence is a time when kids need to learn a lot about close, intimate relationships.

## WHAT'S A PARENT TO DO?

Twelve-year-olds are in no way equipped to talk to someone of the opposite sex, let alone have a mature dating relationship—regardless of what they may think. Seventeen-year-olds, on the other hand, are ready to pursue (and are often desperate for) relationships with just that kind of intimacy. It turns out there is a sequence of phases teens go through from early to late adolescence that helps them build each step toward ultimately establishing a mature, emotionally intimate relationship as an adult.[1]

---

1    This discussion is based on the development of typical, heterosexual dating relationships. The fundamental nature of relationships between people does not differ based on the gender of their beloved

When parents know something about these phases, it enables them to set boundaries that can help their kids develop relationship skills while also protecting them from being thrown prematurely (or rushing headlong) into situations they aren't yet prepared for. For these efforts, a parent will be seen as a prude, out of touch, fascist, bitter and jealous of the kind of love you can never understand, and a monster. So what's new?

On the other hand, parents who set boundaries will be able to help their teen keep some kind of balance in life as well as minimizing the kinds of decisions that can lead to lifelong responsibilities.

**Same-gender groups.** In the fifth and sixth grades, kids remain almost exclusively in same-gender groups when relating to the opposite sex. While there is a lot of long-distance scoping out of the opposite sex, kids this age aren't equipped or predisposed to deal directly with their counterparts. There is a lot for kids this age to learn about the differences between boy and girl communication.

Communication between girls and boys begins through a third party (usually a girlfriend of the girl). Even hand-holding can seem overwhelming at this phase. Kissing, and especially anything more, is way beyond their ability to manage. Friends continue to be the most important close relationships during this phase.

At this age, parents should make sure that kids stay in fairly large (three or more of each gender) mixed groups of boys and girls so that each has the protection of their own herd. Smaller groups can create discomfort and force kids to interact beyond their skill level. Group activities should only occur in very structured, public situations (bowling, skating, movies, etc.) with adult monitoring. While kids may "go steady," nothing even resembling a serious rela-

---

or their own sexual orientation. However, the tremendous influence of socio-cultural factors on the development of non-heterosexual relationships results in minor to major differences in the development of these non-normative dating and intimate relationships. You can find resources about non-heterosexual kids and their relationships on the Reference page located on the book website.

tionship should be occurring at this age. Make it easy for them by making it clear that they are not allowed to go on dates until they are sixteen.

**Mixed-gender groups.** Seventh- and eighth-grade teens are beginning to be interested in the opposite sex. Puberty is beginning to unfold, so they feel compelled to begin to figure out how to relate to this alien—yet fascinating—species. However, there is not a lot that boys and girls have in common at this age. The interests, verbal abilities, and same-sex socialization of boys and girls have been very different. During the previous phase, they each did a lot of watching and speculating about the opposite sex. Now they will need to learn how to talk to each other, and it won't go smoothly at first.

The best way to learn how to communicate with the opposite sex, with the least amount of embarrassment, is to interact as a moderately-sized mixed group of girls and boys. Girls will be frustrated at boys' inability to talk, and boys will be frustrated at not having a clue how to initiate or respond to girls.

At this age, there will be a few brave (and hormonal) souls who will attempt to date. Nevertheless, friends continue to be more important than boyfriends or girlfriends. Activities will consist of hanging out where members of each sex will trade off making brief attempts to talk and interact. Boys will mostly show off physically and girls will mostly stand back, whisper to each other, and laugh.

Parents can facilitate this phase of relationship development by limiting their child's activities to mixed groups of kids (odd numbers of five or more are ideal, to minimize the pressure to pair off). The groups should interact in public places during daylight hours with adults monitoring from the sidelines. Any nighttime activities should be time limited, structured, and highly supervised. You don't want "early blooming" kids jumping to a higher level of intimacy.

Leaving kids this age unsupervised for long periods of time (more than an hour or so), even at the mall, can be an invitation to trouble. It is also not a good idea for teens at this age to spend "date-like" time with their boyfriend/girlfriend; no coming over to the house (or going over to their house) to watch movies, no having them over to dinner, no treating them like they are anything like a couple. There is much they have to learn about how to communicate before that kind of intimacy should be encouraged.

**Pairing off within mixed-sex groups.** Teens in ninth and tenth grade are able to have more genuine interactions with the opposite sex after time spent safely working on these skills in the preceding mixed-group phase. They have just entered the world of high school, where everything is possible. They are now completely grown up and they still have no real responsibilities! Dating begins to be a real interest, though there is still much they have to learn (and to control) for relationships to be healthy.

While mixed-sex groups continue to be important, couples will increasingly begin to pair off within a mixed group. Friends continue to be equally important to a girlfriend or boyfriend. The desire for a relationship is great enough to overwhelm any other interests or priorities in many kids this age. But serious relationships now can throw development in other areas off track.

Parents of teens this age can help keep a relationship in perspective by requiring their kids to do things in groups of at least three people, as opposed to doing things as a couple. One-on-one dating should be postponed until they are at least sixteen years old. Instead, teen couples at this age should do things together with friends; school events, church, movies, hanging at the park, videos at the house, etc.

Day and nighttime activities are more appropriate for this age group, but mixed boy-and-girl overnight parties or access to late-night private places are bad ideas. It is also important to set limits on the time spent in the company of a girlfriend or boyfriend; the more time spent continually together, the greater the perceived intimacy, which can lead to physical intimacy.

In general, it is important to set limits on the length of unsupervised time boys and girls can spend together. It is a good idea to lay eyes on them every two hours or so. When they are together, require your kid to spend time hanging out with their girl/boyfriend in the public areas of your house (rather than always at someone else's house or in a private room in your house). Insist that your kid balance time spent with their girl/boyfriend with other activities and relationships. Part of maintaining that balance is to make sure your kid sometimes does things *without* their girl/boyfriend.

This discussion of the developmental phases of teenage dating brings you right up to the phase of actual dating as a couple.

# DATING RULES

When your teen is old enough to start dating, they will need a very clear idea about the rules.

This chapter covers:

- Dating and the importance of emotional intimacy
- Rules for dating that help your kid maintain perspective

## WHAT'S A PARENT TO DO?

**1-on-1 Dating.** Real dating should not begin before age sixteen. As eleventh grade approaches, adolescents have had enough experience with the opposite sex to be capable of more meaningful interactions and to begin to exhibit elements of true emotional intimacy. By this age, teens have been in high school long enough to know what it takes to manage the academic demands of their class load. They have also begun to think of a future after high school, which helps put the complications of a long-term, committed relationship into perspective (namely, that such a relationship would greatly complicate matters).

An increasing capacity for intimacy makes teenagers ripe for falling head over heels in love. It is not the infatuation of a first crush, it is a feeling of romantic love, the kind of love you get lost in (and, this includes girls *and* guys). Experiencing romantic love is a very important task of adolescence. Indeed, it can be useful for teens to fall in love a couple of times, to help them learn that romantic love is not all it takes to have a mature, lasting relationship.

Despite the emerging ability to develop an intimate romantic relationship, adolescents are still not equipped to effectively deal with the conflicting emotions, negotiations, and demands of intimacy. A mature relationship is marked by balancing the glory of love with competing interests and agendas, work, and dealing with the mundane details of managing finances and a household. Relationships have to be able to survive the stresses and strains of the demands of the real world. The adolescent version of this is balancing true love with maintaining friendships and family ties, schooling, and personal activities like sports, personal hobbies or interests.

That doesn't mean that teens will necessarily recognize the importance of maintaining this balance—which, of course, is where parents come in.

Parents should expect their kids to maintain a balance between a romantic relationship and the competing priorities of friends and family, school, and personal interests and activities. This would include limits on dating frequency (such as once a weekend) and requiring your kid to continue to invest time and energy into other relationships, such as their friends and family.

This kind of balance can even be structured as a trade-off; before they can go out on a date, they have to spend an evening with the family or do things with friends *without* their girl/boyfriend. During the early dating phase, consider having the couple hang out together at the house with the family (which should be sufficient to kill any feelings of passion). They can work up to actually going on dates. While private time is important, there should be an expectation that people may "pop in" on them, just to see if they need anything.

Grades need to be maintained at acceptable levels. Involvement in sports or other activities of interest have to continue. When one of these areas suffers, opportunities for dating should likewise suffer.

**Age requirements.** Even when teens are following a normal developmental pattern of dating, problems can arise when there is too great a difference in age between them and the person they are dating (or going with). Parental limits should help minimize this kind of age pressure.

Seventh- and eighth-graders should only be going steady with someone who is their same grade and same age. This means that eighth-graders should not be going out with anyone in high school, even ninth-graders. There is a significant psychological difference for kids who have started high school that can translate into pressure on the ninth-grader to have a more grown-up relationship, or pressure on the eighth-grader to prove they aren't a "child." (The first big statistical jump in sexual intercourse occurs at this age.)

For teens in ninth grade, there should be only one grade or year difference in a dating partner. They have enough difficulty negotiating this new environment and the demands of high school without adding dating pressure to the mix. Tenth- and eleventh-graders should be separated from their dating partner by no more than two years or two grade levels.

The idea here is that kids need to be dating people who are facing the same developmental tasks. When the gap is too wide, the relationship can become an exercise in sacrifice rather than an experience in age-appropriate emotional intimacy.

**Caveat.** This framework for the development of teenage dating is intended to be a way to think about important skills in the formation of intimate relationships. For some kids, just a discussion of the importance of these issues will be enough; for others, parents will need to create a formal structure that ties dating to other expectations.

Don't think only in terms of limiting and denying. Encourage and celebrate both your kid finding someone worthy of their affection as well as being someone worthy of affection. The goals are 1) to help kids avoid being pressured (by themselves or others) to behave in ways that are beyond their developmental level; 2) to make it difficult for them to give free rein to their natural desire to experiment; 3) to build trust; and 4) to learn how to balance their romantic love with other relationships and responsibilities, while also maintaining a degree of individuality.

# SEX: THE TALK(S)

**D**ating and sex are two of the more sensitive issues parents face while raising their teens. Few topics are prone to cause more tension, embarrassment, and concern. However, that need not be the case.

This chapter presents some ideas about:

- How to talk about sex
- Talking about sex with teens of different ages
- How to set sexual limits

## WHAT'S A PARENT TO DO?

How do you have the first talk with your kid about relationships and sex? You can minimize the tension and angst by following these guidelines.

**Make the time.** Don't count on the perfect moment showing up. You will have to create your own opportunity. When you do, make sure you are protected from interruptions by choosing a time and a place with some privacy. Typically, if you will be talking with a girl, find a place where she can kind of curl up while talking; with boys, it can help to be on the move walking a trail, circling the block, etc. Finally, avert your eyes. Talking face-to-face with teens about serious or personal subjects freaks them out, so position yourself side by side or at an angle.

**Wade right in.** Once you find the time, just start. Consider phrases like "We need to talk" or "I want to talk about some important things ... " or "You are getting to age where ... " Emphasize the importance of discussing dating and intimacy. Tell them to plan on having more of these little chats as they get older.

**Speak to their developmental level.** It is pretty easy to traumatize your kid with information that is too far above their current level of thinking or experience, so try to get a sense of their developmental level before launching into discussions about relationships and sex. Here are some ideas about adolescents' general developmental levels, along with information, skills, and decisions they face at different stages.

If your kid is at the age right before or at the onset of puberty, they need information about the development and functioning of the adult male and female body. A general explanation about the role of body parts in reproduction is also important, especially about sexual feelings and orgasms. Discussions about relationships should be very general at this stage with an emphasis on overall character qualities of a good person and how to get to know someone.

As teens approach fourteen years of age, it is time to talk about what qualities to look for in a potential dating partner. Teens this age also need to begin thinking about how to treat and be treated by a dating partner. It can even help to talk about adults and peers they may know who have these characteristics.

This is an important time to make sure your kid has general information about unwanted pregnancies, sexually transmitted infections, and any other information that can scare them about casual sex. In addition, kids this age need to understand how each step in physical intimacy can easily lead to the next, as well as the importance of decision-making in setting limits.

They will need to practice dealing with someone being mad at them for not doing what they want (and not just about potential sexual pressure). The more you can get your kids to talk about these things, the better.

By the time your child is sixteen, they should be able to identify when they expect to be physically intimate (including sexual intercourse) in a relationship (e.g., first chance I get, when I'm married, if

I really like him/her, after my parents are dead, etc.). It is important for them to have some clear ideas about what they expect from a dating partner and from themselves and to know what they will put up with and what they won't put up with.

They also need to know how to enforce limits on a relationship as well as what to do when they are feeling pressured. Teens this age need to know very specific information about pregnancy risks, sexually transmitted infections, and typical reactions to first time (or ongoing) sex. Reciprocal communication between parents and children becomes very important as a way for kids to think through major life decisions, including those regarding relationships.

**Ask questions before giving answers.** Asking questions is a gentle way to enter into discussions about what your kid is thinking and what they know. Questions that begin with "Have you ever thought about … " or "What do you know about … " or "When do you think is the right time … " can help start a discussion. This allows you to get a feel for what they know or have thought about and how comfortable they are in talking to you. It also demonstrates your interest in this being a conversation rather than a lecture.

Since this topic is emotionally charged, don't assume that an initial lack of response means they aren't going to answer. Sometimes, kids are thinking and sorting things out in their head, so watch and wait before you forge ahead with the answers.

**Validate before you respond.** It is really important for your kid to feel like you respect them and the fact that they will be making choices for themselves. Be sure to express your respect for their opinions and to communicate your admiration for answers that are values-based. ("I'm really glad that you are thinking about what you consider to be morally right and are taking the other person's feelings into account.") Acknowledge how complicated and confusing it can be to sort out this relationship stuff.

**Talk about values.** To be human is to base your actions on a set of morals or values. To talk about relationships is to talk about right and wrong: the right and wrong way to treat others, the right and wrong way to allow others to treat you, right and wrong actions. Have your kid talk about their moral code and how that will guide their actions in a relationship.

**Anticipate.** One way you can help your teen negotiate the treacherous (and thereby thrilling) waters of a relationship is to help them anticipate things that will be coming over the horizon. When it comes to the emotional part of the relationship, it can be useful to think in terms of three categories: lust, romantic love, and commitment. These categories can give you a way to talk about keeping a relationship in perspective: "Yeah, she gets you all hot and bothered (lust). Who knows whether it will end up being real love (romantic love), though? It takes a whole set of qualities to have a relationship that really can last (commitment)."

It is also important to anticipate the lure of increasing physical intimacy. A time-honored categorization of physical intimacy is the baseball metaphor: first base (kissing), second base (above the waist), third base (below the waist), and home plate (sexual intercourse). Whatever way you talk about it, help your teen understand that just spending increasing time with someone in a close relationship may draw them into increasing physical intimacy through comfort and curiosity. Help them figure out what they want and how to make sure things stay at a comfortable level of intimacy *before* they are faced with the situation.

**Set limits.** It will be important for both you and your kid to identify your limits regarding relationships and sexual intimacy. Your limits will be the rules you have for dating: when they can date, under what conditions, and with whom. Their limits will be about having standards for a dating partner and levels of physical intimacy (when and under what conditions).

Finally, it will be important to have an agreement about how your kid will keep you informed about their relationships, especially when they are becoming serious (emotionally or physically). If they can't talk to you about being in love or deciding to have sex, then they aren't ready for the responsibility. (This argument won't stop them, but it makes your point.)

**Don't push.** Since you are going to have many talks about relationships and sex, don't try to say everything in one sitting. Look for signs of overload such as sobbing (you or them), dazed expression, putting in their mp3 ear buds, curling up in the fetal position, etc. Keep your discussions to thirty minutes, max, unless there are clear signs they are into the conversation. Remember, there will always be another time.

**Wash, rinse, repeat.** Make sure there are other times. Once you have the initial conversation about relationships, future conversations are monumentally easier, although you may still have to pursue the topic. Initial awkwardness has been overcome; you have already talked about intimate issues, so now it is just another conversation with their annoying parent.

# ABSTINENCE

Abstinence is a part of the conversation about sex that deserves special attention.

This chapter looks at:

- The importance of talking about abstinence
- How to talk to your teen about abstinence
- What you can do to prepare for this conversation

Talking to teens about the decision to have sex is remarkably complicated. On the one hand, it can change the course of a kid's life. On the other hand, sex is a powerful and rewarding physical experience. It is an inevitable expression of emotional and physical intimacy, and it sets in motion a cascade of emotional and social conflicts.

Sex is a mind-blowing opportunity for physical pleasure, and it has the capacity to take over thinking and cast a shadow on real intimacy. With that in mind, it is pretty clear that adolescents should remain sexually abstinent until they are capable of assuming the responsibilities that accompany sex, in the same way that they should not drink or do drugs until they are mature enough to handle the possible consequences.

It is also pretty clear that your kids will eventually have sex— almost certainly sooner than you think they should (and most likely with someone you object to).

# WHAT'S A PARENT TO DO?

So how do you get your kid to make a fully informed commitment to sexual abstinence? Here are a few things that will improve your chances when you talk with your kid about the role of sex in a relationship.

**Commitment to abstinence.** For abstinence to work, adolescents have to be committed to it. Start by having your kid clarify their stance on sexual abstinence. If they are committed to abstinence, it is helpful to talk about these issues as a way to reinforce this view and better arm your kid to maintain their commitment. If they are not committed to abstinence, then it is important to talk about these issues as a way to influence their thinking. Don't forget to be clear about your own belief that abstinence is the best course (even if you don't carry it all the way to "until you are married"). Teens need to work on learning how to be in relationships (they can work on the sex part after you are dead).

**The cost of sex.** Here's the part of the discussion where you bring up factual information about the potential consequences of sexual intercourse. The number one potential cost of sex is unwanted pregnancy. Unwanted pregnancies present teens with hard choices: raising the child, abortion (and guys don't get a choice in these two, by the way), or adoption. The decision to raise a child profoundly affects freedom, finances, responsibilities, and pursuing professional and career goals. Decisions to end a pregnancy or offering a child for adoption result in different—but equally significant—emotional turmoil, self-identity, and long-term internal conflicts. Finally, teenage parents place a huge burden on their families due to their lack of ability to assume complete responsibility for child rearing and their own lives.

Sexual intercourse is also a factor in various medical issues. There is a significant possibility of acquiring sexually transmitted infections (including the human papilloma virus; look it up together), increased risk of urinary tract infections in girls, and the necessity of making decisions about birth control, either through oral contraception, condoms, or emergency contraception (the "morning after" pill).

Being a sexually active teen still has social consequences, even in this age of sexual excess. Being sexually active can change peer perceptions of your teen (their reputation) and alter expectations of continued sexual behaviors in future relationships. Sex can also throw a close and satisfying dating relationship off track because the pressure for ongoing sexual intimacy. And, finally, confusion, ambivalence, guilt, shame, and regret can be generated when sexually active kids are not ready for sexual intimacy.

As challenging as this may sound, don't shy away from these issues. Spend time talking through the many ripples of that one decision. Do your homework and inform yourself about these issues so that you can speak knowledgeably with your kid.

**Positive model of sex.** It is important to talk nice about sex too. You will lose your kid if you characterize sex as either a roiling cauldron of disease, pregnancy, and the ruination of personal aspirations or as a sacred union of souls through the joining of physical bodies for the sole purpose of procreation. Sex might be those things, but it is also fun and sloppy and raw and intense and physical. Your kid needs to have an idea that there is a whole range of healthy sexual expression (and experimentation) between two consenting, *responsible* adults as a way of making a place for this wonderful way to relate to another person.

Let your teen know that sex should be enjoyed without anxiety or shame—in other words, with forethought, in the right circumstances, at the right time of life, with the right person.

**Clarifying values and decisions.** Living a meaningful and fulfilling life isn't possible without a foundation of morals or personal values. Decisions about sexual intimacy, as with any important aspect of one's life, should be guided and shaped by a moral code. Have your teen identify their personal value system. Talk about how their morals influence decisions about sex and the consequences that might arise from sex. Have them state clearly, to you, how committed they are to their moral code. Discuss how they plan to deal with friends who have differences in personal beliefs and values.

Finally, talk about the costs of having a moral code. (It really does get in the way of fun, at times!)

**Establishing personal goals and future plans.** Having clearly identified personal goals and future plans is associated with the decreased likelihood of early sexual behavior. Have your kid talk about their career aspirations, their educational goals, and how they imagine their early marital relationship might be. Ask if they've thought about the point at which they envision having children. Then have them imagine *lugging a baby around* while trying to accomplish these goals.

You can paint a vivid picture of the responsibilities of being the parent of a newborn. You remember what it was like. (Just remember not to be completely negative.) The more elaborate your teen's visions and plans for their life course, the greater the likelihood they will make responsible sexual decisions.

**Counter arguments.** Teens report that the reasons they become sexually active include love (or it's the right person), everybody's doing it, curiosity, pressure from their partner, and trying to gain (or maintain) their partner's affection. You can help inoculate them against the influence of these reasons for sex by helping them think through whether the risks of sex are worth it.

It's most important to talk about these influences before your kid actually is faced with making a decision. If you are coming to the decision-making process late in the game, you can help your teen learn from mistaken assumptions as they decide about the role of sex in future relationships.

**Refusal skills.** Teens need practice dealing with social (and internal) pressure to violate personal commitments or morals. They will need to be capable of defending their decision to be abstinent when peers give them a hard time. "What would you say if someone said ... " is a way to help them think through what to do in different situations. Teens (both girls and boys) need to have some ideas about how to handle being pushed to cross personal boundaries about sexual intimacy. How do you say "no" in different circumstances and to different people? Personal stories of situations you experienced, even ones that turned out unhappily, can be a powerful way to present potentially difficult situations and how to deal with them.

**Safety plan.** Sexual behavior leads to more sexual behavior. If teens are kissing, they are more likely to engage in above-the-waist petting. If they engage in above-the-waist petting, they are more likely to engage in below-the-waist petting. If they engage in below-the-waist petting (or engage in oral sex), they are more likely to engage in sexual intercourse.

The transition from no sexual intimacy at all to above-the-waist petting is relatively slow, but the pace of moving from above-the-waist petting to sexual intercourse is considerably faster. Knowing this and deciding specifically where they are going to draw the line will help your kid avoid this snowball effect.

Pornography can desensitize and distort your kid's views of sexuality. Talk about the problems of having a sex-as-sport mindset on how they may begin to view sexual partners, sexual expectations, and sexual intimacy. Finally, talk about how to use the environment to help them stick to their decisions regarding sex. It is useful to anticipate high-risk situations: swimming in a public pool is low risk, but getting into a hot tub at a private residence without adults around with your girlfriend while wearing only your underwear to celebrate your one-year anniversary is high-risk.

You can help them figure out how to minimize temptation, avoid risks, and think through strategies for taking care of themselves if they end up in risky situations.

What is the ultimate safety plan? Maintain open lines of communication with your adolescent and have an agreement to talk when they decide they are ready to have sex. If they can't discuss it, adult to adult, they ain't ready.

Once your teen has started dating and you realize you need to talk to them, what do you say? Before you say anything, consider doing some background prep. It will help you feel more confident as well as increasing the likelihood that your discussions will be successful.

**You first.** Before you begin discussing teenage relationships with your kid, it is important for you to give some thought to what *you* want for your kid in a relationship. Love? Happiness? Money? A really hot boyfriend or girlfriend? Take a moment to clarify your own ideas so you can communicate these to your kid. This includes views about the role of sex, morals, motives for dating someone, and fun in a dating relationship. It is also important to respect your own personal limits. There may be some things that you just aren't comfortable discussing. Even then, you don't have to just avoid the issue altogether. You can still help your teen by providing a good book or enlisting the help of a trusted friend or relative (or, sometimes, a therapist).

**Homework.** Do some research in order to have useful information already in mind. Look up statistics on teen sexuality and dating, review information on puberty and technical information on sex, give some thought to what qualities your kid should be looking for in a dating partner, and know something about what makes a good relationship. These are all things that you can help your teen think through.

**Moral code.** It is also useful for parents to clarify the morals or values they expect their kids to use to guide their behavior and decision-making. A moral code identifies right and wrong actions. Morals and values are an important part of making any decision, especially decisions about relationships and sexual behavior. Be prepared to talk about it.

**Bullet points.** Decide what points you want to make, to keep from rambling. These might include the link between morals and behavior, what a good relationship should look like, abstinence, identifying and setting personal boundaries, decision-making about intimacy, the importance of being informed about sex and sexuality, and the importance of open communication between you and your child.

**Equipment, mechanics, and heart & soul.** When parents try to talk to their kids about relationships and sex, it often turns into a conversation just about sex. There are three separate elements that teens need to know about: the development and functioning of male and female bodies, how sex works, and the emotional intimacy of relationships. The most important of these is relationships.

While it is important for your kids to know about safer sex and the risks and responsibilities involved when teens become sexually active, they also need help figuring out how dating relationships should work. This information is almost completely absent in their lives except when they talk to other teens or pick up tips from the media. If that doesn't scare you into finding a way to talk about this with your kid, nothing will.

**Language.** It is generally best to stick to the biological names for equipment and mechanics. It helps educate your kid and also creates a little bit of scientific distance to buffer any awkwardness there might be in talking about the subject. But kids also need language to think about and discuss relationships. It is important to use words that capture the richness of relationships as well as of emotional and physical intimacy. Having a close, intimate relationship with someone is glorious and wonderful and fun. It is also risky, it can be painful, and it carries with it responsibilities. The language you use will also be shaped by the teachings of your faith traditions, which also can be an important source for guidance and decision-making.

**Expertise.** There is only so much any one person can know about a topic, even if they have a degree in the subject—so don't expect to know everything. Not knowing something provides the opportunity for you and your teen to find the answer together.

**Keep your cool.** The scope of sexual information and behavior our kids are exposed to can be difficult to appreciate. If you don't discuss relationships, emotional intimacy, and sex with your kids, they will be forced to make sense of these complex and powerful experiences on their own. You need to know what your kid has been thinking about, exposed to, or doing. How else will you be able to help them put things in perspective? But if they reveal something upsetting, stay calm and ask questions (without screaming, if possible). If it is something serious, you can shift into your "we'll get this figured out together mode." And, you will—either by working through it together or by finding the right professional to help.

# DISCIPLINE AND PRAISE ISSUES

# CORRECTION
# & CRITICISM

## Part 1:
### General Issues

Making mistakes is part of life. The key is for mistakes to become opportunities for improvement. This is where you come in.

This chapter explores:

- The purpose of correction and criticism

- General issues related to constructive correction and criticism

Kids can't get everything right the first time (or, for some, even after the twentieth time). Parenting teens requires praising, encouraging, guiding, and directing. Teens also need correction (redirecting their actions or thoughts) and criticism (evaluating and judging the quality of their products, actions, or thoughts).

Personal growth and improvement requires the recognition of problem areas and a change in behaviors and attitudes. True feelings of accomplishment come from struggling with and then mastering or accomplishing something difficult. Parental correction and criticism is, after all, for your kid's own good!

## WHAT'S A PARENT TO DO?

Since you are saddled with this terrible responsibility, there are some general issues related to effective criticism and correction that are worth reviewing.

**Expect mistakes, poor judgment, and failure.** It is important for kids to know they won't get everything right. This does not mean you should teach them that life is filled with failure and despair. It means that screwing up is a part of learning. You try to avoid it as much as possible, but when it happens, don't waste the opportunity. Teach your teens to ask, what did they learn from it? What would they do differently next time?

**Learn to take criticism.** Teens also need to learn how to take criticism and correction. (This is also known as being able to take direction or being coachable.) It is important to teach your kid how to accept mistakes and respond appropriately. Responding appropriately to criticism and correction requires them to listen—not argue. It also includes accepting responsibility for their role in the problem situation instead of blaming others, being defensive, or trying to redirect the focus on some other issue. Require your teen to acknowledge "I messed up." Finally, taking criticism and correction means teens should recognize that others have something to teach them.

**Will that be on the test?** It helps for them to know what standards to use in evaluating their own actions or decisions. This can be in the form of criteria for a specific task like, say, cleaning up their room (all clothes put up, floor clean, bed made, carpet vacuumed, shelves dusted, trash emptied, etc.).

There are also general principles that underlie a task well done or an attitude appropriately expressed. This is where morals or ethics come in and the values of honesty, kindness, generosity, etc. Make sure you regularly talk about the morals and values you expect of members of your family. "In our family, we (help people in need/tell the truth/finish what we start/do our best/keep our word)."

A family creed is another useful guide. Consider having phrases you repeat over and over until your children finish the sentences for you. "Never give up." "Be polite." "Well begun is half done." "Do unto others ... " These maxims have an important place in guiding and shaping your kid's actions and decisions.

**Self-correction.** Ultimately, you want your teen to self-correct. While telling your kid each step to take is efficient, doing so interferes with them internalizing the lesson and drawing on it in the future. Ask them questions you want them asking themselves: "What did you learn from this?" "What went wrong here?" "How do you fix this?"

**Correct actions, not qualities.** The one thing kids have control over is what they do. Even when they are cruel and you want them to be kind, focus on what kindness looks like. People's self-concepts are influenced by their own behavior ("If I did something kind, I must be kind.") and by the feedback they receive. A kid who is a "screw-up" can begin to fulfill that expectation. Have your teens do what they are supposed to do and it can lead to a change in attitude. If you have to label them, label them as what you want them to be instead of what they are, if what they are is disappointing.

**Recognize personal limitations.** If you criticize your kid for doing poorly in math when they have a learning disability in math, helplessness and giving up are not far behind. Be sure to respect personal limitations. On the other hand, if they are *not* trying in math—with or without a learning disability—that is another thing altogether. Identify limitations as challenges to be overcome, not as excuses to quit.

**Avoid social comparisons.** The important things are what your kid did or didn't do and how they are developing and maturing. Whether there are other kids who are better or worse is irrelevant and can distract your kid from focusing on establishing their own, internal standards. Don't compare them to others. (And don't let them use comparisons to others to justify their actions. "But Johnny gets away with ... ")

**Highlight the positives.** It is equally important for your kid to practice recognizing the successful or effective aspects of their actions. What did they like about how they handled a situation? What did that show about their personal values? Help them learn to assess a situation in a more comprehensive way by seeing the good and the bad, rather than just what went wrong.

**It is what it is.** Don't try to make it better so they don't feel so bad. Kids need to feel bad sometimes and learn how to deal with it. This does not mean you are supposed to find ways to make your kid feel bad on purpose—there will be plenty of natural opportunities to deal with mess-ups without you setting them up. Mistakes are a part of life, something you and your teen should expect. You can also expect them to learn how to handle mistakes well. Failure is a natural outcome of trying something difficult (or not trying hard enough). Your kid should face that reality and learn from it.

**Be matter of fact.** At the same time, don't be overly dramatic. They didn't destroy their life. They didn't bring shame upon everyone from their grandparents to their unborn children. (And if they did, you need to consult with a mental health professional.) They did something incorrectly. They did something wrong. Their responsibility is to recognize it, take guidance, and do better next time.

**Keep track of improvements.** Make sure you notice how your kid has improved since the last time you commented on (or criticized) their progress. You want them to improve their skills, judgment, priorities, and actions. The more you criticize or correct, the more you need to highlight progress (see the 5-to-1 rule, below).

**5-to-1.** The ratio of positive to negative interactions with your teen should be five positive interactions for every negative one, including correcting and criticizing. Maybe you have a difficult kid. Maybe you have high aspirations for your kid. Maybe you are not praising them enough. Whatever the reason, you might have to get the ratio of positives up. If it is less than five to one, your kid is much less likely to take your feedback seriously (because you are always criticizing them). They also might be more likely to feel inadequate or just give up, because they can never do anything right.

With these general issues in mind, there are some specific techniques for correcting and criticizing teens to be found in the next chapter.

# CORRECTION & CRITICISM

## Part 2:
### Effective Techniques

What's the best way to give your teen constructive criticism and correction?

This chapter looks at:

- Elements of effective criticism

- Specific steps of effective correction and criticism

- Teaching your kid how to respond to correction and criticism

## WHAT'S A PARENT TO DO?

There are countless ways parents help their kids recognize mistakes and learn the correct way to do something. It's important to remember certain guidelines when you let them know that their efforts are in need of improvement.

**Maintain their dignity.** Teens are extremely susceptible to humiliation and embarrassment. Be sensitive to the surroundings. Criticisms or corrections are a personal interaction between you and your kid. Take them aside to a private space and have siblings or relatives leave the area. Close the windows to your house when screaming suggestions for improvement. It is important to avoid making a scene in public (purely for the sake of your child's dignity, of course).

**No name-calling.** There is no place for insulting or degrading your kid by using terms like stupid, idiot, hopeless, worthless, useless, wussy, etc. Name-calling is hurtful and unhelpful, and it tends to encourage immature replies from teens. Worse, your kid will need to stop caring what you think in order to feel protected from the pain this causes.

**Start with what they did right.** Any formula for correcting or criticizing should begin by clearly identifying the things your kid did well or got right. Remind them of their better self. Show them you still see what they *can* do well. Implicitly, you are teaching them that there is good and bad, better and worse, competence and incompetence in every situation. What did you like about their decision? What did they do that was positive or desirable? Praise and compliments highlight the aspects of a situation you want them to repeat. And, if you happen to have a kid who is overly self-critical, this will help them maintain a balance. Always start with praising your kid (see the chapter on Praise for suggestions). Consider presenting all the positive stuff together rather than jumping back and forth between compliments and correction. (Making a list can facilitate this. Also, see the 5-to-1 section, above.) Then talk about the problems, mistakes, improvements, additions, inadequacies, alternatives and shortcomings they will need to address.

**Language of change.** Avoid words that characterize things in absolutes such as always, never, every time, etc. Introduce the concept that they can change—and that you expect them to change. Imply future improvement. "You'll get it if you keep working on it." "Next time, it will be important for you to ... " "How are you going to do this differently in the future?" "This needs to be the last time you ... " "From now on ... " Assume they are going to fix it and keep going. Presume change with words like "You will," "When you," and "Haven't done it, yet."

**Ask leading questions.** The goal of correction and criticism is both improvement and the development and refinement of personal standards. This will involve guidance as well as insistence that they conduct their own self-evaluation. Ask questions that require this kind of review. "Where did things go wrong?" "Are you proud of this?" "Did you give it your best?" "Is this how you want people to think of you?" (If they respond "Yes!" to that last question, you might need to reply, "Well, I guess we've got some more work to do, because that is not how we do things in our family!")

**What's the goal?** To succeed at some task, it helps to know what you are striving for. Don't forget to identify the long-term goal. This can be task-specific (learning to solve equations, having a clean room) or a way of being (hard-working, kind, etc.).

**Provide specific feedback.** Be clear and direct about what they did or did not do. Focus on the issue at hand. Avoid bringing up the fifty times you have already corrected them or all the other ways they have screwed up in the past. Then ...

**Give direct instruction.** Corrections and criticism start with clearly stating what your kid should or should not do. "I want you to ____." "Don't ____." "This was not done correctly because ____." It is surprising how often parents are vague, overly complex, confusing, or imprecise in expressing exactly what they need their teens to do. Clear, direct instructions help kids avoid mistakes or screw-ups due to a misunderstanding or lack of knowledge of what is required.

**Break it into steps.** Too much information about what your kid did wrong or how they need to improve can be oppressive and discouraging. Focus on initially presenting an overview of what needs to be accomplished and then identifying the next couple of steps needed to improve or keep things on track (or get things back on track) toward accomplishing a goal. If it is more than three steps, stop there. Save the next three corrections until these three have been addressed.

**Focus on effort and actions.** Statements that comment on what your kid did or didn't do ("You didn't ___." "You need to ____.")

are preferable to statements about basic qualities or characteristics ("You are a _____." "You disgust me."). It is easier to change what you *do* rather than who you are. Kids tend to live up to how they think you perceive them. If you think they are "lazy" why should they try? So ...

**Personal values.** Identify how their behavior reflects on their personal values. "Did you try hard? Did you do your best? Is that really the impression you want people to have of you?"

**End on a positive note.** Parents can provide a reservoir of hope and promise when kids are frustrated, struggling, or despairing. Offer encouragement. Make sure you help your kid realize they can do it. "You just have to keep at it." "It will take some work, but you'll get it." "Don't give up now." If the screw-up is serious, remind them of all the qualities you admire in them and of the other areas where they have succeeded. Make sure they know you haven't forgotten those positive qualities.

**Responding to criticism.** Finally, your kid needs to know how to respond to correction and criticism. They should, first, be required to just listen (without arguing). Then they should ask questions so that they thoroughly understand the feedback you are giving them. Finally, they should consider thanking you for the feedback (it's worth a shot). If the critic is sincere and seems to be trying to help rather than looking for a chance to put them down, their thanks is an acknowledgement of the critic's intent. If the critic is a jerk, thanking them is a disarming response. Your kid needs to know that jerks won't know how to respond to gratitude, and it makes your kid look good to others who are watching or will hear about it. They may as well practice this with you.

If there is any way to address the issue through praise—focusing on what they did right as a way to reinforce this in the future—do it. Correction and criticism is important and necessary, but it can be hard to take. Use criticism sparingly and with respect for the dignity of your kid.

# GROUNDING

**G**rounding is a time-honored way to indicate to your kid that they have screwed up. The challenge is to make sure grounding is effective.

This chapter examines:

- The reasons to ground your kid
- The basic components of effective grounding
- When grounding may not be enough
- Creative variations
- Turning grounding into an accomplishment

There comes a time in most teens' lives when they are just not getting it. It becomes necessary to shut everything down and start from scratch. They may have committed a major violation, like taking drugs, sneaking out at night, or shoplifting. Or they may have committed one minor to moderate violation after another; as a parent, you'll find yourself saying, "How many times have I told you ... ?" Grounding provides a way to reel your teen in, keep them close, and provide a time for you to review and reeducate.

Grounding mimics arrest and incarceration. It discourages misbehavior by presenting clear, negative consequences; it provides incentive to avoid breaking rules in the first place; it establishes a new beginning; it facilitates quality time to get acquainted with each other again; and it creates a little break in the momentum toward problem behaviors that may be building. You can do all this by parking their butt in the house.

## WHAT'S A PARENT TO DO?

**Basic formula.** Grounding needs to have a clear beginning and ending. Leaving it open-ended ( "I'll let you know when you can have your life back!") only really works on kids who were going to shape up anyway. Kids who need to be grounded more than once during the teen years are more likely to see an open-ended grounding as stretching out forever and think, "I might as well sneak out because I'll never be able to get off this grounding."

To be effective, grounding must:

- Begin at the time of the infraction.

- End at a specific time on the day following the specified grounding period—for example, grounding for one week will end at 8 a.m. on the eighth day following the infraction. (You'll be pleasantly surprised at how providing your teen with this little bit of extra time gets on their nerves.)

- End with specific criteria.

**Length of grounding.** Think of time periods that will result in your kid missing at least two rounds of things that are important to them. Grounding should curtail their sense of freedom, a very important issue for the little darlings. Some kids have a normal social calendar (meaning they hang out with friends every weekend or so), while others are more socially active, texting more than eighty times a day, constantly online, etc.

- Ground in one week increments (even if it causes them to miss more than two important things).

- Stick to two weeks maximum for most groundings and other consequences. With all the connectivity kids have through electronic media, one month can seem like an eternity to them. You actually want them to successfully complete the grounding. It makes it possible for them to take responsibility for their misbehavior and for you to express your admiration for the way they have taken responsibility by fulfilling their punishment.

- Specific events, days, etc. Grounding doesn't have to be in unbroken periods. You can tailor it to the crux of the problem. For example, they can be grounded for four straight weekends (Friday through Sunday) when the problem was associated with them being out and about. The rest of the week remains unaffected.

- Task completion. Don't forget that you want them to gain some level of understanding, growth, or awareness from the grounding. Often, the restriction of activities is sufficient to get their attention. Grounding can also be tied to the acquisition of a specific skill or the accomplishment of a specified task, which you expect to be completed within the period of grounding. This is also an excellent time to have long talks about important issues, since they are stuck in the house with you anyway.

**Misdemeanors and felonies.** For regular teenage infractions, grounding can be a self-contained punishment. Nothing else is required. But for special circumstances, grounding is part of a more elaborate attempt to address the problem.

- **Regular**. For typical teenage infractions, you want grounding to sting—not crush. It is intended to get their attention. Regular infractions would be issues like curfew violation, persistent chore avoidance, misuse of vehicle (through reckless driving, too many passengers, etc.), irresponsibility, ignoring texts or calls from parents, not being where they say they were, or getting into trouble with their friends.

- **Special circumstances**. Grounding can be part of a larger intervention strategy for infractions like alcohol or drug use or shoplifting, or it can be backup punishment when they are already being punished. In these circumstances, grounding is the necessary but least important aspect of addressing the problem. It will be important to consult books, reputable online experts, or mental health professionals for effective strategies to get your kid back on track from a truly serious offense.

**Grounded from what.** Be very specific about what they can and can't do when grounded.

**Deprivation.** There are lots of things you can take away or limit: visiting others, having visitors, electronics (TV, computer, cell phone, texting, video games, mp3s), extracurricular activities, their job, attending school functions, use of a vehicle.

**Growth and development.** Some kids don't do very much, so traditional grounding doesn't have enough impact. Other kids need to demonstrate that they appreciate the significance of their infraction for its effects on other people, morals, or reputation. In these instances, consider requiring your kid to accomplish something during their grounding, other than silent suffering. Manual labor, quality time with family, contribution to the household, reports and essays, volunteering, or any kind of skill development can be added to the grounding.

**Protected activities.** There are some activities that you may consider important enough to be protected from grounding. These often include activities that make a positive contribution to your kid's life, such as sports, skilled activities (e.g., art, music, dance), and employment. While there might be times when restricting involvement in these kinds of activities is necessary to make your point, it is important to weigh carefully the potential negative effects of including this category of activities in the grounding. Don't forget that you can still put constraints all around the beneficial activity to make them suffer.

**Time off for good behavior.** There are some circumstances when it can be useful to allow your kid to earn back some of their freedom. If they have dug a deep grounding hole or there is some really important event (a concert they already had tickets for, a significant school event, etc.), it is appropriate to have a system by which they can earn time to attend an event or to shorten the length of grounding.

- **Minimum time served**. Grounding doesn't work if they can get out of it before it hurts. Make sure they serve at least five out of seven days of grounding. Make sure some of the five days extends across the weekend.

- **Special time off.** You might allow your kid to subtract time from the end or allow them to apply it to some approved event in the middle (such as three hours to attend a school event).

- **Time off is earned by good works.** Allow them to complete undesirable tasks that aren't already their responsibility. They should not get time off for chores they are already required to complete. Need a new flower bed? That messy garage need straightening? Here's your chance. If your kid is grounded because of their attitude, sustained periods of having the right attitude or behavior can earn them some time off. Be specific and require proof. ("Name five situations in which you said supportive or encouraging things to your sister. Did anyone observe Sara being complimentary?") Earning time off should be voluntary. It is fine with you if they just serve out their time.

- **Prison wages.** Don't be generous in providing time off. You can do hour for hour. You can do two for one. Be clear with your kid about the formula of how much work equals how much time off, as well as the maximum amount of time they can earn.

**Grounding as a learning experience.** Taking away all the fun electronics and the chance to spend time with friends may be satisfying, but it is important for your kid to learn something from this experience. If they just sit around and suffer, they aren't gaining anything except punishment. Consider assigning tasks or activities that provide them with an opportunity to have a personal growth experience, increase their knowledge, or develop some sort of skill.

For example, if your kid is grounded for not responding to a parent's texts or calls, you may want to require them to have seven straight days of responding to your texts or calls within fifteen to thirty minutes. The clock starts over if they miss it. (For fun, you can text them when you are in the same room. It annoys them and it makes a point.)

You might find a book they can read on the issue that led to the grounding. Require them to learn some specific skill and demonstrate mastery before they can get off grounding. Set them up to volunteer for a worthy organization.

**Acknowledge their accomplishment.** Make sure you let them know you notice their efforts. "I appreciate how well you are handling being grounded." "You have really taken responsibility for screwing up by making the best of your grounding."

Don't overdo it (no "You are doing *so great*" statements). Don't use guilt or shame. Teens need to be able to recover their dignity and reestablish their honor. By successfully completing their grounding, they are making up for their mistakes or infractions. Guilt and shame will interfere with the process of internalizing the lessons you want them to learn.

**Adding more time to the grounding.** Be very conservative about adding time to their grounding. Extending their grounding out into the future *ad infinitum* is demoralizing; teens will be more likely to just give up and try to get around it. If you have to tack on more than another week or so, it is probably time to consult with a mental health professional.

Grounding is the foundation of parental discipline for teens. Make sure you get the most out of it by not overusing it.

# PRAISING TEENS

## Part 1:
### Effective Techniques

Teenagers need a lot of encouragement. It is important to get every-thing possible out of the times you praise your kid.

> The first section of this chapter covers:
>
> - The basics of praising teenagers
>
> - When to praise and not praise

Praising your kids is curiously complicated. Praise is the most effective way to generate and sustain your kid's internal motivation to complete a task. It helps kids identify what parents think is most important. It makes you feel good.

But praise also can be a sign that you think someone isn't quite up to the task—for example, if you say "That was really good, honey!" as though you are surprised. It can be taken as an insult. ("Who knew you could add and subtract?") It can cause a kid to focus on personal qualities that interfere with future success. ("You are so pretty!" "You are so smart!") It can give your kid an unrealistic self-perception. ("You are the most wonderful person in the whole, wide world!")

# WHAT'S A PARENT TO DO?

**Be positive.** Praise begins with providing positive and productive feedback that communicates approval ("I really like that."), information ("You got that one right."), admiration ("I'm impressed!"), compliments ("You did a really good job of proving your point in that paper.") and encouragement ("Keep at it. This is really coming along well."). Avoid offering backhanded praise ("That wasn't the worst performance I've ever seen."). It's funny but not very supportive.

**Be sincere.** Kids can tell when you don't mean what you say, so be sure your praise is genuine. Fake pride or false admiration can send the message that you think your kid is kind of a loser who needs boosting up. Find real behaviors or qualities to praise. If you can't seem to find anything praiseworthy about your kid, it is time to get them involved in something they can excel at—and consider consulting with a mental health professional to gather some suggestions.

**Be specific.** Praise is most effective when it is specific. "You did a really good job of picking up all the clothes in your room." "I really liked the way you described the main character in your paper." When parents praise their teens using broad, general statements (That was a great paper." "You are such a smart kid."), their kids can end up dismissing the praise as just something said to make them feel better. Or, worse, they may believe those general statements, which can lead to trouble down the road when the statements turn out to be wrong—like when the teacher disagrees with you about the greatness of the paper, or your kid realizes he's unlikely to be smart in every life domain.

Try identifying individual instances of excellence that focus on content, effort, persistence in the face of challenges, completion, creativity, morality, personal character traits, or early promise of later excellence. It also helps to focus on individual parts of a larger product or steps in a process, since waiting for the final product may take too long (and it might not end up as successful as you'd like).

**Praise behavior, not your kid.** Focus your praise on things your kid can control, like working hard, persistence, improvement, learning, etc. One formula that captures this idea is represented by the words "that is" rather than "you are." (Say "That is really interesting." instead of, "You are really creative.")

**Tell them why.** Adding an explanation of *why* something is praiseworthy to the feedback enables your kid to know what you want them to repeat in the future. It also makes it clear that you have paid attention to what they were doing. Keep in mind that telling them what is praiseworthy is not the same as telling them why they should do well or excel. Saying that their work is admirable because they need to really do well in this class—because otherwise they will never get into college—is likely to generate anxiety and unhelpful pressure to perform.

**Focus on internal standards.** The developmental goal for your child is to continue growing and improving. The best comparison for praise is their own past performance, skill level, aspiration, or ambition (for example, "You know, you are getting much better at summarizing the stories you have read. You used to have much more trouble with that."). Your evaluation and praise should not be based on whether they are better than other kids.

**Keep it realistic.** Your kid doesn't have to be any further along than they are. Progress builds on a realistic view of their current level of mastery, so don't exaggerate their competence or abilities. If you praise them for something that is beyond their capability, failure is right around the corner. Either they will think they know more than they do, or they will know they don't measure up and feel pressure to try to fake it. Both paths can lead to blaming others and avoiding challenges.

**No "buts."** "I am so proud of how hard you worked on that project, but you could have …." Combining praise with correction, criticism, or even suggestions can strip the praise of its meaning. Group all the praiseworthy statements together. Then—and only then—talk about improvements, additions, inadequacies, alternatives, and shortcomings. This keeps the "needs improvement" portion of your talk from poisoning the "praise" part.

**Let some things pass.** Make your praise count. You don't need to find the silver lining in every single cloud. Kids don't need to be praised all the time. Take some successes for granted. If you are constantly searching for something to praise, you might make your kid self-conscious. They may also begin to expect to be praised for things they should just be doing as a matter of course. Kids need to be able to make their way in the world without someone constantly telling them how wonderful they are. On the other hand ...

**5-to-1.** Strong, healthy relationships are characterized by a ratio of five positive interactions for every negative interaction. (This ratio was first revealed by John Gottman and his colleagues who studied long-lasting adult relationships.) Praise is one kind of positive interaction with your kid (though not the only kind). Keep an informal tally of the ratio of compliments, praise, and agreements to corrections, arguments, and criticisms you give your teen. If you drop below the five-to-one ratio, you've got some work to do.

**Praise, don't pay.** Letting your kid know about your pride, admiration, and appreciation is much more powerful than paying them for desirable behavior. Paying them for success has been found to have a funny way of actually undermining their natural interest in doing well. When the money runs out, so does their effort. Pay your teens for manual labor but not for doing their best or for obligations like grades and chores.

**Normalize failure.** Kids need to struggle. They need to fail sometimes, so don't sugarcoat it. ("Yeah, you really blew that one! What are you going to do about it?") Make sure they know that trying and coming up short is part of life. Help them use failure or struggle as a way of getting more information about areas that need attention.

**Praise them for the qualities you want them to exhibit.** Praise is a very effective way to let your kid know what is important to you. Be sure to praise them for the qualities you value. Look for the smallest indication and comment on it. ("You know, I noticed how considerate you were of your brother yesterday when he was upset.") Kids will become, in part, what you expect them to be. Focus on larger issues to praise within a particular task such as your teen's character traits, morality, ability to set goals and work to achieve them, etc.

Now all you have to do is integrate each of these concepts together into a brief, spontaneous response—and your kid will turn out to be perfect. And if they don't, as everyone knows, anything that goes wrong is always the parent's fault.

# PRAISING TEENS

## Part 2:
### What to Praise

O nce you know *how* to effectively praise your adolescent, it is important to know *what* to praise.

This section of the chapter looks at:

- Using praise to encourage

- What to praise in your kid

- Avoiding praise that sends the wrong message

## WHAT'S A PARENT TO DO?

When it comes to praising your teen, the key is to find ways to build your kid up by encouragement and support—regardless of their ultimate success or failure at a task. Your basic task in deciding what to compliment, praise, or encourage your teen about is to focus on:

○ things your kid can influence by their actions (instead of attributes that they have or don't have)

○ identifying the positive (instead of pointing out the negative)

○ building on successes (versus pointing out failures)

○ pursuing personal goals (instead of responding to external pressures, motives, or shoulds/oughts/musts)

○ the *way* they have done something (instead of just the outcome)

○ mastery in the form of knowledge and skill acquisition (instead of performance in the form of grades or victories)

○ important values and character traits (instead of success at any cost)

**Success.** Praising success and excellence is important and rather straightforward. Most success is its own reward. But if you stop at praising a desired outcome like success, you miss the opportunity to highlight other qualities you will want your kid to develop, and you risk your kid thinking the only thing that matters to you is success—regardless of how it is attained.

Here are some praiseworthy qualities exhibited by your teen that are relevant whatever the final outcome:

**Effort.** One thing that kids control is how hard they work to complete a task. More importantly, effort has a direct impact on success; the harder you work, the more likely you are to succeed. This makes it an ideal focus for praise. Praise your kid either for overall effort ("You really worked hard on that paper.") or for their effort on particular components of a task: "I was impressed by how you put everything away after you finished with the yard work [even though the lawn looked like it had mange once you finished]." Note: Bracketed remarks are better left unsaid.

**Skill.** This is a tricky area to target for praise. Skill is a combination of practice and talent. The talent part is a natural ability. If you praise kids for their innate abilities or qualities (like musical talent, physical attractiveness, or exceptional intelligence), they might begin to attribute success or competence to a quality they can't do anything about (talent) rather than to something they do or don't do (practice). You don't want them relying on talent; you want them focusing on practice. Try to separate out the talent part from the *acquired skill* part in your praise. Say "I can remember when you fell every time you tried that kick flip. All that work you put in on it has paid off," instead of, "You are so coordinated (a talent) that those tricks just seem to come easily to you." Say "You've gotten to where you don't even hesitate when you have to solve polynomials. All that time you spent practicing sure has made a difference," instead of, "You're just a math whiz."

**Character.** Character is a particularly praiseworthy quality. You want your kid to be thinking in terms of character when they make decisions in life. Character is an important factor in every kind of task, and it forms the foundation for a meaningful and satisfying life. Create a list of the most important morals or character traits you want to encourage in your kid, to keep them fresh in your mind. Consider integrity, responsibility, compassion, kindness, honor, honesty, generosity, courage, hard work, leadership—the list can go on and on. Find ways to praise your kid for showing these character traits. "I am very impressed by the way you took responsibility for getting the house straightened up without my having to say anything."

**Initiative.** Taking initiative is a double-edged sword. On the one hand, it is important for your kid to make things happen. On the other hand, your kid can really screw things up if they try to do something that's far beyond their expertise. Like skill, you may have to separate out the intent (seeing something that needs doing and trying to take care of it) from the outcome (destroying, breaking, or ruining something in the process). "Thanks for taking your dirty dishes back to the kitchen without my having to remind you. It means a lot to me." "I appreciate your wanting to help me out by trying to fix the toaster, son. I really do. (Our homeowners insurance will probably pay for most of the damage)."

**Persistence.** Kids need encouragement to keep striving in the face of obstacles, hurtles, or outright failure. Praising your kid for continuing to try when things are going badly is an important way to make it difficult for them to quit. "I'm really glad you are not giving up on this. I know it is frustrating." "Even though this didn't turn out like you wanted, I am very proud that you kept working on it right to the end."

**Risk-taking.** Taking calculated risks is an important part of an interesting life. There are times when your kid will need encouragement to reach for something requiring a real stretch, which could result in them falling flat on their face. Give your kid the encouragement and recognition they need for taking the right kind of chances. "I can't believe you actually tried out! That was awesome!" "I am so sorry she turned you down, but it was *so* worth the risk. You just never know."

Some caveats:

- Praise works best in combination with other kinds of feedback. It is, ideally, part of a more complex combination of praise, support, encouragement, evaluation, constructive criticism, and even sometimes accepting disappointment.

- Be careful about trying to make your kid feel better by blaming things on other people ( "It's all politics." "He just didn't like you.") or other things ( "It was just an off day for you." "The sun was in your eyes."). There are times when we just don't measure up. Those are the times to pick yourself up, dust yourself off, and start all over again. The appropriate response is to sympathize with their disappointment ("That sucks") and help them figure out what they can learn from the experience that will benefit them in the future—but don't expect them to figure this out right after they have suffered a devastating failure or rejection.

Motivating kids through fear of judgment, failure, humiliation, shame, or the displeasure of others leads to poorer quality work, the death of creativity, lack of personal enjoyment and investment in a task, loss of intrinsic interest, and feelings of anxiety and inadequacy. Kids can end up giving up altogether or discarding those pesky morals that interfere with winning at any cost (and begin to think, if you can't beat 'em, join 'em).

Praising your teen for doing something right is a valuable role you play in shaping their future successes.

# PUNISHMENT

Punishment is only partially about making your kid suffer for violating rules or misbehaving. It is also about helping them think first—and clearly consider the cost of their decisions. It's also about helping them learn to respect boundaries (family, personal, legal, etc.)

This chapter deals with:

- The basic formula for punishing teens
- Repeat offenders
- Punishment through addition (rather than subtraction)
- Finding the joy in parenting

Many parents who come from a family of spankers recognize the inherent problems in using corporal punishment to discipline their kids. The biggest challenge for these parents is figuring out what to do instead. For adults who had harsh or even abusive parents, choosing not to follow the same path can mean they end up without much of an idea about how to enforce their expectations. Unfortunately, when you are creating a new tradition, you have to think through each situation. Thinking takes a time and creativity—something that can be in very short supply these days.

## WHAT'S A PARENT TO DO?

Here is a formula for punishing your kids that is flexible, straightforward, and effective. It teaches a lesson but doesn't require getting out "Mr. Spoon."

If your teen commits a first-time offense, consider tying the consequence to the violation. If they have poor grades, the punishment should include more studying. If they haven't cleaned their room, then they are grounded until the room is cleaned. If they abuse a privilege (such as using a vehicle, cell phone, or the internet), remove the privilege until they have demonstrated appropriate respect for your rules.

However, if that doesn't get results—or if it's a first time offense that is serious—you can take punishment to the next level. More serious punishment has a couple of elements:

1. Start by finding something your teen will dislike or even hate. Teens need to actually suffer when they screw up because their suffering will:

   a) Help them build character—because all suffering builds character

   b) Up the ante of any natural consequences, decreasing the likelihood that they will repeat the misbehavior or lapse in judgment

   c) Help them develop a sense of responsibility and accountability for their actions ("Ain't nothin' free, baby")

You want the punishment to be related to the area of troublesome behavior. If the problem is a dirty room, the consequence could be about cleaning something up (in addition to the room). If it is about responsible driving, the consequence could be something related to driving. If it is defiance of authority (yours or others), the consequence could be giving them one arbitrary, meaningless task after another until they show the right attitude when being bossed around.

2. Don't forget, you can add misery to your teen's life rather than just limiting yourself to restrictions or deprivation. Parents might naturally think first of taking things away. ("You're grounded until you're eighteen!" "I'm selling your X-Box!" "I'm shaving your head in your sleep!") But there's also a whole, wide world

of punishments based on "active" suffering. For example, digging a hole in the back yard and then filling it back up; weeding the garden; volunteering at the local food kitchen; writing essays on important topics; or running laps at the local track. The list is limited only by your imagination.

3.  Don't forget lecturing. You might be surprised by how miserable you can make your teen by scheduling regular lectures on the area he or she is driving you crazy about—long, boring lectures with quizzes for understanding thrown in.

4.  Find something that will provide you with evil glee. (Please note, this only works with sane people. You should *not* get a sense of evil glee by humiliating your child.) Evil glee is when you discover a punishment that leads to you experiencing a deep, gut laugh at the thought of implementing the consequence. It often turns out to be just the right punishment for your kid to get the message so everyone can get back to the business of getting things done and enjoying life. There isn't any reason parenting shouldn't be fun! If they have once again neglected to do their chore of cleaning the bathroom, you might have them get two plastic bags and gather up all the doggy-doo in the backyard. The possibilities are endless; having to spend hours in conversations about religion with one of their religious leaders, riding the bus to school, meditate together using a guided instruction tape. Anything that makes them miserable and makes you chuckle to yourself because of what you know about how your kid would react.

The main thing to remember is that punishment is about guiding and directing. It is about demonstrating to your teen that it's in their best interest to consider the consequences before choosing to do something wrong. Ultimately, punishment is about helping your teen grow into a more self-disciplined young adult.

# DRIVING ISSUES

# DRIVING

## Part 1:
### The Learner's Permit

So let's say you are crazy enough to consider allowing your kid to take the first step toward getting behind the wheel of a car by obtaining a learner's permit—a temporary, conditional license that will let a teen practice driving in traffic when another adult driver is with them in the vehicle. Your teen will need your help developing the awareness and skills needed to become a responsible and safe driver.

This chapter addresses:

- How to prepare them to be apprentice drivers

- Important criteria if they want to get (and keep) a driving permit

- Ways to promote safe driving skills

- Ideas for teaching your teen defensive driving

They've nagged. They've whined. They've schmoozed. Desperation oozes from every pore. A child turning fifteen years old is (yet another) parent's worst nightmare, the age when teens in most states qualify for the dreaded learner's permit.

With no clear rites of passage in our culture, obtaining a permit and then a driver's license takes on mythical significance. Freedom.

Independence. The open road. This perception might explain why motor vehicle accidents are the leading cause of death for teens. Add passengers in the car to an inexperienced driver and you increase the risk of fatal accidents. On the other hand, having a kid who can drive is a great advantage. They aren't the only ones who obtain a little freedom.

## WHAT'S A PARENT TO DO?

**Start early.** It helps if you have begun to nag, harass, and lecture them about the dangers of driving before they even get their permit. (You need at least a two-year head start, so let's say around age thirteen.) This includes beginning to talk about the serious responsibility represented by the privilege of driving, pointing out examples of good and bad driving when traveling together in the car, and quizzing them about what they would do in driving situations you encounter. For reasons discussed later, have your kid make suggestions if they notice potential hazards (or careless driving on your part).

**Practice with vehicles they already operate.** If your kid has a motorized vehicle like a dirt bike, go cart, golf cart, or riding lawn mower, require them to be a responsible operator and tie it directly to the opportunity for them to drive a bigger vehicle in the future. Bicycles, rollerblades, and skateboards will also work. Consider giving them a mock driver's exam with a test of driving skills for the use of their vehicle. It is funny and makes a point, especially if you "revoke their license" for reckless driving or for violations of rules of the road.

**Model responsible driving.** It is also a good idea for you to do a quick review of your own driving habits. Set an example and avoid hypocrisy by being as responsible as you will ask them to be.

**Familiarize yourself with local driver's license laws.** For example, there are school attendance and satisfactory academic progress requirements for getting a license in many states. Knowing the laws will provide the starting point for your expectations about your teen's driving and the use of your vehicle. Driving between the ages of fifteen and eighteen might come with restricted driving hours, initial restrictions on the number of passengers in the car, the required presence of an adult licensed driver, and consequences for motor vehicle accidents or moving violations and mandatory seat belt use (except for New Hampshire). Your kid should be familiar with these requirements, which means you will also need to know them.

**Establish the criteria to obtain a learner's permit.** It is a good idea to let your teen know what will be required of them before they can get a learner's permit. You might insist on:

Dedicated time studying for the exam. They can't take the exam until they can pass a parent-administered test with 90 percent accuracy. It's a waste of time to take the test if they haven't studied, and they need to indicate to you that they take this seriously. Study with them. Use driving time to teach practical lessons, such as what to do when you come to a four-way stop.

Grade point average of B or higher. Most insurance companies provide a "good student" discount for insuring licensed drivers. Even though your kid might have a learner's permit without being insured, grades equal money when they get a license. Get them used to the idea that this will be one of the criteria for driving when they obtain a real license.

**Create a "graduated learner's permit."** Think in terms of gradually exposing your kid to the conditions they will encounter as a licensed driver.

- **New learners.** Begin by allowing only the two of you in the vehicle. No passengers. No radio. No distractions. Progression to the next level of responsibility is earned once they automatically demonstrate good driving habits. This would begin with pre-ignition checklists (seat belt, adjusting seat and mirrors, checking to make sure passengers are wearing seat belts, etc.). It would also include safe driving habits; they must be able to come to a full stop at stop signs, accurately identify posted speed limit and observe that limit at all times, stop for yellow lights rather than gunning it, maintain proper distance from other vehicles, be courteous to other drivers, and react with empathy rather than anger to discourteous drivers. When they are comfortable behind the wheel and you have little to say about their driving, they will be ready to move to the Experienced Learner phase. (Note that in some states, drivers with a learner's permit who use a cell phone—with or without a hands-free device—may be fined and may receive delayed eligibility for the next license type. Since texts and calls have a time stamp, it's easy to check.

- **Experienced learners**. Teens who have had more time behind the wheel should demonstrate the driving behaviors you would expect from them as licensed drivers. Introduce distractions at this phase: radio, a sibling as a passenger, suddenly screaming at the top of your lungs (just kidding about the screaming). If the quality of their driving slips, take them back to the New Learner phase for at least two weeks. It might be the distractions or it may be overconfidence. Regardless, driving is serious business. By the end of this phase, you should be confident that your kid would be a responsible driver without you in the vehicle.

**Develop driving safety skills.** It is useful to give your kid experience dealing with a number of threats to safe driving. When they get to the Experienced Learner phase, inform them that you will be randomly testing their ability to drive safely under a variety of circumstances. Be sure to let them know that you will be doing this; it's not a good idea to just spring it on them. You actually want them to succeed. Note: initially, introduce these distractions in less stressful driving situations (not on the expressway at seventy miles per hour).

- ○ **Distraction**. Turn on the radio. Gasp and act like you are about to be killed in a head-on collision (something your spouse may still be testing you on). Have a sibling act annoying (but without touching the driver). Get mad at them about something. Nag them. Continue just past the point where they appear to be affected. They should be able to stay focused on their driving in the face of these distractions.

○ **Disruption**. Reach for the steering wheel. Grab their arm. Do things that will actually disrupt their driving. (Does it need to be said again that you should only practice these with caution?) Have them drive off the shoulder of the road and then steer back onto the pavement. (Again, practice this very slowly at first and then build up to faster speed.) They should have some experience responding to things that directly disrupt their driving.

○ **Incitement**. Make suggestions that require violating safe driving practices. Try to get them to run a yellow light. Try to get them to hurry up. This one will be more likely to be a farce, but it will make the point.

○ **Skillful copiloting**. Require your kid to notice when you are violating any safe driving principles. Research suggests that kids will rein in their driving in response to pressure from same age passengers. Train them to be that kind of passenger by making this skill an explicit part of your kid's driver training. They should notice unsafe driving and learn how to suggest safer driving.

Review your kid's reactions to the challenges you presented after the drive. Make sure they have developed some effective responses, including how to tell passengers to back off. This might even require stopping the vehicle to make their point. You will learn a lot about your kid's readiness to deal with challenges when driving. The development of these coping skills could be life-saving, but be sure to have fun with it. The lessons will still be effective.

**Amateur defensive driver training course.** One final skill to develop is how to respond-to unexpected events that occur outside of the vehicle. Find an isolated area that can mimic paved road conditions, such as an unused parking lot or a paved street in an uninhabited housing development. You will need two or three large, rubber garbage cans, tennis balls, a stuffed animal, and water balloons or water guns. The objective is to have your kid operate the vehicle under distracting or dangerous road conditions. These lessons are lots of fun. You can even gather several of your teen's friends and put them all through their paces.

○ **Developing a feel for the vehicle**. Set up the trash cans so that your kid has to swerve in between them. Have them start out slowly. Increase speed so that they develop some confidence in handling the vehicle if they have to swerve suddenly. Then, set a couple of the trash cans up and have your kid accelerate toward them and then brake at the last moment. The goal is to get as close as possible to the trash cans without hitting them. Finally, have a couple people get behind the trash cans lined up along the street. One of them will toss the stuffed animal out (from a safe distance) in front of the vehicle, requiring a sudden stop. This helps the driver get a feel for braking suddenly and how far the car travels at different speeds.

○ **Responding to sudden noises**. As your experienced learner drives by, throw tennis balls at the side of the vehicle. The goal is to give them experience with hearing sudden, loud noises without reacting.

○ **Losing visibility**. You and your assistants are going to throw water balloons or shoot water guns at the windshield as they drive by. This will give your kid some experience responding to a sudden loss of visibility. Be careful as you do this, because inexperienced people tend to jerk the wheel when the water hits. You don't want any accidents—but you do want your teen to have the first experience under these conditions to be in a safe, controlled environment instead of out on the highway.

The learner's permit provides a controlled opportunity to help your kid begin to develop more skill and confidence in their driving. Have them go slow and earn it. The sooner they get their license, the sooner someone is going to have to start paying through the nose to insure them.

# DRIVING

## Part 2:
### The Driver's License

"Let's roll!" Teens pour out of your front door onto the lawn arguing about who gets to ride "shotgun" and talking over each other about who's going to be at local hang out as they pile into the car. How could you help but smile? Then suddenly it occurs to you that none of those kids crammed into your car have any common sense and their lives are in the hands of your idiot teenager, who gets distracted when flushing the toilet. As they start the car and begin to back out of the driveway, you break into a run, throwing yourself onto the hood of the car screaming "Stop! Stop!"

This section of the chapter addresses issues that come up once the license is in hand, or nearly there. It discusses:

- The law for getting a license
- Rules for driving and using a family vehicle
- Driving expenses & how they will be handled
- Consequences for messing up

Obtaining a driver's license is a rite of passage for teens in this country. Motor vehicle accidents are the leading cause of death for teens. Passengers in the car increase the risk of fatal accidents (except when girls are passengers in a car driven by a boy; then the risks go down for fatalities but up in other areas). Despite all the risks posed by teenage drivers, a kid who can drive is a great advantage when family members need to be in several places at once.

## WHAT'S A PARENT TO DO?

Let them get a driver's license, that's what—but with conditions.

**Driver license requirements.** In most states, at age sixteen, your kid can legally obtain a restricted driver's license. The question is, what will they need to do to prove they deserve that license? Teens should not only fulfill the legal requirements for a license, but also demonstrate that they will operate your vehicle responsibly.

**Legal requirements.** It should be easy to check the driver's license laws in your state. In some states, the first level of independent operation of a vehicle is the "intermediate restricted driver's license." To qualify, a teenager must be at least sixteen years old, possess a learner's permit for at least six months, and successfully complete the driving exam, among other things. After one year of successfully maintaining a valid intermediate restricted driver's license, teens can obtain an intermediate *unrestricted* driver's license.

**History of responsible vehicle operation.** It is also important for parents to set some criteria of their own. At the very least, your kid should demonstrate six consecutive months of responsible driving with their learner's permit—just possessing a permit for six months doesn't qualify. Responsible driving is reflected by safe driving habits, consistent use of driving safety skills, no auto accidents, and not receiving any moving violations or citations of any kind. Restart the six-month clock if they violate any of these criteria.

**Expectations of licensed drivers.** Sit your kid down and have a talk about what you expect from them as a licensed driver. Be sure to include a review of the laws, your feelings about texting and cell phone use while driving, their responsibilities for errands, and your grade expectations.

○ **Legal restrictions.** Some states have intermediate restricted driver's license laws that limit driving only during daytime hours (except for school, work, or hunting—and these require carrying a parent permission form). There are often restrictions on the number of underage passengers and other restrictions. Know your state's driver permit law.

○ **Texting and cell phones.** Texting while driving is eight times more dangerous than driving drunk. Cell phone conversations are statistically as dangerous as drunk driving. It's also against the law in more and more states to drive while either texting or talking on a cell phone. Increasingly, states are enacting laws that will fine drivers for texting or cell phone use on the road. Insist that your kid not text or use the cell phone while driving. Since texts and calls have a time stamp, it's easy to monitor.

○ **Errands.** All children with a valid driver's license should be required to run whatever errands their parents assign them. No questions. No whining. If they don't like it, have them hand you the keys.

○ **Grade expectations.** Car insurance often costs less when a teenager maintains a "B" average. This requirement ties driving to the larger arena of life and to long-term financial planning.

**Driving Expenses.** Someone has to purchase the vehicle your kid will drive as well as pay for the fuel, liability insurance, and maintenance and repairs. If you require your kid to be responsible for everything from buying the vehicle to covering the cost of upkeep, they will already be learning the life lessons this responsibility presents. These lessons include a) things are more expensive than you think and b) you never have as much mad money as you figure. Unfortunately, the financial pressure of purchasing and maintaining a vehicle can cause some teenagers to shift their priorities to making enough money to cover these expenses and still be able to buy stupid stuff. Grades can suffer. Keep an eye on this kind of short-term thinking. You may have to intervene to refocus their priorities.

If your kid is lucky enough to have parents who can make a vehicle available to them, it will be useful to build in some financial responsibility for this privilege. Few kids have a realistic idea of the cost of living, even in families with limited means. Any opportunity for parents to help their kids appreciate the hidden costs of everyday items will give the teens a better perspective on what life will be like on their own. (On the other hand, they may also just decide to mooch off you for the rest of their lives.)

Typical expenses associated with driving include the cost of the vehicle, fuel, insurance, and vehicle maintenance.

○ **Vehicle acquisition.** Your kid may have to purchase a vehicle, either because of your values system (work to earn what you have) or because of limited family finances. For some reason, kids who have to purchase their own vehicles seem to be much more protective of those cars than kids who are given a vehicle. This alone can reduce many of the risks associated with teen driving. If they will be using a family vehicle, require them to make some kind of contribution to offset the expense of the vehicle or its upkeep. This can help instill a greater sense of responsibility.

○ **Auto insurance.** Car insurance for teenagers is EXPENSIVE! You can be looking at around $2,200 a year per kid. That amount approaches 50 percent of the income for a teenager working twenty hours a week at minimum wage. If you don't require your kid pay for car insurance outright, this is another expense category to which they can be required to contribute. It is extremely frustrating to have your money go for unsexy things like automobile insurance (and health insurance and home infrastructure repairs and taxes). They might as well learn this lesson now.

○ **Fuel.** If your kid is responsible for providing their own fuel, they will readily come to understand the unpleasant reality of hidden expenses. It would be so much more fun to buy something cool with that money. If you provide funds for fuel, consider establishing a set amount to be provided on a given day each week. This requires them to manage this money and monitor their mileage. Hopefully, they will mis-allocate the money ("Dude! I'm starving!") or do too much driving around and run out of gas before the next installment. That is a really useful lesson.

O **Vehicle maintenance**. Like insurance, vehicle maintenance is expensive. Unlike insurance payments, it crops up unexpectedly. This expense category is just chocked full of lesson-learning.

**Trust, but verify.** Every now and then, when your kid drives off, get in your vehicle and tail them. You don't have to tell them, if all goes well (although there is some value in your kid knowing that you are not above sneaking around to double-check on them). Regardless, spying is a perfectly legitimate parenting technique. It's especially justified if you *do* discover problems.

**Violations.** Finally, it is important to clarify what will happen if your kid violates your rules for operating a vehicle. Here are some suggested guidelines for consequences that are consistent with a view that your job is to help your teen become a responsible, safe driver.

O **Texting and cell phone use while driving.** It is so convenient! And, besides, what could go wrong? Confiscate the cell phone for a week. If it happens again, confiscate the cell phone for two weeks and drop their driving privileges down to a learner's permit for one month. If it happens a third time, permanently cancel their cell phone service.

O **Traffic citation**. While any traffic citation your kid receives should be taken seriously, moving violations carry the greatest risk and potential cost. The consequences will have two levels. First, the state will assign points for the violation that will determine whether your kid will be driving in the near future. Second, you will also have something to say about their poor driving habits. Actions have consequences. Consider holding your child responsible for any related increase in automobile insurance costs, if they are not already paying for their own insurance. It will also be important to review their driving habits. This can be best accomplished by reducing their driving privileges to the learner's permit level for one month, to enable you to observe them and correct any poor driving habits. It will also be a great opportunity to spend quality time with your kid.

○ **Police but no ticket.** Some kids have the great good fortune of being stopped by a police officer who remembers what *they* were like as a teen. While your child has technically broken the law, officers will occasionally decide to let parents address the problem rather than writing a citation. This would also warrant reducing their driving privileges to learner's permit level for one month, to enable you to review their driving habits.

○ **Automobile accident for which your kid is responsible.** Taking responsibility means that if you screw up, you fix it. They wreck the car; they pay for the damages. If insurance costs increase, they are responsible for those costs, too.

○ **Neighborhood watch.** Sometimes you will be informed of problems with your kid's driving by friends and neighbors. These complaints are the equivalent of being stopped by the police without being ticketed.

○ **Driving under the influence.** Zero tolerance. This kills people. First offense, revoke all driving privileges for at least six months—or permanently, depending on how strongly you wish to make your point. Second offense, permanently revoke driving privileges in any vehicle you own and consult with a mental health professional; your kid has a substance use problem.

As with all parenting, if the system ain't broke, don't fix it. By paying close attention to early driving habits and your kid's attitude, you can usually tell if you need to provide more structure. When you add more structure, most kids will come right into line. Happily, confiscating those keys is a remarkably effective consequence.

# FAMILY MANAGEMENT ISSUES

# THE FAMILY CONTRACT

**S**ocial contracts underlie all aspects of human interactions. Most of the time, such contracts are invisible. Parenting often involves helping your kid(s) understand these social contracts and recognize the obligations they have to important social partners like their parents and siblings. Mostly, though, teens just need to do their chores.

> This chapter considers:
>
> - Signs you need a family contract
>
> - Techniques to make the process go more smoothly
>
> - Step-by-step instructions for creating the contract

The family contract is a way to prepare your kid to live with people in the real world. It keeps the household running smoothly by establishing a clear, rational structure that identifies everyone's responsibilities and obligations. A contract fosters communication and minimizes arguments and conflict. Depending on how you approach the contract with your kids, it can also improve relationships, teach negotiation skills, and help your kids appreciate what they have. Like all parenting, creating a family contract imitates the real world without the permanent costs of mistakes (because you might get mad at them and make them shape up, but you won't evict them).

## WHAT'S A PARENT TO DO?

Many families can get along quite well without laying everything out in a formal contract (at least, rumor has it that these families exist). Remember the maxim: if it ain't broke, don't fix it. How do you know if it would be worth formulating a family contract? Here are some signs you may need a more formal understanding of every-one's responsibilities and the costs for neglecting them:

- Lots of arguing over whose job is what or whether someone is being treated fairly

- Kids who won't just take care of something when you tell them to ("Hey, would you take out the trash?" "Not now, Mom, I'm busy.")

- A complicated family structure (blended families, people coming and going from week to week, multiple generations living in the same house, etc.)

- Repeated conflict over particular issues ("I had to do that last week!" "I'll do it in a minute.")

- Family members who are overscheduled, so that free time is hard to find and things get ignored

- Families undergoing transitions (a recent move, movement from one developmental stage to another as in childhood to adolescence, etc.)

There are a few techniques that are important if you are developing an effective contract while having your kids learn from the experience.

**Take your time.** Set aside a block of time to sit down and get the contract set up. The process is as important as the outcome, so don't rush it. If you run out of time, table the meeting and schedule the next time to finish up. Be sure to have the follow-up soon, so you don't lose the initiative.

○ **Discussion.** Make proposals. Ask questions. Talk—really talk. Insist on opinions from everyone. Watch your body language, because subtle cues could cut off discussion.

○ **Fairness**. Kids don't have to *like* the contract, but they do need to think it is fair. Everyone needs to actually believe the rules are reasonable and that it's possible and practical to accomplish them.

○ **Flexibility**. Make room for creative solutions. You will need to have an idea of where the contract generally needs to end up, but you don't have to have it all mapped out ahead of time.

○ **Compromise**. Go into the meeting ready to make compromises. Each kid will need to have the experience that they have been able to both contribute and to gain some concession. If you are normally agreeable, take an initial hard-line position on something so you can compromise. If you are normally a hard-line person, let some things go. It's a great way to motivate your teen and help them feel some ownership in the contract itself.

○ **Rules of conversation**. Listen. Don't interrupt or let others interrupt. People are allowed to disagree, but they have to do so politely and without criticizing—and that includes you. Be pleasant. Summarize to indicate understanding. Highlight areas of agreement to keep from feeling like everything is terrible.

○ **If it ain't broke ...** Only make rules for the things that aren't working. Leave everything else alone.

## FAMILY CONTRACT OUTLINE

**Make a list of important areas to be addressed.** Look for repeated arguments or areas of chronic punishment. Add areas where things are going well so you can cross them off the list. Solicit suggestions from everyone for topics that need to be reviewed.

**Address one area at a time.** Finish with each rule before you move on to the next. This is harder than it may seem. People are always throwing in other things when conflict is being addressed. The rules and consequence for the first area will be the most difficult. Take your time with it. Don't give up, no matter what. The remaining areas will get easier. Take a break if things get too heated. This part of the process has huge implications for teaching kids emotional self-regulation (meaning that nobody can yell or leave in a huff), persisting in the face of frustration (because you will continue to discuss the issue until it is resolved, no matter how many meetings it takes), and productively resolving conflict—they won't like some of what you require, but you are going to compromise to let them have the experience that persistence and reasonableness pay off.

**Make each rule clear, specific, and detailed.** If you have to create a family contract, it is because a more general, situational understanding of responsibilities isn't working. Agreed-upon tasks, curfews, etc. are scheduled to the minute. ("All cleaned dishes are to be removed from dishwasher and put up where they belong." "Curfew is eleven p.m., sharp.") Eliminate anything that requires interpretation by specifying wherever you can (A "C" average is 70 or higher, not 69.9; clean is determined by the parent, not when the kid thinks it is good enough; etc.).

**Specific consequences for specific rules.** Link consequences to the rule violated. Unfinished chores mean standing in the area of the required chore with no eating, watching videos, urinating, etc. until the task is completed. Grounding should be the consequence for direct defiance or refusal. ("No, I'm not going to do it!")

**Reward compliance.** Make sure you notice when they do what they are supposed to do. You can acknowledge it casually ("Thanks for taking care of the trash." "I appreciate you cleaning up your room.") or formally ("It means a lot to me that you are taking care of your responsibilities without my needing to get involved. That is a sign of real maturity."). The point is that you are going to nail their butts to the wall if they don't do it, so you need to also let them know that their desirable behavior is noticed and appreciated.

**It ain't over 'til the annoying kid agrees.** The contract isn't complete until everyone says, "Yes, I agree." Hint: "I don't care," shrugs, and mumbles don't count as agreement. Wear them down. Don't end the meeting until agreement is achieved. This is the continuation of your demonstration that you will not just let this go. It is a lesson in being required to participate and be held accountable for their agreements.

**Write and post rules.** Make hard copies for everyone. The contract (not the parent) is the final arbiter; is it there or isn't it. If a rule is not there, it may be time for another meeting to update the contract. Note: Parents still have the parental override privileges, but should use them very sparingly.

**Enforce the rules.** Don't agree to a contract if you aren't going to enforce it. Be calm, firm, and unmoving; they agreed to this. Only renegotiate a situation after the original consequences have been imposed. Feeling sorry for them isn't enough. That also means that if your kid finds a loophole, you still follow the contract—but then immediately have a meeting to close the loophole for the future. An agreement is an agreement. If they keep finding loopholes, you may have a naturally gifted litigator—or it might be time to consult with a mental health professional.

**Review and revise.** Review the contract within two to four weeks of implementation (or right after your kid has found a loophole). You can change anything you want at any time because you are the parent—but it is a very bad idea to change things outside of the negotiation process. If contract changes appear arbitrary, you lose credibility and your kids won't have a reason to follow the contract.

Specific strategies to address specific areas of concern—such as alcohol and drug use, poor grades, chores, TV/media screen time, family time, and curfew—can be inserted into the contract. The contract is meant to provide an overall structure for establishing family rules and consequences.

# ALLOWANCE
# AND MONEY

L ife goes much easier when you know how to manage money. Unfortunately, kids are given very little training in this area.

This chapter explores:

- The value of giving your kid an allowance
- Family finances as a teaching tool
- Requiring your kid to save and charitable giving
- Limiting "fun" money
- Reasons not to pay your kids to do chores

Many Americans at all economic levels have expectations for possessions and luxuries that far exceed their income. America is, after all, a culture shaped by consumerism. As with so many other aspects of adult life, there are many things your kids can learn from you before they are forced to confront the realities of the cold, cruel world. One of them is that money can be used or abused.

Most kids start learning about money with an allowance of some sort. Should we even give our kids an allowance? Yes. The most obvious reason is that it helps teach them how to manage money and how money can begin to manage you, if you don't keep an eye on it. An allowance provides a means by which parents can help their kids experience the reality of how much (read that as "how little") disposable income you really have when you have to live within your means. Managing money also requires kids to delay gratification, plan, anticipate, and work toward a long-term goal.

## WHAT'S A PARENT TO DO?

**Step one.** To begin, parents will need to determine what they can afford when it comes to allowance. It can be useful to include your kid in this step, to provide a reality check for your ongoing discussions about managing their money. A general discussion about family finances helps identify what it takes to have the lifestyle your family enjoys. For this, family finances need to be translucent (providing general information on income and expenses) rather than transparent (giving a detailed accounting for all of your income and expenditures). It can be maddening to have your kid try to tell you where you could shift money from one expense category to another—namely, into their pocket.

**Step two.** Once parents have determined how much allowance they can afford, it is important to specify how your kid is to allocate any income they receive, whether it's from allowance, gifts, or employment. This will be the core mechanism for helping them develop good money management habits. First, establish a set of non-discretionary expenses. Some teens have a problem with this. "You can't tell me what to do with my money! I earned that." Well, yes; except that the list of nondiscretionary expenses you provide for your kid out of the goodness of your heart is quite a long one. (Let's see, there is room and board, utilities including access to the internet and other media, medical expenses, transportation, school expenses, unexpected maintenance expenses like repairs and replacement costs, clothing, supplies, extracurricular activities, bills for cell phones and other media, vehicle expenses like car payments, insurance, and fuel, gifts, and personal care like haircuts, makeup, etc.)

Since adults have non-discretionary and discretionary expenses, it is a good model to use for your kid to divide up any income they receive. Non-discretionary expenses can be anything you decide. Some universal elements would include boring and frustrating expenses that pay off in the future like savings (at least 15 percent of any income), "taxes" for some future goal like saving toward a vehicle or college (at least 15 percent), and support of charitable or religious organizations (10 percent often comes to mind).

As your kid gets older (or if your ability to provide an allowance is limited), it can be an instructive strategy to shift the management of some of the non-discretionary money into their hands. In this way, their allowance may increase but so will their responsibility for expenses. Things like fuel, car insurance payments, clothing, cell phone and other electronic media expenses, and personal grooming would fit into this category. Run out of money, lose access.

**Step three.** Establish expectations for discretionary spending. Discretionary expenses would be anything your kid wants to purchase. As you try to calculate the amount of money to provide for this category, it can be useful to consider what you think is a reasonable amount to be spent on non-essential purchases. Think in terms of an "entertainment outing." Examples would be the cost of going to a movie, one-third to one-quarter the cost of a video game, a school sporting event, or eating out at a fast-food restaurant. Then decide on an acceptable number of times a kid their age should have an entertainment outing (and if you think it is every week starting in middle school, you are giving your kid an unrealistic view of what they should expect in the early part of their work life). A starting place can be one outing a month for sixth- to eighth-graders; two to three outings a month for ninth- and tenth-graders; and four to five outings a month for eleventh- and twelfth-graders.

You might also consider calculating the basic cost of the outing rather than including all the trimmings (cost of the movie and a drink but not popcorn or candy, a fast-food meal for a reasonable adult rather than a teenage boy, etc.). Finally, identify acceptable and unacceptable uses of expendable income.

**A final note.** Generally, kids should not earn their allowance by doing the chores. Money for chores is usually predicated on the "chores are like work" concept. The problem is that some kids will actually quit their job (do without the money so they don't have to do chores) and decide to live off "the government" (their parents).

Chores are an obligation that kids have as part of contributing to the family, the price they pay for sharing a common living space (like when you have roommates or a spouse/partner). Not doing chores is not an option.

If you are still worried about providing enough for your kid when it comes to discretionary spending, here are few statistics to keep in mind. Kids with $25 or more a week in spending money are nearly twice as likely as those with less money to smoke, drink, and use illegal drugs, and more than twice as likely to get drunk. According to the 1996 Rand Youth Poll, kids five to fourteen years old spent $24.4 billion and directly influenced another $117 billion spent on their behalf! This is a boatload of money from people who don't even have a job. Tell them to read a book (that they can get from the library).

Note: The chapter on Jobs and Employment also has information on money and finances.

# CHORES AND OTHER HOUSEHOLD RESPONSIBILITIES

U nless you have one of those naturally fastidious kids, it almost seems easier to just do chores yourself than to persuade your teen to help out. But if you do that, you'll miss out on teaching your kid some important lessons about self-sufficiency, obligations for a shared living space, assuming responsibility for your own mess, consideration for the preferences of others, and contributing to the family for all they provide.

This chapter provides information on:

- Identifying and assigning chores

- Making the distribution of chores fair

- Reasons for having a Family Contract

- How to create a Family Contract that works for everyone

## WHAT'S A PARENT TO DO?

How do you know if you should go to all the trouble of developing a structured system with charts and happy face stickers and rewards? Ask yourself a few questions. Do your kids already willingly help out? Can you count on your kids to do what you ask (like take out the trash or pick up their room) without having to nag them? Other than a little huffing, does everyone think the current assignments are fair? If the answer is "yes," don't mess with it.

But if you are like the rest of us, a clear, specific, flexible, and fair system can help minimize arguing and more easily hold kids accountable for their responsibilities. The following are some of the components of a successful household responsibility contract.

**Make a list.** Start by identifying all the various household maintenance tasks. List *everything*, including tasks done by parents. This helps kids see how relatively little they are actually doing. Be sure to include an estimation of the time for completion and the frequency required for each task (daily, weekly, monthly, seasonally, etc.). Many tasks fit into maintenance of a few geographical areas: personal space (room, clothing, vehicle for licensed drivers); common areas (bathrooms, living, dining, kitchen, family); general household maintenance (setting and clearing the table, cooking, laundry, trash, dishes and cleaning); and yard maintenance (mowing, raking, weeding). Other tasks will fall under home repairs, pet care, and vehicle maintenance. Decide which of these will be kid chores.

**It's an obligation, not a job.** As a general rule, parents should avoid paying kids for household chores. While the argument can be made that chores are the equivalent of work, unlike work, these "employees" can't quit—hopefully, you are going to make your kids complete the chores anyway. Arguments and resentment will then ensue. Kids should recognize their obligation to pull their own weight, which is a way to prepare them for communal living as an adult. You don't get paid for taking care of your own living space. It is an obligation.

**Have family meetings.** Once you have determined which chores are kid chores, gather the family together to create a household responsibility contract. It can be informal or it can be written with exacting detail. As you follow the remaining steps, write out the agreement. Plan on regular family meetings to celebrate success or modify the agreement as situations change or responsibilities shift.

**Make it fair.** Fairness has several dimensions. By identifying the time and frequency of specific chores, it is easier to ensure an equitable distribution of total time per week each person will have to spend completing chores. This also allows you to make the point of how little actual time chores take. When there are tasks no one wants to do, establish a system by which kids trade off the responsibility. (Note: Keep an eye on your naturally sweet kid. They might willingly take on a disproportionate amount of work.)

**Specify days and times for chore completion.** It is important to identify a day and time for the assigned chores to be completed. Solicit lots of input from your kid on this. Take their schedule seriously. Be flexible. Be very specific. "I will clean my room by noon every other Saturday." There is no confusion; there is nothing to argue about. They are giving their word that their chore will become a priority at the agreed-upon time (if it hasn't already been completed by then).

**Life stops if chores aren't completed.** Once the day and time are set, nothing more need be said—nothing, that is, until the agreed-upon time arrives. Your kid can complete the chore any time they want *before* the deadline. However, if the chore has not been completed by the agreed-upon time, their life comes to a halt until the chore is completed. If they are about to attend a sporting event, if they are out doing things with their friends, if they are sitting on the toilet—back they go to complete the task.

The value of this plan to you as a parent is that the chore will be addressed at a specific day and time, with no constant arguing about doing it *now*. The benefit for your kid is you don't nag them. That's right. In fact, don't even mention the chore. Don't ask if they are going to do it or remind that time is almost up; it will either be done or not be done by the designated time. If it isn't done, completing the chore becomes your kid's sole priority—no eating, watching media, talking to friends, texting, nothing. An agreement is an agreement.

**Teach them to negotiate.** There are several places in this agreement where kids can practice negotiation skills. The first is identifying a day and time by which the chore must be completed. Since your child's life will come to a halt at the agreed-upon time if the chore has not been completed, they will need to pick a time that will work for them. Help them think through when the best time will be, given their schedule. Planning, goal-setting, and prioritizing are all contained within this process.

Another area for negotiation is in the assignment of chores. They might benefit from direct instruction about how to negotiate with a sibling (or even with you) regarding who gets assigned which chores. Then, they are held to their word. The contract is followed to the letter even if it turns out to be inconvenient or unfair is some way. Renegotiations can take place at the next family meeting that occurs *after* the chore is fulfilled under the agreed-upon contract.

**The "If Momma (or Daddy) ain't happy, ain't nobody happy" rule.** Last but not least, parents determine whether a chore has been satisfactorily completed. Inform your kids that any arguing about whether the task is complete will result in additional detailed requirements for completion. A room can be straightened. It can also be straightened and vacuumed. It can be straightened, vacuumed, dusted, drawers organized, windows washed inside and out, clothes arranged by color, carpet cleaned—the list can go on and on. Nip complaining in the bud, because complaints are the source of the majority of tension and conflict in the home. Besides, listening to complaints is incredibly annoying.

Going through the process of setting up obligations for chores is as important, if not more important, than getting the actual chores done. So take your time and don't skip steps or dole out assignments just to get it over with.

# CURFEW

Curfew serves a number of purposes. It helps kids learn how to balance fun with responsibility. It limits opportunities for trouble. It can help keep them safe. Curfew ensures that kids pay attention to self-care (things like sleep, rest, and recuperation). It also helps you sleep easier because you know they are safely in the house.

This chapter takes a look at:

- How to set curfew
- Rules for maintaining contact when they are out and about
- Making exceptions to the curfew
- Curfew during overnights and holidays
- Suggestions for curfew at different ages

**The law.** A good place to begin when establishing family rules is by reviewing the local law. While laws do differ from one community to another, in many states, curfew for kids under eighteen is between midnight and five a.m. unless they are going directly to or from a lawful activity, on a legitimate errand, or in the company of a parent or guardian. For kids sixteen and younger, a curfew might be 10 p.m. on weekdays and 11 p.m. on Friday and Saturday. Kids in this age range are to be home until six a.m.

For seventeen-year-olds, curfew might be eleven p.m. on weekdays and midnight on weekends. Parents may not knowingly allow their kid to violate curfew laws. Police can issue a warning or court summons, or even make an arrest for a curfew violation. The point is, follow the law.

**Establishing curfew.** Here are the basics of setting up a curfew for teens:

○ **Start with a family discussion**. While it is more efficient (and fun) to just deliver the Laws of Curfew from on high, teens can benefit from the process of determining a rational curfew. This will model how you want them to make decisions about play versus work when they are on their own. Some of the more important elements that should enter into the equation are how early they have to get up the next day, how much sleep they need (not how much they can do without), and how much time they need to fulfill other important responsibilities—such as studying, maintenance of their environment, and family relationship maintenance (and of course, updating Facebook). Curfew should also take into account the evening agenda (Do they have plans? Or are they just looking for trouble?), safety and, of course, how important (or fun) the activity will be. Finally, make sure you touch on how trust builds on trust. When they follow curfew, it makes it more likely you will consider special exceptions for them in the future.

○ **Set the times**. Once you have talked about why they have a curfew ("Because I said so") and identified important factors to weigh in determining a reasonable time to return home (usually right before they start to have fun), set some specific default times. This will help minimize arguments each time they want go out. Have one curfew for weekdays (Sunday through Thursday) and one for weekends (Friday and Saturday).

○ **Decide what counts as a violation**. This is kind of tricky. On the one hand, when you say ten o'clock, it means ten o'clock. Responsibility and keeping commitments are important character issues. On the other hand, time isn't set in stone. I would recommend that you identify a time *after* the curfew when consequences will begin (for example, "At 11:10, you will be considered in violation of your curfew").

○ **Decide on consequences**. One minute past the specified time is a violation. Consider having a formula that increases consequences for increased time past curfew. For every five, ten, or fifteen minutes past curfew your teen returns home, one hour will be deducted from curfew on the next most-desirable night out (a happening weekend). If they are going to be late, they must call at least thirty minutes before their curfew. If they don't, it counts as being one hour past curfew. This encourages them to keep track of time and be responsible rather than avoidant, and it helps them respect that other people's schedules are affected by their timeliness. If they return home more than one hour past curfew, they can be grounded for one or two weeks. If they are more than two hours past curfew or haven't called by one hour after curfew, they can be grounded for one month. Make the point that they are not to mess with your agreements or your emotions.

○ **Rules for renegotiating a curfew**. It is useful to have a mechanism that identifies how your kid can discuss the need for a later curfew. You may also need a formula for how often curfew can be extended after they are already out—for example, they can initiate no more than one change in curfew every two months). This will encourage your kid to think ahead by having to negotiate before they leave and it will reduce the conflict that can arise when kids try to negotiate every time. It can also help you stick to your convictions rather than being swayed by the pressure of the moment.

○ **Review curfew prior to departure**. Be sure your teen repeats their curfew and their responsibilities to you right before they leave.

○ **Check in upon arrival**. Require your kid to check in when they get home. This is a nice way to greet them upon returning to the bosom of their loving family—and it's also a chance to check for signs of illicit alcohol or drug use, the telltale smell of cigarette smoke (or the covering scent of

Febreze), and the general disheveled appearance that may suggest suspicious activities.

**Rules while out.** Since the main reason they have a cell phone is to be able to stay in touch, they'd better stay in touch. Talking to you helps them remember what they are supposed to be thinking about: safety, sobriety, sanity. When you call or text, they should respond. It is useful to establish a rule that they inform you every time they change locations. This gets them in the habit of keeping you informed. It also demonstrates to them that letting you in on what they are doing won't result in intense interrogations or interventions. This means you will need to intervene only if absolutely necessary. Try to delay dealing with your concerns about risks or appropriateness of locations until the next day.

**Touching base.** The longer kids are out unsupervised, the greater the opportunity for them to come up with some idiotic way to get into trouble. Basically, the more trustworthy your kid, the longer the time to allow in between checking in. This could be accomplished by requiring them to either come home after a couple hours or swing by the house so you can take a look at them and get a report. Younger teens and teens who are building back trust would be required to check in either by phone or in person in two-hour intervals. As teens get older and/or earn more trust, it is reasonable to allow longer periods of unsupervised time—but even highly trustworthy and older teens should be expected to check in at least every eight hours or so. The greater the opportunity for trouble (such as time spent in urban or high-density-population areas), the more strict you need to be about touching base.

**Special circumstances.** There will be special circumstances that justify modifications to the curfew. Requiring your kid to negotiate exceptions to curfew will force them to weigh the costs and benefits of the activity in order to justify it to you. Depending on how argumentative your teen is, you may have to limit the number of exceptions up front (no more than one exception every six weeks, for example). Negotiating special exceptions—rather than letting your kid just come and go as they please, regardless of curfew—also provides an opportunity to acknowledge and reward trustworthiness. Is this kind of trust and responsibility deserved? Unfortunately, when it is, this means you have to give in, but it's for the right reason: they earned it. It is worth an occasional sleepless night worrying for them to reap the benefits of establishing and maintaining trust.

Special circumstances are also an opportunity for them to demonstrate how to maintain trust. Make sure you have a talk with them about the cost of screwing up this opportunity. If it goes well, more trust (and subsequent freedoms) follows. If they blow it, they will take a step backward and have to rebuild trust.

**Overnights.** Since the best way to avoid curfew is to spend the night at someone's house, you may need an overnight policy. How many overnights on a weekend? How many must be held at your house, so you can see what they do? How many in a month? Again, this is adaptable, depending on your kid's age and responsibility.

**Holidays.** Setting limits on time away from home and how late teens can stay out during holidays and school breaks is more often about maintaining a balanced life. Checking in on a regular basis becomes particularly important if they are going to be out and about for longer periods of time. They have to be much more organized and have better planning skills to get into trouble if they must stop by the house to see if your parent radar is activated.

**Developmental considerations.** One final issue is taking your kid's age into account in determining curfew. The younger the kid, the earlier the curfew.

- **Middle school**. Curfew should be fairly early for middle school kids—seven-ish on weeknights and ten on weekends). Later curfews overlap too much with the times older kids are on the prowl. Adult monitoring should be required for any gathering or activity of middle school kids.

- **Ninth and tenth grades.** Kids in their middle teens can handle later curfews and greater freedom. Nine on weekdays and eleven on weekends can work for them. Regular contact with and checking in with adults should be a condition of being out. Limit their opportunities for unstructured, unsupervised activities in unspecified locations.

- **Juniors and seniors**. Kids in their late teens typically should have begun to earn the privilege of later curfews (eleven on weekdays, twelve and later on weekends) with long periods of time out of the house. (Don't forget, in many states, kids under eighteen will need a note from parents if they are staying out later than twelve.) This sets the stage for you to assess their judgment in maintaining a balanced life. Give them enough rope. If they aren't sufficiently trustworthy, work with them to try to earn that privilege. There is value in needing to rein them back in occasionally. Discuss how to be mature and responsible with their time and identify ways they can demonstrate responsibility to earn the chance to try again. This helps prepare them for freedom at college or independent living.

Curfew serves as a way to set appropriate limits for your kid as well as the chance for them to demonstrate their trustworthiness and responsibility. Be sure you give teens the opportunity to show you the kind of kids they are.

# JOBS AND EMPLOYMENT

Older teens can benefit from increased responsibility for their expenses and luxuries. Earning their own money, with some limits, can be an important experience in preparation for early adulthood.

This chapter will help you:

- Determine if your kid needs a job
- Set limits on work hours and earned income
- Identify alternatives to work
- Recognize signs of job stress
- Teach your kid the right way to quit

"I gave you money for gas two days ago."

"What are all these iTunes charges on my account?"

"Do you realize how much our car insurance is going up now that you have a license?"

"Where do you think the money for a car is going to come from?"

"What, do you think I'm made of money?"

There are conflicting views about the desirability of teenagers having part-time jobs. On the one hand, working gives them something productive to do with their time other than become an expert at video games and updating their Facebook page. A job requires them to make and keep commitments (like following a work schedule) and encourages them to become more economically self-sufficient. Employment gives them the opportunity to manage their school, studying, fun, and work time as well as their money (with your help in taking some of it away).

Jobs require teens to develop a work ethic, learn the value of a dollar, develop people skills, and experience the limitations of minimum wage work ("I can't live on this!"). Finally, teenage employment might provide necessary income for the family.

On the other hand, jobs can interfere with important life areas like studying and sleeping. Working teens might get used to using their money to make frivolous or impulsive purchases. It is not unusual for them to begin to increase their work hours so they can purchase even more unnecessary possessions. Kids with $25 or more a week in spending money are nearly twice as likely as those with less money to smoke, drink, and use illegal drugs, and more than twice as likely to get drunk.

Teens with jobs can come to expect that a big chunk of their pay will go toward disposable income, which differs vastly from the small percentage that's available to adults who are responsible for their own living expenses. Finally, work can cut into unscheduled time that is important for introspection, recharging, and the opportunity for spontaneous experiences.

## WHAT'S A PARENT TO DO?

To start with, decide if your kid needs a job. Here are some criteria to consider. The more you check off, the more useful a part-time job may be for your kid:

○ No extracurricular involvement (all they do is go to school and come home with no honors or AP classes and little homework)

○ Too much free time (twenty or more hours a week doing nothing, with no productive activities like homework, extracurricular activities, or personal growth activities like skilled hobbies, reading, etc.)

○ Longstanding lack of interest in school

○ Lack of constructive, after-school activities (sports, religious involvement, active participation in skilled hobbies like music, art, computer-hacking, etc.)

○ Plays video games more than fifteen hours a week

○ Intends to enter the work force right after high school graduation

○ Doesn't appreciate the necessity of earning their keep (constantly asking for money for luxuries, doesn't seem to appreciate monetary blessings, etc.)

○ Parents have a lot of money and/or provide the kids with a lot of luxuries

If you decide that a job might be a good idea for your kid, it will be important to cover a couple of issues. As with most parenting issues regarding teens, make sure you include your teen in on the decision-making.

**Know the law.** When there is a parenting category regulated by a law, start by following the law. It's pretty easy to check your local laws by using the internet. Just enter "(your state) child labor laws" on a search engine and click on whatever turns up. Government sources (websites whose addresses end in ".gov") are the most reliable sources for information like this.

**Limit employment hours per week.** Research has suggested that kids who work a moderate number of hours perform better academically than kids who work a lot or not at all. A good general rule is fifteen hours a week during the school year, since grades begin to suffer when teens work twenty or more hours per week. During the summer, you can consider letting them work more; even full-time summer work doesn't appear to be associated with negative outcomes. Given the amount of free, unsupervised time your kid may have on their hands while *you* are at work, summer employment can be an important deterrent for trouble.

**Savings.** Require your kid to put a percentage of their income aside for a rainy day. This helps build the habit of saving, mimics the real world limits on money available for discretionary expenses and provides the experience of having only a percentage of their paycheck for fun things. Consider requiring them to contribute at least 15 percent to savings. Get together and create a rainy day list of the only acceptable reasons to dip into savings.

**Charitable giving.** It is important for kids to get in the habit of contributing to those less fortunate. Consider requiring them to put aside money that will be used to support charitable or religious organizations. For some reason, 10 percent seems like a nice round percentage.

**Parent tax.** If having a job is going to prepare your kid for a working life, there is another category worth creating: taxes. These taxes are ones that you impose. Parent taxes can be applied to some future goal like saving toward a vehicle, apartment startup expenses, or college expenses. Think of something in the range of 15 percent of earned income that you collect and keep in a secured savings account.

**Responsibility for at least some non-discretionary expenses.** As your kid gets older—or if your ability to provide an allowance is limited—it can be instructive to shift the management of some non-discretionary expenses into their hands. Things like fuel, car insurance payments, clothing, cell phone and other electronic media expenses, and personal grooming would fit into this category.

**Productive activity as an alternative.** Teenage employment is not necessary for healthy development and later life functioning. Constructive extracurricular activities of all sorts (like the previously mentioned sports, music, skilled hobby, or volunteering) can be equally helpful. In some instances, unpaid activity is even more helpful. If your kid is engaged in productive activities like these, adding paid employment may actually negatively affect important things like grades. However, it will be important that kids not be allowed to opt out of working when they discover it is easier to just sit around in the house you pay for, eating the food you provide, and benefiting from the luxuries your income makes possible. If your kid decides working is not for them, require them to do something else constructive at least twenty hours a week (sport, hobbies, religious involvement, volunteering, etc.). They'll have to choose one or the other.

**Acknowledge their work ethic.** Be sure to let your kid know that you recognize and value their willingness to work at a crappy job for little pay. It can also be helpful to calculate the number of hours your kid commits to school, homework, employment, and productive activities. Some parents discover that they have more free time than their teen does.

**Monitor employment stress.** Some service jobs can be high-pressured. Bosses, coworkers, and customers are all potential sources of stress and conflict. Managing school and work schedules can also be stressful. Be sure to talk to your teen about watching for excessive job stress. Check in on a regular basis to make sure things are going well. You may need to help them figure out strategies for addressing the specific stresses they are experiencing.

**Conditions for quitting.** Kids need to know how to change or end employment. This requires an understanding that your job history will follow you. If you end a job on a bad note, you will lose the opportunity to obtain a reference for future employment. They also need to know the formula for quitting; two weeks of notice is the industry standard. You may have to establish what they lose when they quit their job the wrong way (or at all). If you still pay for luxuries while they work, you may want to make access to things that cost money contingent on them having a job. If they are responsible for some of their luxuries (like their cell phone, gas, etc.), they will need to know that funds for these expenses will not be picked up by you. Finally, you may need to have some deal-breakers. These might include declining grades or picking up undesirable habits like smoking or alcohol or drug use (which are often funded by the money earned from a job). If any of these problems surface, you might need to make curtailing their work (or monitoring their expenditures more closely) part of the package of consequences to address the particular problems.

There is a lot that kids can learn from working, with the right kind of oversight and prioritization by parents.

# TEENAGE PRIVACY

## Part 1:
### The Privacy Issue

J ust because teens *think* they have a right to privacy, that doesn't make it true. However, getting them to understand where their rights to privacy begin and end can be a challenge.

This chapter reviews:

- The *real* right to privacy

- The three big categories of teenage privacy

"You don't have any right to read that!"

"That's *mine!*"

"This is *my* room!"

"I don't have to tell you *anything!*"

"Mind your own business!"

Teenagers often have trouble with the concept of rights. They have a growing awareness of the concept itself. ("That's none of your business!") They focus on fairness and notice that adults have more privacy than they do. Just as they begin to feel the need to individuate and become increasingly independent ("FREEDOM!"), advertisers and marketers encourage them to exercise their "rights" to buy whatever product they are selling. ("I've *got* to get that!") All of these factors conspire to persuade teens to make up a bunch of rights they think they should have. ("Hey, don't we live in *America*?")

While certain rights are universally acknowledged—they have the right to bodily privacy, the right to not be abused, neglected, or exploited, and the right to feel safe and nurtured—other rights are provided at the discretion of adults.

The right to privacy is not guaranteed. It is not a teen's *right* to have a private room (or even a space) to themselves, although it is nice when they can get it. They don't have a *right* to refuse access to their private computer accounts. The privilege of privacy presented here is based on your view of appropriateness and how much permission to have privacy you are willing to grant.

Remember that the *opportunity* for privacy is important for teens and will help them to exercise their independence, think their own thoughts and have things that belong to them.

## WHAT'S A PARENT TO DO?

To begin a discussion with your kid about privacy, you will need to clarify what teens can expect to be kept private. The main categories are personal possessions, personal space, and private communication.

**Personal possessions.** What is your kid allowed to consider their own private property, to do with as they please? Can they sell the video game machine if they want to? Can they give their expensive electronic devices away? Having private possessions help teens practice the responsibility (and consequences) of ownership. If it's broke, somebody else won't fix it. Possessions usually include a percentage of money kids earn or receive as a gift; legitimate purchases made with said money; personal gifts and clothing.

Some very generous parents let their kids act as though many more things are their private property. Some things may be characterized as *theirs* (your car, your bicycle) where the use of the term "yours" is a convention of speech, not a statement of fact (because, for example, they can't sell the car unless you agree).

To have private possessions, the teen also has the obligation to use them appropriately and without impinging on the rights of others. They also might be obligated to be reasonable (meaning they can give you an acceptable reason). It should go without saying that anything obtained through illegal activities—or with money obtained through illegal or unacceptable means—will not be considered a personal possession but rather as contraband that may be seized by The Man (or The Momma, as the case may be).

**Personal space.** Teens need personal space. They want a place to put their things—like a drawer, cabinet, or lock box—as well as a personal living space to retreat to that can't be violated without permission (such as a bedroom or part of a bedroom). Personal space provides a place for teens to chill, explore personal thoughts and ideas, and imagine possibilities.

Their obligation for the privilege of this private, personal space is to keep it adequately maintained (free from damage, insects, germs, odors, and chaos) and to abide by the rules and expectations for appropriate and acceptable furnishings and possessions (no illegal drugs, stolen property, poisonous reptiles unless previously agreed upon, etc.).

**Private communication.** In the old days, a diary was the place for teens to record their private thoughts and feelings. Now it's social networking sites like Facebook, blogs, video capture on phones and computers, texts, chat rooms, forums, voice mail messages, and email. Through these media, adolescents are both documenting personal and intimate information as well as sharing it indiscriminately with "friends" they have never met and don't know anything about (because their "friends" live in Bulgaria). Teens can benefit from the privacy of these communications by exploring personal expression, developing creativity, and maintaining important relationships.

The privilege of private communication obligates teens to use the various media appropriately (as defined by their parents). Cussing when talking to friends is normal behavior for teens. Writing profane, pornographic descriptions of others or themselves, while it is increasingly common, is generally considered inappropriate in any medium of communication that can be forwarded, copied, or distributed. Neither can they use private communication to make drug deals, arrange illicit liaisons, or share grossly inappropriate material.

# TEENAGE PRIVACY

## Part 2:
### Limitations on Privacy

O nce you identify the privileges of privacy your kid can expect, you will need to identify the limits of these rights.

This chapter outlines:

- Basic privacy practices

- Limits to an expectation of privacy

First, privacy goes in both directions. A basic component is obtaining permission before intruding into private domains. It's also important for kids to understand that parents have access to all (non-bodily) private domains.

### WHAT'S A PARENT TO DO?

**Reciprocation.** If your kid expects others to respect their privacy, they must do likewise. This seemingly simple concept can involve years of arguments with and enforcement by parents.

**Knock before entering.** One fundamental issue of privacy relates to a personal space. Teens might be engaged in very personal (and sometimes embarrassing, though natural) activities that require a private space. More importantly, they need some alone time to think, obsess, recharge, and fantasize. Hopefully, you have already instituted a household rule that everyone must knock at a closed door (regardless of whether the door is locked or not) and wait for a response before entering. Knocking as you open the door doesn't count.

**Don't touch what doesn't belong to you.** Private property should not be touched, taken, or used without permission.

**Passwords and IDs.** While your kid lives in your house, you should have the IDs and passwords to every electronic means of communication. There should be no expectation of total privacy. Your kid should expect that you will access their accounts any time you decide. (See the chapter on Violating Your Teen's Privacy for suggestions about respectful approaches to privacy violations by parents.)

**Social networking site friends.** This is the one time a parent and a child should be friends. No friend status for parents, no social networking site. Anything that is open to more than just your kid must have you on the guest list.

**Need to know.** Consider your child's private information as existing on a need-to-know basis. But you will determine whether there is a need to know—not your kid. It is really important not to just randomly or arbitrarily intrude into their privacy. They need to get some benefit from being trustworthy and being a good kid. Allow them the respect they have earned.

**Regular checkups.** Every now and then (at most, every couple of months), sit down with your child and intrude into their privacy. This is especially important for social media, internet, and texts. Let them know ahead of time you will be doing this. Have them be with you when you do it. You will want to keep up with where things are and may be able to head something off at the pass. (See below for strategies to intrude into your kid's privacy.) As you look at your teen's written communications, don't forget to think back about what would have happened to you if your parents had overheard the language you used in conversations with your friends as a teen.

**As long as ...** Trust is crucial to the maintenance of privacy for teens. There are some telltale signs that bring trust into question and should result in your intruding into the private areas of your kid's life. These include the discovery of worrisome behavior (porn sites, signs of alcohol or drug use), withdrawal and isolation, furtiveness or secretiveness, suspicious behavior, friends in trouble, unknown friends, extreme mood swings, extreme reactions to inspections, depression, and volatile relationships with friends or dating partners, to name a few.

# TEENAGE PRIVACY

## Part 3:
### Violating Your Teen's Privacy

Expectations of privacy are not absolute. Just as in our democracy, where privacy rights can be suspended depending upon threats to security and safety, there are conditions under which your child can expect to lose the privilege of privacy. Since you have established privacy as a privilege rather than a right, they must understand that privacy may be suspended.

This chapter covers:

- The importance of asking first
- Developing sources of information
- Keeping your kid informed as a form of respect
- Searching possessions using mutual inspection
- Developing a family policy of respect for privacy
- Ways to help your kid regain the right to privacy once lost

When your kid has violated your trust, demonstrated poor judgment, made bad decisions, or used possessions and personal space inappropriately, their privacy can be suspended. Some of the bigger categories include concerns for their safety ( such as suicide or risky behavior), alcohol or drug use, immoral behavior, illegal behavior, violations of rules and expectations, and mental or physical health concerns.

# WHAT'S A PARENT TO DO?

**Tread lightly when violating privacy.** OK, so first it's "privacy is a privilege you can suspend any time you want" and then it's "don't upset the little darlings when it comes to privacy"? Not exactly. Trust is fragile. If they turn out to be trustworthy and you act too forcefully around privacy, your kid may lose the desire to earn your trust. ("Whatever! It doesn't matter what I do, you are going to suspect me anyway!") Affording them some dignity is appropriate when you intrude into personal areas. You are modeling how to show respect for someone (whether or not they are the spawn of Satan). Make sure your kid already knows what will lead to you suspending the expectation of privacy. Then ...

**Ask.** If you think your kid is hiding something, keeping something secret, or doing something inappropriate—ask them directly. By asking, you show that you expect them to be responsible for their choices and have the integrity to own up to their actions. Don't worry about tipping them off. Asking about something you are concerned about may actually make them rethink their choices (even if they have already slipped up). If you ask and they deny, and it turns out they lied, the truth will come to light (as long as you continue to monitor). This opens up the opportunity to discuss their decisions, the kind of person they want to be, and the damage to your trust in them. (If they do 'fess up, really emphasize the importance of "At least I can trust you not to lie to me." You can feel disappointment in their decisions but pride in their integrity.) Your questions might even open up a discussion the two of you need to have that they wouldn't introduce.

**Knowledge is power.** The more you know, the more you can do to ensure your teen's safety and healthy development. It is important to have access to sources of information about your child. This means access to important adults in their lives (teachers, parents of friends, etc.), peers, communication technology, personal space, and your child themselves. Take advantage of these resources. Let your teen know that you will be checking on them behind their backs.

If they try to throw a fit about this, it is purely manipulation. It is perfectly clear that this is legitimate (even if they don't like it).

**Protect your sources.** Friends, parents of friends, siblings, neighbors, school personnel, social network sites, blogs, and internet monitoring software are among the variety of sources of information available to you about your teen. Be sure to protect your sources. If you get upsetting or disturbing information, use it to be resolute in uncovering the issue for yourself. Now you know where to look or what to push to discover it for yourself. The best rationale for protecting your sources is parent intuition. *"Who told you?"* "Something was just not right, sweetheart. I couldn't put my finger on it. I had a funny feeling ..."

**Fair Game.** Anything in the public domain is the same as an invitation for you to examine it. This includes things left in plain sight, overhearing, POS (no, not that. It is online computer-speak for Parent Over Shoulder, which, by the way, you should be doing), computer windows left open, computer history, and information from concerned others.

**Covert ops.** Snooping, searching, investigative cleaning, secretly opening up electronic communications, reading diaries, and trailing your kid when they go out are all tried and true parenting techniques for checking up on your kid. While they are perfectly legitimate, again, it will serve your larger purposes better if you use these strategies to figure out what to look for. Then you can make it look like you found out another way. If they catch you red-handed, it is awkward and can be mildly to moderately damaging to your credibility. It's better to take a direct approach if you have concerns. (Except for trailing your kid. That is a really good one. And tell them you are doing it.)

**Fair warning.** Let your kid know before you suspend their privacy privileges. "It is going to be time soon for us to review your Facebook page. You might want to look over it and see what needs to be edited." The goal of intruding on your kid's privacy is not to catch them (although that might be a side benefit). It is really about checking to make sure they are safe and engaged in healthy relationships and activities. It is about helping them think about what people (like you, not just their friends and peers) will think of what they are doing.

**Mutual inspection.** Do you think your kid is hiding something? Rather than doing the search yourself, have them do it with you. It is their personal space. If it is a physical space like their room, go with them and have them lift things, open drawers, and shake out clothes while you direct them. Do you suspect that they are making drug deals through texting? Have your kid scan down through the texts while you are looking. Are you wondering what they have been doing on Facebook in the areas that aren't available to you as a friend? Sit with your kid and have them open the pages and go through things together. Even though you already have their passwords and IDs (right?), letting them be present during your inspection is a sign of respect for their dignity and acknowledgement that you are entering a personal domain. Let them be the one who touches their stuff. It's also good to have them present with you if anything surfaces. (The looks on their faces will be priceless.)

**Interrogating friends.** Violating the privacy of your kid's friendship is a risky and rarely successful approach. Accessing this source of information is to be used only when you have serious concerns about the safety and wellbeing of your kid. If things are that serious, it won't take much for your kid's friends to fill you in. Be sure to maintain the friend's confidentiality if your kid doesn't know they were ratted out. "I'm really worried about Marcus. (Insert specific concern here.) If there is something I need to know, you can trust me to keep it between us. I'll make it look like I found out another way, but I really need to know." "If I find out you have kept something important from me like (give a list of only the most important issues, not every nit-picking thing), we will have a problem." Yes, it puts the friend in a bind. Tough. They can talk all they want about what a controlling, unreasonable parent you are. Meanwhile, you will either get information or the word will get back to your kid that you are on their trail. Again, you need to be sure there is a trail to be on—otherwise, you will have driven your kid further back by humiliating them in front of their friends.

**Bodily integrity.** Teenagers have the fundamental right to determine who may see and touch their body. This is a form of privacy that can only be violated for the safety of the person or of other people (such as medical necessity). The transition to this kind of privacy can be bumpy during early adolescence. You may not have needed to be so sensitive to times when your kid was naked during their childhood, but puberty puts a whole new face on this. The earlier you institute respect for this form of privacy, the better. A related issue can be that some people are just not as modest as others. Family members may not want to be exposed to a naked, adolescent body bounding around the house (or peeking out of loose-fitting boxers or sheer blouses).

**Punish violations of privacy and private possessions.** Everyone must knock first and wait for a reply before entering. Everyone must ask permission before entering another person's private space (such as their bedroom). Everyone is required to ask permission before going through another person's private things (drawers, keepsake boxes, etc.). Everyone is required to ask permission before borrowing someone else's possessions (such as electronic devices and clothing).

**Executive override.** Parents have the final say. They can determine the appropriateness of a violation of privacy. Be judicious. If someone has to wait to get permission from another family member, so be it. Use your override only when really necessary.

**Regaining the privacy privilege.** When your kid has abused the privilege of privacy, they need to be able to repair it. Call a family meeting. Other family members can learn by example, and other privacy issues may arise. Make it possible for your teen to regain the privilege step by step. Review your expectations for the use of private possessions, space, and communication. Check every couple of days for two weeks or so. If things are acceptable, have a "Can I trust you to use this privilege appropriately?" discussion. Start expanding the time between reviews across another couple of weeks. Then you can return to "only with cause."

If additional violations occur within two weeks, you have a more complicated problem. You might have a bullheaded kid or a deeper divide between your values and expectations and those of your kids. Increase the frequency of checks to every day (to try to catch them being appropriate). When they have seven consecutive days of appropriate uses of privacy, try the two-week formula again. If they still can't manage it, it may also be time to consult with a mental health professional.

So here it is, the end of a discussion of teens and privacy, with a strong emphasis on the fact that kids don't get to consider privacy a fundamental right and that you can override it any time you want. The final point will throw in a twist.

The opportunity for privacy is very important for healthy adolescent development. Help them see personal privacy (as with so many other things) as the payoff for being a trustworthy, responsible person of integrity.

But keep your eyes open.

# GRADES AND STUDYING ISSUES

# GRADES

O nce school is in full swing and the first progress report makes its way to your mailbox, you may be faced with setting (or revising) some expectations about grades and studying.

This chapter looks at:

- Setting academic goals

- Fostering a sense of personal responsibility for grades

Hopefully, you have one of those conscientious kids who loves schoolwork and sees grades as a challenge to be mastered. In that case, "if it ain't broke, don't fix it." For the rest, there will likely be a need to tweak the system. Because you want your kid to assume personal responsibility for grades and the self-discipline to achieve them, the trick is giving him or her as much ownership as possible over studying and grades while providing enough structure to track their progress.

## WHAT'S A PARENT TO DO?

**Set Goals.** To begin with, it is important to establish the goals toward which they will be so diligently striving. This can be in the form of their overall grade point average, specific grades (B or better in every subject; no F's) or creative combinations (at least one B in a core subject and the rest C's; at least two A's and a C or better in all other classes). Ideally, this should be something you and your adolescent do together. The more directly they link these expectations for grades to their future plans, the more likely they will be to buy into the program.

**Review progress.** Once you establish the goals, set a timetable for reviewing progress. For some kids, it will be report cards; for others, it will be at the end of every two weeks. Whatever it is, once you set the timeline for review, do not ask them about how they are doing in school. That's right—no "Do you have homework tonight?" or "When is your next test?" You can be interested in school. ("What did you do in math today?") You can volunteer to help. ("Do you need help with anything tonight?") Just don't ask about homework or grades. For your kid to feel a sense of responsibility for their grades, they must have some room to exercise that responsibility. This is why setting a time for review is crucial. It gives them some room to do this on their own and it builds in accountability, because you'll be checking on their progress soon enough to intervene if things aren't going well.

When the time for review arrives, get together with your kid and go over their progress. As with most parenting interactions that can lead to making corrections, it is really helpful to lead off by identifying all the possible things that are going *right* and that your kid is doing well on. Then look at the areas that need some attention. If things are going fine, this becomes an opportunity to celebrate your adolescent's increasing independence and responsibility for important areas of their life.

**Encourage personal responsibility.** If there are problems, this review time provides the opportunity to help your kid learn to track their progress, analyze problem areas, and adapt or modify strategies to address the problem. It is a little microcosm of how to deal with challenges in life. Make them take the lead in reviewing progress and coming up with solutions. This sometimes requires asking lots of questions, so be sure to set aside plenty of time. It's much quicker just to tell them what they need to do, but the process of figuring this out is as important as the actual plan. (And, by the way, having to sit down and painstakingly review their academic progress can be one of the punishments for not taking care of their schoolwork.)

The great thing about poor grades is that, in most instances, improvement is simply a matter of expending more effort—another great life lesson. Middle school students should spend approximately one hour a day studying, while high school students should be spending closer to two to three hours a day. These numbers can be a place to start the discussion. Most teens don't devote that much time to studying. Lots of kids seem to have the idea that school is like work; when you leave the office, you're done for the day.

If your teen is studying enough but still has problems, some other factor may be interfering. Learning disabilities, trouble with a specific subject (or specific area), poor or inefficient study skills, attention difficulties, and mood disorders are possible culprits. It may be worth consulting with an educational specialist just to make sure.

Once you have put a process in place to identify goals, clarified your expectations about grades, and determined a timeline for monitoring your kid's progress, it will be necessary to talk about what to do if their goals aren't being met.

Did you notice how the discussion about goals subtly changed from "the goals you set for them" into "their goals"?

# HOMEWORK AND STUDYING

What if your kid doesn't follow through when it comes to keeping his or her grades up?

This chapter covers:

- An examination of study habits

- The establishment of a study schedule

- The development of a set routine

- How to get your kid to take responsibility for their own studying

Come to an understanding with your kids. Have a "study clause" that describes what will happen if grades drop below acceptable levels. The idea is that your adolescent can study however they want, as long as their grades are acceptable. If the grades fall, then they have to study *your* way. And your way will teach your kid to study effectively while motivating them to take charge of their own studying.

Here are some ideas:

**Review study habits.** To begin, review your kid's current study routine with them. This would include how they keep track of assignments, when they do homework, how much time they spend studying, and how much time they spend preparing for tests or big assignments. Problems might become very clear to you at this point.

**Develop a study schedule.** Once you have reviewed your kid's current study schedule and determined that the problem is time and attention to schoolwork (rather than a learning disability), set a schedule for specific days and the amount of time that will be dedicated to studying. Kids should be studying from one hour a day for middle school students up to three hours a day for regular or honors-class high school students. (If you have to establish a study clause for an AP student, they are in the wrong classes.)

Your kid should devote the specified study time daily from Sunday to Thursday and either Friday or Saturday for a total of six days a week. (Here is the part where you apply some misery to get their attention.) They have to spend the time studying whether they have any homework or not. They may actually have to study *ahead*! The agonized wailing, moaning and gnashing of teeth that ensues can be delicious. Whatever arguments your kid generates against this plan, the answer is a variation of, "Well, I guess you should have taken care of this yourself. When your grades improve, you can go back to studying your way."

**Develop a study routine.** Since your kid will be responsible for abiding by the plan, to the letter, it is important to define what studying will look like.

- **Set the time.** The discussion between you and your teen is the most important part of this. It really doesn't matter when they study, as long as it isn't when they are alone or when you are asleep (so you can monitor compliance). They also need to choose the day of their weekend studying.

- **Track compliance.** It is important to require your kid to be responsible for following through with the study clause. Don't remind them; they will pay if they don't keep up (see below). Kids should inform a parent when they begin and when they finish each study period. This avoids the "I already studied when you weren't looking" excuse. Finishing homework at school doesn't count in this system. Again, the goal is both to show them how to improve their grades and to make them miserable enough to do it on their own without all this fuss.

- **Comfort.** It isn't necessary to be a complete fascist about this, but on the other hand, doing homework while lying down on your back with your eyes closed, or while texting or playing video games, is unlikely to result in any great improvement in grades. Material that is directly related to school in some way must be open and in front of your kid throughout study time.

**Resistance is futile.** Be sure to specify what will happen if they don't follow the plan. You may even have to specify the frequency and time of study breaks (thirty minutes of catching some TV and fixing a sandwich is not studying). You definitely need to clarify what will happen if they "forget" to study or try to shave time off the daily total. If they do not complete the time, they will have to spend double the time studying the following day. No exceptions. If they violate the program twice in a seven-day period, they are grounded from everything for a week and the study plan continues. (Note: If your kid violates the new study plan three times in a seven-day period, you have a bigger problem than grades. It's time to consult with a mental health professional.)

**Escape clause.** Finally, clarify how your kid can work their way out of the program. The easiest way is to assess grades from a progress report or report card. When grades meet expectations, your teen is free. If grades don't improve initially, or if they begin to slip again in the future, add time to daily studying and double the length of time required to escape from the program. If grades still don't improve, something more complicated is happening. It's time to consult with a mental health or educational professional.

This program should be effective without you having to ask every day about homework or grades. Don't micro-manage. Don't make yourself crazy by monitoring the online grade books available at some schools. Whatever measurement period you set to assess grades, don't check in between. Remember, the task is for kids to assume more responsibility for setting and then monitoring their own grades, so they will acquire the fund of knowledge and intellectual skills that will carry them forward into the exciting world of adulthood (and out of your house).

# LEISURE TIME ISSUES

# PARTYING

Teens are going to attend parties. Either you will know about them or you won't. It is better to know about them to make sure your kid knows how to have a good time in large groups of teens without getting wasted, out of control, or arrested.

This chapter examines:

- Responsible partying

- Appropriate parties for kids at different ages

- Clarifying how you expect your kid to behave at a party

- The issues of hosting a teen party

- How to help your kid anticipate the cost of taking risks

## WHAT'S A PARENT TO DO?

**Talk about partying responsibly.** Your kid's views about parties and partying will be directly affected by what you say. Have a conversation with your kids about the right ways to enjoy yourself at a party. Talk about fun and the problems of excess. What is too much? How do you make sure that your fun doesn't mess up other important areas of your life (like your relationships, job, or freedom)? How far is too far? How do you decide? What responsibilities do you have to others in setting limits on yourself (considering the possible embarrassment or inconvenience to a spouse or significant other, friends, or the community)? What is right (and wrong)?

These are the decisions your teen is (supposed to be) making as they determine their own limits. This is not the time to brag to your kid about the drunken, drug-fueled revelry of your youth—or, worse, of last year. (Save this for when they are twenty-five.) If your kid needs to get wasted to have a good time, you have failed them. But talking ain't enough.

**How you party matters.** Your kids are watching. It is difficult to maintain credibility if you violate the guidelines you have promoted as healthy and appropriate. Follow your own guidelines. (Yes, this Adult Role Model thing is a real pain when you want to just cut loose and violate a few social norms. It was a lot easier when they were young kids, and you could just put them to bed and hire someone to babysit).

**How young is too young?** You're never too young to have fun. Your kid can, however, be too young to attend an unsupervised party. Setting limits on your kids at various ages is for their own good and can save you trouble in the future. If you let your kid participate or just be present at a party where people are celebrating as adults, don't be surprised when they begin to think they can also make other decisions like they are an adult (like determining their own curfew, deciding whether to follow rules, and having sex).

**For kids younger than sixteen,** parties should be organized (and monitored) to require appropriate behavior. Fourteen- and fifteen-year-olds can even benefit from being given responsibilities as role models for younger kids. Mixing kids under sixteen with kids over sixteen is a recipe for trouble. You might have to set up an appropriate party for kids under sixteen with adult supervisors. The point of partying at this age is to learn to have fun in a big group without using recreational substances.

**For sixteen- and seventeen-year-old kids** (high school sophomores and juniors), think in terms of opportunities for them to practice balancing fun with responsibility. This would mean giving them greater freedom but with limited access to extremes of party behavior and with intermittent monitoring. This is the age where teen parties should be loosely (but responsibly) supervised or limited to a small group of teen friends who don't have a history of alcohol or drug use or major mischief) on their own. Your kid should be required to check in regularly throughout the evening. It is generally a bad idea to mix teens younger than eighteen with young adults (such as college-age kids). What is typical for a young adult could mean trouble for a teen. They also have a whole different set of responsibilities and priorities. Unfortunately, your older teen may be *desperate* to party with the young adults. They'll just have to wait.

**Review expectations for parties.** So you have decided your kid can go to a party. Talk about what you expect of them. Tell them what will happen if they step across the lines you have drawn. Important categories for discussion include:

O **Expectations** about alcohol or drug use.

O **Dealing with temptations** like alcohol or drugs, sex, property destruction, rock and roll, etc. Make them demonstrate they know how to refuse an invitation to use alcohol or drugs or to engage in risky behavior. (Role-playing is a fun way for you to make teens prove they can turn down drugs and sex and property destruction. They can't say later that they didn't know how, *and* practice is either a chance for both of you to be funny or it really ticks them off! Either way, it's very funny.)

O **Friends.** Who they are with and where will they be? What are your rules about teens wandering around at night (and making mischief)? They should let you know about any change of plans or locations.

O **Checking in.** Your kid needs to be where they are supposed to be and be with the people they are supposed to be with. They should be required to check in at least every two hours or so (to interrupt them at just about the time they are getting into trouble). Let them know what will happen if you don't hear from them (like you might suddenly show up and start hollering their name).

O **Emergency exit plans.** How are they—with or without your discreet help—going to deal with a situation that starts to turn bad while still saving face? What if the police show up? What if the party turns dangerous (fights break out, things start to get broken, etc.)? What are the indications that things are beginning to get out of control (but before gunfire erupts)?

○ **Post-party alcohol and drug testing**. Let your kids know that if you have any suspicions of recreational substance use, there will be testing (the kits are readily available at your local supermarket or online).

**Host a teen party.** If you are *insane*, the best way to keep an eye on your kid at a party is to have it at your place. This is extremely risky because you are responsible for anything that happens to the kids who are there (including injuries) and liable for anything that happens after they leave (if they under the influence and get hurt, for example). In any case, don't plan on much fun for yourself. On the other hand, someone's got to do it.

If you do decide to let your teen host a party, here are some things to consider:

- **Give your kid** as free a hand in the planning as possible.

- **Serve greasy**, high fat, junk food and high-sugar (and, oddly, high-caffeine) beverages. Remember, this is not a healthy eating event (unless your kid and their friends are into that).

- **Think in terms of activity stations**

  ○ **Interactive video games** (guitar hero, anything with a Wii or Xbox Kinect). It's structured. It's active. It's social. It doesn't require conversation. First-person shooter games should be banned unless there is more than one video game station—not because of any personal objection to violence, but because it is boring for others to watch for any length of time and some of the guys will become hypnotized.

○ **Movies, especially slasher movies**. Have a movie going on one of the TVs. It needs to be a movie that doesn't require you to follow the story line too closely and that people can scream and react dramatically to.

○ **Music, the louder the better**. Keep the music going at a high volume. You might even find a teen band willing to play a set during part of the evening.

○ **Active games** that can be mildly competitive but played by anyone, like ping pong (buy or borrow a table), foosball, pool table (if you have one), Twister (yes, Twister, male and female bodies twisted into provocative positions), a dart board, etc.

• **Fireworks.** Include fireworks (where legal). Some idiotic (typically) boy is going to try to shoot a projectile firework at another (typically) guy. Think safety if you'll have fireworks: hose already linked to the faucet, non-projectile fireworks, etc.

• **Fire.** Bonfires, fire pit—you just can't go wrong with a fire. Add s'mores and you automatically have a party, even with jaded teens.

• **Establish ground rules** for substance use, coming and going, conflict, respect for neighbors, etc. Announce it early on, when most kids have arrived.

• **Clarify with your kid** what you will do if you discover someone is under the influence. (The answer to this may end the discussion for having a party before you begin.)

• **Have a plan for unwanted guests**. Older party crashers can cause real problems.

• **Monitor** from a distance.

• **Let your teen know** you expect them to intervene if there is a problem. (This is part of their practice for becoming an adult and asserting themselves in awkward or difficult situations.) Call them aside and decide what they need to do if you see a problem arise. You may still need to get involved if your kid doesn't address the problem, needs you to be the heavy ("My dad is such a jerk!"), or is in over their head.

**Expect risky behavior.** If there is a teen party, there will be at least some of the teens under the influence. There will be some kids looking for some kind of excitement. One of them may be yours. Allowing your kid to attend a teen party is an exercise in trust and responsibility. Your kid needs to know what you will do to them if they use drugs or alcohol. Alcohol and drug screens upon return from the party are quick, easy, and relatively inexpensive. But parties can also lead to destructive behavior. It's one thing to toilet paper a house; it's quite another to destroy property. If your teen gets arrested for something, will you bail them out? Be sure you go over your limits and how you expect your kid to take responsibility for their actions.

The best protection against your kid partying inappropriately is to keep them in the house while you remain sober and constantly vigilant, to suppress any attempts at inappropriate frivolity or socializing. This is unrealistic and naïve in the extreme. Help them develop the right attitude toward fun and learn to be responsible for their actions (while hopefully using good judgment along the way).

# SCHOOL BREAKS

Your teen might have a lot of down time during the different breaks throughout the school year. He or she might need some help finding something to do.

This chapter examines:

- Ideas for fun and productive activities during school breaks

Overheard at a teen's house:

"I'm bored." "There's nothing to do." "This place sucks!" "We don't have anything to do in this house!"

While your first thought may be, "You'll *wish* you were bored when I get through giving you chores to do! Here I am having to work my fingers to the bone..." your teen's problem may be a combination of lack of imagination, lack of experience, lack of motivation, and insecurity about doing something that might be perceived as uncool (even though it turns out to be fun). Teens also tend to think that fun has to cost a lot of money.

## WHAT'S A PARENT TO DO?

With some ideas and a little push (in the form of planning, arranging transportation, and providing a little pocket change), you can help something fun materialize. Here is a list of activities for teens on break from school.

O **Burn something**. Nothing says fun for a teenager like setting things on fire. Consider organizing a bonfire. The fire can be anywhere from a barbecue grill to college-game-day size. All kinds of things can be added, like campfire foods (hotdogs, s'mores, popcorn) and music (recorded or provided by a local teen band). Remember to inform your neighbors and check with local authorities regarding relevant ordinances. This can provide a little lesson on the importance of being a good neighbor and a good citizen.

O **Drop them off at the park**. You might be surprised at the number of parks in your area. Pack some snacks, gather up a couple of your kid's friends, and dump them off at one of the local parks. Establish the pick-up time and warn them what will happen if they cause any trouble.

O **Abandon them in the wild**. Hiking! It's perfect. You just drop them off on the edge of a wilderness area with a few supplies in a backpack and return hours later to pick them up. It's kind of like the mall but with more dirt and less shopping. If they are really outdoorsy, you can make it an overnight camping trip.

O **Fatten them up.** It is difficult to go wrong with food. Look for unique eating establishments that combine eating with a challenge. Is there a place that serves a burger so large it can't be consumed by one person or a dish so spicy no one can finish it? Think in terms of gourmet twists on traditional foods like hotdogs, hamburgers, chicken, or sandwiches. Eating establishments around college campuses will have a certain appeal (and may fulfill some of these criteria for challenge eating). Finally, the challenge can be brought home by having kids create their own food (such as nachos, ice cream, pizzas, etc.) from ingredients you provide. Keep in mind that teens tend to say they don't want anything until you put it out; then they're like a swarm of locusts.

O **Have them go at each other**. Competitive activities are great for two or more kids. In addition to the inherent enjoyment of the sport, competing against each other can add another level of interest. The range of possibilities is extensive and includes darts, Ping Pong, billiards, basketball, flashlight tag, and disc golf. There are also pickup games of ultimate Frisbee, touch football, soccer, or any other team sport. Some competitive activities that have fees or require equipment include bowling, laser tag, paintball, miniature golf, bocce ball, croquet, volleyball, horseshoes, and golf.

O **Dangle them off a cliff.** Rock climbing facilities can be found in most communities. They provide the opportunity to either climb a wall (with a safety rope) or clamber over large, boulder-like formations.

O **Turn them loose.** There are places teens can go to just wander, like museums, zoos, sports complexes, science centers, planetariums, and public libraries.

O **Family Feud.** Don't forget about card and board games. While Monopoly can be fun, it can also go on forever. Think about Risk (a board game where you battle with other players to conquer the world), Password, Tangram brain teasers (which can be downloaded from the internet), and Trivial Pursuit, to name a few. There are card games at every level of complexity, any of which are worthy of consideration because they could start a family tradition (or a huge family argument following defeat).

O **Expose them to loud, obnoxious music.** Your community may have a music venue is teen-oriented or where local teen bands perform. Some places host all kinds of bands but are committed to providing a safe environment.

O **Just around midnight.** Star-gazing, watching the sunrise, or pulling all-nighters are all ways to introduce something different into the nightly routine. Star-gazing and watching the sunrise are probably best accomplished with you. All-nighters can be arranged and supplied, and then you can go to bed.

Remember, in addition to making your children do things because they are supposed to, you can also make them do things on the outside chance that they might like it. If you are hesitant to just let them go, join them; become invisible and observe from way out on the sidelines. Regulate potential for trouble by limiting the time they are unsupervised; the younger the teen, the shorter the time between checking in. If they enjoy it, great; even if they don't, they are more likely to either stop whining or come up with their own ideas.

# SPRING BREAK

There is apparently a tear in the space-time continuum that makes time fly faster when you have a day off compared to a day when you're working or in school. It has something to do with not having specific tasks or activities. When spring break approaches, you may want to consider encouraging (or requiring) your kid to fill their break with both free time and specific activities. It's for their own good, after all.

This chapter reviews:

- Decisions about leaving teens home alone
- Developing a plan
- Establishing clear expectations
- How to keep them accountable
- Transitioning back to school

## WHAT'S A PARENT TO DO?

**Age and independence.** When can you safely leave your kids alone during the day? How long is too long to leave your teen unsupervised? The law is a bit murky.

You will be held accountable if you knowingly expose or fail to protect a child under the age of eighteen from neglect (as well as abuse) that results in physical injury or that adversely affects their health or welfare. From a developmental perspective, kids begin to demonstrate higher-order cognitive processing around the age of twelve. Around this age (ages eleven to thirteen), parents can reasonably leave their kids unsupervised for three to four hours in a familiar environment like the home.

Younger teens (ages thirteen to sixteen) can reasonably be left unsupervised for periods of six to eight hours. Overnight is chancy, at best. Older teens (seventeen and older) are capable of managing many of the issues (and emergencies) that might arise if left unsupervised for a day and a night, although it depends on the experience and maturity of your particular kid.

In all of these instances, it is important to review basic safety issues and how to deal with various potential emergencies like fire, minor injury, serious injury, responding to strangers at the door, etc. (See also the Siblings Watching Siblings chapter.)

**Make a plan.** Time can really slip away as kids stay up late and sleep into the day. They may consider this a great way to spend their break. On the other hand, they may also end up with a sense of disappointment and wasted time (as well as not getting some important things done). You would do well to help them have a combination of doing nothing and being productive. What do they need to accomplish by the end of the break in terms of school assignments, spring cleaning, and personal growth? Be specific or general, but have a plan. Check on their progress about halfway through. Let them know up front what they can expect from their break. It will also be necessary for them to obtain permission for whatever plans they have.

**House rules.** It is probably a good idea to review the house rules, especially if your kids are going to be left unsupervised during the work day. This would include policies on leaving the house, having visitors over, mixing volatile chemical agents, checking in with you, and all the ways they will suffer if sibling conflict breaks out.

**Supervision.** Just when kids can be safely left alone at home, they become more likely to get into trouble. Make sure your kid is accountable to a responsible adult. The possibility of having someone stop by to check on them can go a long way toward having them think twice about getting into trouble. The value of good neighbors is that you can have someone check on your household if you have to be at work. If there isn't someone who can take this role, then it is important to be in ...

**Regular contact.** Regular contact with you should be expected of teens left at home while you are at work. At the very least, you can check in by phone. Don't forget that most phones have the capacity to take both still pictures and video if for some reason your parent radar is going off. ("Hey, take a quick shot of the clock in the kitchen and send it to me. I just want to make sure you are still in the house.")

**All work and no play...** Many parents are tempted to have their kid tackle a few tasks they haven't quite gotten around to, like cleaning up the garage, digging a new perennial bed, or giving those carpets a good steam cleaning. If you do have work-like tasks for your kid to complete during their break, be sure to balance them with time for play. Think about activities that allow you to drop teens off and pick them up, or things they can do (or you can do with them) in the evenings.

**Constructive activity.** If they are going to do something constructive during spring break, consider having them do it in the middle of the week (or the middle of their vacation period). This also goes for any school assignments. That way, they have the initial time to wallow in the delicious freedom of being on break and then squeezing in the final, waning moments of joy at the end of the break. Besides, early activity will get all the screaming and arguing out of the way rather than saving it for the night before school resumes. If you make your teen do something constructive in the middle of their break, things will have time to settle. This will also have the psychological effect of making their break seem longer!

**Day trips.** Consider taking a day or two off from work to have a mini trip (or two) during spring break. Look for hiking trails, camping sites, parks, rivers, lakes, and other interesting places to visit. Many cities and towns have publications with information on activities of interest in the area. Check them out to see what is available near you.

**Transitioning back to school.** You may want to help your kids slowly begin to reorient on the day before school resumes. No farewell to arms parties or wild, last-minute adventures; it is time to review any school assignments that will be due, get things organized, and get to bed early, since their sleep/wake cycle is likely to be all out of whack.

With all the movies (and exaggerated stories) about wild times during spring break, teens can end up expecting some epic debauchery. With a little planning and a lot of perspective, you can help them have an enjoyable, relaxing, and realistic break from school before the final push toward end-of-year exams.

# SPRING BREAK
# (HIGH RISK)

Spring Break at the shore. The sound of waves breaking onto white sandy beaches, blue skies, lazy days reading and swimming and boating, and nights spent with family, friends, and food. What could be more relaxing? Spring Break at the beach! Drunken teens vomiting in the sand, packs of wild-eyed kids hunting for a hook-up, all manner of lascivious behavior both in the shadows and right in plain sight, and the abandonment of rational thought, self-restraint, and morality. What could be more horrifying?

This chapter will provide some ideas for:

- Reining in your teen's expectations
- Clarifying expectations and setting ground rules
- Identifying some important safety skills
- Clarifying the cost of trouble

## WHAT'S A PARENT TO DO?

**Spring Break is not a fundamental human right.** For a surprising number of kids, this bacchanalia at the shore has assumed the mantle of a fundamental right. But this *wasn't* what the founding fathers meant by "pursuit of happiness." They were talking about a philosophical concept derived from a life spent in pursuit of contentment, not carnal pleasure!

Spring Break is a privilege. Teens should be clear that the opportunity for Spring Break arises from the fruits of hard work.

Even if your kid is paying for a Spring Break trip, the money is available because they don't have to use it for rent, food, and other necessities.

Generally, making indirect references will suffice. ("It sure is nice we can afford to do this." "Is it going to be worth spending money for this trip? I just want to make sure that everyone is going to make it worthwhile.") A really useful ploy is to be a bit unsure about the trip—with a little implied threat thrown in for good measure. ("I'm not sure this is a good idea. I don't know if you are really ready to handle this. Maybe I should just work this week and have your *grandparents* come for a visit to keep you company during the day.")

**Review expectations.** Have a family meeting to remind everyone what will be expected of them while on the trip. This is particularly important if your kid will be traveling with another family. If another kid is traveling with you, include them (and their parents) in the meeting. Go over the rules for checking in with you, personal and water safety, dealing with various situations that might arise, family time, and what happens if rules are violated (see below). Have them discuss their moral code as it relates to decisions, choices, and behavior (see below). Require each kid who will be going on the trip to give their word to abide by these rules. This is useful later to add shame for lacking integrity, untrustworthiness, etc. to the outright suffering you will be imposing if they violate the rules.

**Morals and choices.** Making a public commitment to a set of beliefs or a plan of action can be a powerful inducement to follow through with the commitment. Spring Break can be another opportunity to have your kid talk with you about what morals they use to guide their behavior. What are the things they consider right (and wrong)? What are their views on drinking and drug use? What are their views on intimate physical contact (like kissing, heavy petting, sex)? What should they do if someone is doing something wrong, is in trouble, or gets hurt? When should they come to you (or contact you) for help? What commitments will you make if they bring a problem to you? (This last provision is important so they can know how much they can trust you to help rather than make things worse.) What will you do if they *don't* bring problems to you?

**Supervision.** Would you turn your teen loose at a college frat party? If you answered "yes" there probably isn't any need to continue reading this chapter. For everyone else, it is important to make sure your kid is accountable to a responsible adult throughout Spring Break. If another kid's parents are hosting the vacation, be sure to find out their position on monitoring, alcohol and drug use, curfews, and punishments for breaking the rules. If you get to pick the adult supervising your child, consider the following characteristics: teetotaler (i.e., doesn't drink or use drugs); devout Mormon, evangelical or conservative Christian, Sikh, Buddhist (though Buddhists may be a bit too tolerant), Muslim; clergy in an established religion (excluding New Age religions, pagans, Rastafarians, etc.); Catholic nun; present or former high school attendance secretary (these folks are *tough*); alcohol and drug counselor; or an engineer. You might even want to cultivate a relationship with adults who have one of these characteristics in the hopes that your kid will become friends with their kids.

**Checking in.** You are asking for trouble if teens younger than high school seniors are given much free rein during Spring Break. All younger kids are going to want to act like they are part of the college crowd, with potentially disastrous results. Middle school kids should not be out of sight of a responsible adult for longer than an hour. They shouldn't be out at night without constant adult supervision. Young teens (ages fourteen to sixteen) should physically check in (they come to you or you go to them) every two to three hours. Legal curfews (from home) should be imposed for night-time wandering. Teens of all ages should only be in populated areas—not exploring in the sea grass back off the beach.

**Personal safety.** Review basic safety rules. Don't go off with someone you don't already know. Stay in populated areas. Don't take shortcuts in areas you don't know well (like anywhere on vacation). Don't change locations without making sure someone knows where you are going. Avoid stairwells and dark, isolated places. Come up with potential situations where your kid might ignore these safety rules so you can help them figure out how to problem-solve ahead of time. (See information about *Refusal skills*, below.)

**Water safety.** Your kid needs to have some basic knowledge about staying safe. Make sure you review the signals provided by the flags on the beach (red = stay out of the water, yellow = use caution, green = ok, blue = ocean creatures are nearby). They also need to know how to get help when a lifeguard is and isn't present. The three most important beach rules are:

1. Always face the water (to see waves that may be coming in)

2. Know what to do in a rip tide or undertow

3. Don't dive into the surf

**Swim buddy.** Teens should not be wandering alone in a town filled with all manner of normal and deranged people—like, say, a beachside town during Spring Break. Groups of three or more teens exploring together and watching out for each other are preferable. This allows one kid to back up the other while the third runs for help. They must all agree to stay together, no matter what. Use peer pressure to your advantage. Let them know that they sink or swim together, so to speak. Everyone will be punished if one of them messes up. If you are taking one of your kid's friends on vacation with your family, it helps if one of them is likely to be the voice of reason (or is hesitant and afraid). If, as is often the case, you aren't blessed with one of these kids, consider renting one from another family.

**Risk assessment.** Your kid needs to have some idea about how to tell if things are potentially dangerous or getting bad. When should they leave a group of people, even if they are friends? When should they worry about someone they just met? How can they make sure it is safe to use an ATM (the most frequent site of robberies)? Go over potentially risky situations and ways to respond to them with your kid before you leave.

**Refusal skills.** A surprising number of teens end up in trouble because they lack skills at refusing to go along. "I couldn't say no. I'd look like a loser." Take some time with your kid to figure out ways they can sidestep things that make them uncomfortable. This would include what to do about pressure to sneak out, engage in illegal behavior, or put themselves in potential danger—as well as pressure to use alcohol or drugs or engage in sexual behavior—this is for both girls *and* boys. (If you think boys aren't being pressured into sex these days, you are perilously uninformed about the pressures that young teen boys are encountering. Happily, many guys are not open to sex with just anyone, but they might suffer from not knowing how to deal with the pressure to be sexually promiscuous.) Go through as many scenarios as you and they can imagine.

**Family time.** If this is a family vacation, require family time. Think about board games and beach games (throwing, tossing, flinging objects at each other, kite-flying, boogie-boarding, body-surfing, sand castles, etc.). Take at least one sunrise and one sunset walk along the beach.

**Cost of trouble.** What if they break your rules? Mild infractions should lead to constant supervision for four hours during the next prime time (early afternoon, right around dark). This would mean having to shadow you as you do activities that are interesting to you. Make sure the activities are excruciating to them (shopping for beach cover-ups or jewelry, reading, putting sun tan lotion on you while you are lying in the sun in full view of everyone on the beach, wearing embarrassing swimming attire while you go out in public with them, etc.). Major violations like drinking or drug use, sneaking out at night, or major personal safety violations—or anything that results in police involvement—should result in 24/7 supervision for the remainder of the trip or being sent home. The curtailment of privileges should continue when you return home. They will obviously need to be protected from their own bad judgment, even at home. They will obviously need more guidance at home on the small things like what movies to watch, going out without supervision, etc.

Any place that has large concentration of adolescents and recreational substances constitutes a high-risk setting. Take some time to put the pieces in place so that high-risk Spring Breaks can be a wonderful luxury rather than a horrible disaster.

# SUMMER BREAK

Police hate summer. Think roving bands of disaffected (or at least bored) youth who are out day and night, looking for something to occupy their time. All the things kids get in trouble for increase as unsupervised time increases: crime, drug use, and consumption of high-fat foods and sugary drinks. First-time marijuana use peaks during summer vacation. Sexual activity increases.

> This chapter presents:
>
> - The main components of a productive summer break

Kids lose a month of learning across the summer. Some kids can lose up to three months of reading comprehension. Kids gain body mass twice as fast in the summer, compared to the school year. Parents stress over finding something for their kids to do. Kids consider being responsibility-free during this block of time as a fundamental human right. What's not to love about this hallowed tradition? While some school districts are rethinking providing a three-month annual break from education and supervised activity, parents are still faced with the dilemma of finding something to do with the kids during summer.

## WHAT'S A PARENT TO DO?

**Read.** A real book. (OK, it can be an ebook.) There are fundamental differences between reading a book and watching a movie, even a movie based on a book. Reading is an active mental process requiring you to construct your own images and elaborate your own ideas. Watching movies is a passive mental activity where all information and images are formed, interpreted, and pre-processed for you. Reading also differs from video game play. Playing video games is an active mental process that promotes planning, multi-tasking, and reaction speed while having all concepts, imagination, and cognition fed to you by the game developers. Players are still spoon-fed the mental activity rather than it being a self-generated, imaginative process, as it is in reading. The pace of change and the increases in information from year to year have made life-long learning a fundamental aspect of competitiveness in a global economy (as well as just keeping up with the person in the next cubicle). Kids need to have experience actually thinking for themselves.

Require your kid to set aside reading time each day to exercise their mind. Half the battle is won if they already have summer reading assignments from school. If your kid has an allergic reaction to reading, consider instituting a family reading time (such as thirty minutes at night when everyone is home—yes, that means you have to read too). Take your kids to the book store. Stop by the local library. Librarians can be very helpful in making suggestions. Consider having everyone read the same book. If nothing else, pull out your religious texts to kill two birds with one stone. Some things *are* worth getting into an argument over, and requiring your kids to read is one of them. If they try to give you too much grief, make them do some math problems too—just for good measure.

**Exercise.** Every day. (Insert the endless articles and media pieces on the rise of obesity here.) The real reason to require your kid to exercise is that it will wear them out, channeling some of that energy that would otherwise be used to argue or get into trouble. It is also healthy for them and associated with virtually every kind of mental and emotional health. (And, again, it makes them tired.) Give them a Frisbee, make them a sandwich, and drop them off at the park. Have them get their skateboard or rollerblades and drop them off at the skate park. Have them get their bathing suit and drop them off at the pool or the lake. Drop them off at the river. If all else fails, make them exercise with you to make sure they do it. The benefits of exercise are evident at every age.

**Contribute.** Summer break is not a fundamental human right. Kids can mistake the necessity of scheduling time off as a culturally-supported opportunity to lie around, play video games, and update their Facebook page.

There are things your kids can do to pick up the slack while you are off working to put bread on the table. When they were in school and you were at work, there was at least some equity. With this extra time on their hands, they can help contribute by doing things that need to be accomplished around the house or in the community. Consider having them fix dinner once a week (a useful skill to learn). Require them to take on a chore you typically complete. People who have extra time on their hands and a right spirit will also seek out opportunities to give to others through volunteering. Every community has charitable organizations that could use some help. Look them up and sign them up.

**Participate.** Sitting alone in the house watching TV, surfing the net, or playing video games is just not stimulating enough. Summer is the ideal time for your kid to participate in family and community activities. Consider having family night where you get together and play games (even if it has to be through interactive video like Wii, Kinect, or the like). You can also go to movies, visit parks, have a picnic, or do any of a number of other things as a family. Kids benefit from participating in activities through your faith organizations (church, synagogue, mosque, temple, meeting house, etc.). Kids should participate in something on a weekly basis.

**Work.** Employment is a fact of life for productive people. It is important for kids to develop the skills needed to be able to tolerate and make the most out of drudgery and monotony. (This is not to say that this view of work is what they have to look forward to.) Your goal will be to help your kid find a profession that brings them satisfaction, challenge and joy. However, that isn't always possible. A dead-end teen job can be a great help in motivating your kid to aspire to some more satisfying way to support themselves and their future family. Consider requiring your working age teen to get a job. (Volunteering is a good substitute.) If employment isn't possible, assign household tasks that are not a part of chores (e.g., clean the garage, weed the garden, etc.). You have to work, and they should, too. Most US workers only get two paid weeks off a year!

**Play.** All work and no play ... There are lots of benefits to play for teens. During play, kids can risk failure in ways they might avoid when someone is watching and evaluating. Play can provide a means of discovering interests and talents that might otherwise have gone unnoticed. Playing is fun. Encourage your kid to have some fun. Have them expand their horizons and pursue something they are really interested in doing or knowing. Summer can be a time for a concentrated tutorial (if your kid finds that kind of thing interesting). Your teen might enjoy developing specific skills in a specific sports ability, foreign language, music, dance, or special skill of some sort. There are a variety of summer camps that can provide this kind of experience for your teen. There is even a role for video games as a fun activity. Remember, play is defined by each person. Your kid needs to be the one to identify what they consider fun. There is a difference between encouraging and pressuring.

Now that you've identified the important categories for summer break activities, it is easier to build some structure around their days. Help your kids make the most of the summer.

# SUMMER PLANNING GUIDE

Once you consider what you want your kid to get from their days in the sun, it will be time to get things set up.

This chapter presents:

- Ideas for creating a summer calendar

- Important ground rules to put in place

- The many forms of monitoring the little darlings

- Ways to promote productive and responsible behavior

- The importance of working in at least a little fun in their summer

## WHAT'S A PARENT TO DO?

**Inclusion.** By January, teens have begun to construct an elaborate fantasy of the ways in which they will spend the endless hours of time in the sun, free from responsibility or any other consideration except relaxation, socializing, and fun. It's a good idea to closely involve your kid in the thinking and planning for the summer they will actually get. They should be clear about all the things they will need to work into the twelve or so scant weeks until school begins again.

**Review expectations.** Start with what you expect them to include in their summer. Have them talk about what they want. Make it clear what you require.

**Make a calendar.** It can help to lay out everything your family is planning for the summer. It also helps your kids anticipate various trips or events. In families where kids divide their time between separate households, the calendar can help clarify all the transitions. Calendars are particularly important if your kid has a summer job. It helps them identify when to request time off and provides a way to set up some deadlines for any summer reading assignments, not to mention any requirements for intellectual stimulation you may have for them (e.g., books, skill development, etc.). Finally, the calendar can help you realize all the things your kid is trying to squeeze into the summer (or how much more planning you may need to fill large blocks of unsupervised time).

**Rules of the house.** No matter how clear the rules have been, it is always a good idea to review what is and isn't allowed. This is particularly important if your kids will be spending time relatively unsupervised (see Supervision, below). When can friends come over? When can your teen go over to a friend's houses? What are the requirements for hanging out in the neighborhood? What is their curfew? When are they expected to check in? What are the expectations about leisure time (including video games, updating Facebook, etc.)? What about chores?

**Structure.** While there is real value in having a flexible schedule that can accommodate unexpected opportunities for fun and excitement in small doses—like a vacation, for example— it's not such a good plan for long stretches of time (like the entire summer break). It is useful to have a regular schedule for the days, weeks, and months of summer. Kids should get up and get to bed regular times. Their days should have at least a general routine to them. You should expect them to do specific things on certain days (bathe and brush their teeth every day, do regular chores, maintain responsibilities, participate in productive activities and personal education, etc.).

**Interval planning.** A widely practiced strategy for organizing the teenage summer is interspersing formal activities (like camps and vacations) with more open-ended or individualized activities. This might be a good way to maximize the benefits of highly monitored (and costly) activities like camps as well as the less costly fun, like time with relatives. It also breaks up extensive periods of free-flowing time with friends that can end in trouble born out of boredom (and limits the time they have to talk themselves into doing something really stupid).

**Supervision.** Leaving teens to their own devices for extended periods of time is usually an invitation for trouble, but providing supervision can be an issue when you can't provide it yourself. The bottom line is that teens need to be accountable to an adult throughout the day.

**Monitoring.** The more time kids spend without checking in with a responsible adult, the greater the risk they will end up doing something stupid, risky, or self-destructive. (This doesn't mean they WILL do something stupid, risky or self-destructive—it just means the odds increase if they don't have the accountability that comes with monitoring.) Young teens should check in with you (or your designee) at least every two hours. Middle teens should check in every three to four hours. Older teens (i.e., graduating seniors) should check in every six to eight hours or so.

The safest, most effective way to monitor your kid is to have them be physically present. They can stop by in between activities or take a break and let you get a good look at them. This presents the opportunity for you to ask them the questions they should be asking themselves (e.g., "What have you been doing?" "What are you planning on doing?" "Don't take me for an idiot, what are you *really* planning on doing?" "How are you going to have fun but not get arrested, use drugs, or have someone end up pregnant?") At the very least, they should contact you by phone to give you an update, explaining where they are and what their plans are for the next block of time.

**Spot checks.** It is always a good idea to trust but verify. As your kid earns more trust, becomes more responsible, and is more often found where they are supposed to be, it is appropriate (and important) to allow them greater self-determination in their plans. Let them know that you will still be double-checking periodically, just to make sure things are still as they seem. Act like you trust them, but keep your eyes open.

**Consequences.** And, then, you will need to give some thought to how you will make your kid suffer if they try to get around your expectations. There are lots of ways to accomplish this. (See chapters in the Discipline and Praise section for more on this.) If the infractions are small ones, consider having a limited punishment. For example, if your kid doesn't check in when they are supposed to, they are grounded for the next (most desirable) day. Help them see the connection between trust and freedom. You don't have to pull out the sledgehammer for every issue. On the other hand, if it is a big problem (alcohol or drug use, or a major violation of family values like lying, stealing, etc.) be prepared to shut down their freedom. Then start again from square one using small tests followed by small increments of the restoration of trust.

**Morals, leadership, and serious trouble.** Finally, don't forget to review what your kid considers right and wrong. There are hopefully going to be opportunities for your kid to be more independent; it is summer, after all. Alcohol use, drug use, premarital sexual intercourse, crime—all these increase during the summer. Your kid is going to be faced with temptation. They are going to be confronted with the necessity of choosing right from wrong. Don't miss the opportunity to talk about morals, values, and leadership. Find out what they think. Let them know what you expect of them.

**Productivity.** Every religion, philosophy, and program for personal growth emphasizes the importance of productive activity as a component of happiness. Productivity arises out of labor. When we had to grow our own food, productivity was built into the day. These days, it requires some planning (and prodding) to help a teen stay active. Consider requiring your kid to do some kind of work during the summer, like a paid job or tasks around the house that aren't part of their regular chores. Being productive provides a source of satisfaction (and a contrast, which gives them a greater appreciation of leisure time).

**Personal education.** One goal of education is to prepare kids to become lifelong learners. Summer is a good place to practice, since there aren't structured educational demands. Establish requirements for some self-directed (which is to say, parents-directed) learning during the summer. It can be anything that requires gaining knowledge and includes reading of some sort. What do they care about? What do they want to know more about? See what you can do to help your kid become more knowledgeable about something that interests them.

**Responsibility.** Summer is a great time to help your kid develop an appreciation for the value (and limits) of responsibilities. To be responsible, they have to be given the opportunity to follow through with commitments, complete tasks, and demonstrate reliability and trustworthiness. This is not only accomplished through more traditional responsibilities (also known as chores) but also through increased freedom to be accountable for themselves. Curfew, more time out before having to return to the house, and staying alone without supervision are all opportunities for kids to demonstrate responsibility. Start off small and build toward greater responsibility. Make sure you let your kid know that how they handle the smaller responsibilities (like coming home at or before curfew and checking in on time without complaining) will lead to increased freedom and responsibility. Then, make sure that you keep track and reward them for being responsible.

**Fun.** All right, they should also have at least a little fun. (See the School Breaks chapter for some ideas.) Play is important. (See the chapter on Play for a discussion.) Daydreaming has value. Unstructured time—when they are not watching TV, playing video games or updating personal webpages—can lead to the discovery of lifelong interests. (But don't let them overdo it, or they might start expecting life to be full of joy, excitement, and meaning. Then where would they be?)

Teenagers with long periods of unsupervised, unstructured time (when not in the natural environment) often end up in trouble. The key is to find ways to break these periods up into small blocks of time. Summer planning is essential to make the most of the time they have off while making it less likely that your teen will get into trouble.

# VACITIONS

I t is always a gamble to take teens on any outing that involves the family. But vacations? Spending a stretch of time with your whole family when it includes a teen can become anything from a wonderful bonding experience to a miserable journey through hell. There are a few things parents can do to increase the likelihood that their family vacation experience will be at least tolerable (and maybe even down right fun).

This chapter presents ideas on:

- Planning
- What to anticipate
- Maximizing teen "buy in"
- Reinforcing the potential cost of misbehavior and rule-breaking

## WHAT'S A PARENT TO DO?

**Include them in the planning.** If teens have a say in where you go and what you do, it reduces the probability of conflict. They may jump right into the discussion with ideas. On the other hand, you may have to provide a little structure. ("I was thinking about this or this. Which do you think would be more fun?") Then put the choice to a family vote. If your teen is out-voted, it is reasonable to consider having them get priority next time (or this time, if they were also out-voted last time). In this case, definitely make sure there is …

**Something for everyone.** When you are planning vacations for children, you can pretty much make all the decisions and they'll be happy enough. But figuring out what teens might find enjoyable is a much more difficult task. Make every effort to include something of interest to each person, even if it requires significant adjustments. The greater the variety of activity choices, the better off you will be with teens.

**Make it memorable.** Give some thought to including something that would be out of the ordinary. The qualities of memorable moments include activities with some degree of perceived risk, excitement or thrill (like bungee jumping or white water rafting); something never encountered or done before (which could be as simple as room service or a visit to a water park); something that produces an experience of profound awe or wonder (like seeing Niagara falls or the Mall of America); something they thought you would *never* let them do or experience (That doesn't mean alcohol or drugs!); or something *extremely cool* (which is difficult to define because it is different for each kid). Ask yourself, would your teen find a proposed activity worth talking about to their friends? Consider making it a surprise. Just one experience during the trip can be enough to accomplish this. Shoot for enjoyable; see if you can accomplish memorable.

**The journey and the destination.** We all know someone whose parent, spouse, or friend made them ride in a car for twenty-seven hours straight with only two restroom breaks to reach the vacation destination. This kind of hurry-up-to-get-there attitude can set off a downward spiral of miserable vacationing. Break the trip up into meaningful chunks of time or experience. Instead of the vacation being about spending as much time as possible in San Diego (and so driving 2,000 miles straight through to get there before fun starts), make San Diego just one part of the vacation. There are plenty of potential sites of interest along the way.

**Trains, planes, and automobiles.** It is important to anticipate the frustrations and limitations inherent in the means of travel to your vacation destination. Create travel packs appropriate to the potential unpleasantness for whatever transportation you are using. This would include distracting activities, snacks and drinks, and clothing changes (in case of potential spills) to name a few.

**Don't over-schedule.** If you try to do everything, your teen might not remember anything. ("There's a picture of Mount Rushmore. It's blurry because we could only drive by if we were going to fit everything in.") Leave room for unexpected discoveries. Really experience the things you do.

**Chill.** An important part of vacations is to have time to relax and refresh. Build in time for everyone to just hang out. This is an important use of some of the time you gain by not scheduling yet another memorable activity. This would include breaks during the day, in between activities, and opportunities to sleep late.

**Roaming.** Teens love to explore. Try to arrange things so that it is possible (and safe) for your teen to wander around and check out the local flavor. A swim buddy is preferable. Frequent contact by phone will do if there aren't any other options. Remember to talk about the dangers of an unfamiliar area.

**Local teen activities.** Most cities have online or paper publications that list concerts, venues, and other happenings in the area. If there is a band your teen loves, check to see if they will be in the area during your stay. Buy tickets. See if you can find a local band that performs the kind of music your kid likes. They may want to check them out. If you are unsure about safety, go with them. (Bring ear plugs and plan on standing outside or completely out of the way. Don't make eye contact or indicate in any way that you know your kid while you are there.)

**The more the merrier.** Vacations can be instantly more enjoyable for teens if they have a friend along. Of course, more preparation is required (as well as more money). Before the trip, you should consult with the friend's parents and go over the rules and consequences, including the conditions under which friends will be sent home or kept under lock and key.

**Money. management.** Make teens responsible for managing their money while on the trip. This is a great opportunity to teach them about making wise money choices. Have them think through expenses, set spending limits for themselves, and prepare for unexpected expenses. Hopefully, something will happen (losing money, running out of money, etc.) that provides a (small) life lesson.

**Down-time activities.** Give some thought to things your teens can do during down time. Pack some board games, card games, books, magazines, or music—anything but electronic communications (texting, surfing the internet, and video games).

**Emergency supplies.** You may want to consider tucking some things away that can be distributed during emergencies. This might include pocket-sized travel games, a CD your kid has been wanting, or even—God forbid—a video game or hand-held video game system. You can reveal the surprise if there is a significant delay during the trip (when you are stuck at an airport, if the car breaks down, etc.) or act of God like a hurricane, flood, or plague.

**Snack bags.** Food and drinks are essential means of shutting up teens. Pack some of their favorites and keep them handy.

**Rules.** As always, take the time to review your expectations on the vacation. These include curfew, appropriate use of money, wandering alone, checking in, required family time, alcohol or drug use, conflicts and arguments, whining and complaining, and general risk-taking.

**Consequences.** It is good to give some thought to how you will punish misbehavior before you set out. It keeps you from having to improvise on the spot (which might result in too much or too little). The best punishment for teens is to make them stay right by your side for some extended length of time following an infraction. This is especially delicious if they have to go along while you do things with their younger siblings. Grounding them (to the room) may be possible. Don't forget long (thirty to forty-five minutes) lectures on why what they did was wrong. Similarly, deliver lengthy, emotional, guilt-inducing rants on the dangers of what they did. Warn them that further problems will spill over into curtailments of freedoms back home, since you can't trust their judgment or their word. (Make sure they know they are responsible for paying back the bail money you might have to spend to retrieve them from jail.)

The goal of vacationing is fun, relaxation and family camaraderie. Don't let that get lost in all the details.

# LIFE SKILLS ISSUES

# ANGER MANAGEMENT

## Part 1:
### Dealing with Angry Teens

Teenagers are going to get angry. They will need help learning how to do it right.

> This chapter deals with:
>
> - How to tell if anger is a problem
>
> - Conducting a personal anger management checkup
>
> - Ways to respond
>
> - How to talk to them about their anger
>
> - Establishing rules for being angry

When you throw together hormones, exciting new opportunities for fun, and the perception that "I am *not* a child"—and add the role of parents in setting limits—teens are going to get mad. Most teens have their little fits now and again during early adolescence and then learn how to keep their tempers in check. However, a significant minority of teens continue to struggle with managing their anger and frustration. Some teens are more emotionally intense than others. Some are more impulsive or strong-willed or self-centered. Some teens just get angrier than others.

# WHAT'S A PARENT TO DO?

Start with a quick assessment.

**Typical anger problems.** Even though angry outbursts peak somewhere between early to mid-adolescence, they nevertheless stay within a tolerable range. Getting mad now and again is part of being human. *How* you get mad is what's important. Start with a quick assessment to see if your kid has a problem managing their anger. These are the signs:

O  Frequent loss of temper over small issues

O  Doesn't calm down, even if it costs them something important

O  Yelling and screaming as a way of communicating anger or frustration

O  Slamming things (doors, books on a table)

O  Throwing small or non-dangerous objects like pencils of pillows, although not at people

O  Mild name-calling ("stupid," "crazy," etc.)

O  Short fuse or similar angry intolerance of frustration (demonstrated by road rage, exploding over video game play, etc.)

**Is it serious?** Some teens end up with serious anger problems. If any of the following are present, it would be a good idea to consult with a mental health professional.

O  Anger problems persist beyond 6 to 12 months despite your attempts to address the problem

O  Attempts at intimidation (getting up in your face, standing over you); physically threatening harm; or actually assaulting people when angry

O  Destroying or damaging property (breaking things, putting holes in the wall, etc.)

O  History of persistent temper tantrums and ongoing anger problems continuing from a young age

O Saying deeply insulting or demeaning things to intentionally hurt other people's feelings

O Serious name-calling (profanity, vulgarities, etc.)

O Unable to clearly remember what they said or did after an angry outburst

O Suicide threats or self-injury (cutting, burning, biting, head-banging, etc.)

Before you try to help your kid get better at managing their anger, there are a few things to consider.

**Do a personal anger control check-up.** It might seem pretty obvious, but it's worth saying that you will need to have your own anger under control. If you introduce anger or match your kid anger for anger, things are going to go downhill. If you have any of the criteria for anger problems or serious anger problems listed above, it is time to consult with a mental health professional for yourself.

**Avoid unnecessarily provoking your kid.** As a rule, parents of adolescents should never use physical coercion, physical aggression, or corporal punishment. It won't work, it will make things worse, and it will have lasting effects on your relationship, your kid's view of her/himself, and how they handle anger. Name-calling or insults hurled at your kid in the heat of the moment are both immediately emotionally damaging and will build up resentment and rage that can escape from kids in later interactions. There is a surprisingly diverse range of parenting strategies you can use to make your kid suffer for breaking rules while at the same time teaching them the lessons and skills you were originally intending to impart. If you can't come up with any strategies that work, it is time to consult with a mental health professional.

**Stress instead of anger.** Stress or trauma can lead to frequent angry outbursts. When kids are emotionally overwhelmed, they will lash out at anyone or anything around them. One source of stress is suffering a significant loss (the death of someone close, the end of a significant relationship or friendship, parents' divorce, inability to participate in a valued activity, rejection by a potential dating partner, etc.).

Major stressors also include a recent move; conflict with friends; and increasing difficulty, challenge, or competition in academic classes or sports. In these situations, the strategies to help kids deal with their anger may be more about helping them manage stress rather than giving them full-blown anger management training. If the anger your kid shows seemed to have come out of nowhere, look for possible stressors rather than just assuming that your kid has run-of-the-mill anger management problems. (There is an extended discussion in the Stress Management chapters.)

**Identify triggers.** Look for the situations or events that set your kid off. You are going to use these when you talk to them about recognizing when they get mad for the anger management steps presented later.

**Video games.** The jury is in on video games: guilty. Like exposure to aggression on television (which also has been conclusively proved), all kids who play aggressive video games demonstrate more aggressive behavior, aggressive thoughts, anger, decreased empathy, and lack of helpful and concerned behavior toward others. If you have a kid with an anger problem, video games need to go. Tell them why. If they get their anger under control and act like a civilized human being, you may reconsider. In the meantime, hand them a good book.

**The louder they get, the quieter you become.** This formula can be very effective in changing the emotional direction of an interaction. Depending on how things turn out, your kid will begin to associate a low voice with things getting serious (and potentially going bad) for them.

**Validate the feeling, if not the underlying belief.** Give your full attention to your kid when dealing with anger. Make it clear you are listening. "I'm glad you told me." "I understand how mad/hurt/frustrated/unhappy/disappointed you are." Anger can often be diffused when the other person feels like they are being heard and taken seriously. But be sure to give them *more* attention when they are expressing themselves calmly and reasonably. If they start to escalate, make them wait to calm down before you will continue.

**Have a sit-down about dealing with anger.** Arrange a meeting to let your kid know you will be working with them on their anger problem.

- **Identify the problem.** Let them know that you are worried and unhappy about how they handle their anger. Give examples that illustrate your point without berating them.

- **Discuss** how their anger problem messes things up. "We have to find a way for you to be angry and still make your point. When you blow up, it throws everything off track, you get in trouble, and people won't take you seriously in the future." Remind them that you are not going to accept that behavior.

- **Tell them you will be working with them** to develop better anger management. Let them know that you are going to work together to help them figure out how to handle their anger better. This will include some specific steps everyone is going to use when angry.

- **Raise their awareness** about their anger. Find out what *they* notice when they get mad. How often does it happen? Do they see it as a problem? Do things usually end up well?

- **Identify triggers.** Are they most likely to blow up when someone tells them "no"? When they are tired and hungry? The mere existence of their sister? What makes it hard for them to manage their anger: thoughts, actions of others, situations, or events? Let them know what you notice that seems to trigger them.

- **Identify signs of growing anger.** What are the body sensations they notice when getting very angry ("My face gets hot and I clench my fists")? What do they begin to think to themselves ("I shouldn't have to put up with this")? What do they begin to think of the people around them ("I start to think that the other person is trying to make me mad on purpose")? These kinds of signs and thoughts play a big role in anger going over the top.

**Establish the rules for anger.** Set some ground rules for acceptable and unacceptable ways to deal with anger.

- No yelling (yeah, right). Yelling and hollering gets everyone hyped up. Use your inside voices.

- No name-calling, insulting, blaming, cursing, shaming, judging, demeaning, demoralizing, ridiculing, or criticizing. Being "mean" might make you feel better in the moment, but you feel worse in the long run.

- No destruction or aggression.

- Kid stops when parent says stop.

- Use appropriate language (no profanity, vulgarities, cursing, etc.).

- Conversations (or arguments, as the case may be) will continue (with possible time-out breaks) until the issue is resolved or the limits of negotiation have been reached.

- Issues can be brought up again when kids are calm and reasonable by asking "Can we talk some more about ___?"

Once you have covered these issues, you can begin to help your kid learn the steps to effectively managing their anger. That will be the topic of the next chapter.

# ANGER MANAGEMENT

## Part 2:
### Teaching Anger Management

I f you have determined that your kid has an anger problem and you have laid the groundwork for anger management (see previous chapter), there are some strategies they need to learn to rein in that temper. You can help.

This section of the Anger Management chapter teaches you how to help your kid:

- Identify when they are angry

- Express anger appropriately

- Keep anger from sneaking up on them

- Manage their emotional intensity

- Learn to accept without making things worse

### WHAT'S A PARENT TO DO?

First, this is one of those parenting situations (like conflict resolution, negotiating, and assertiveness) that will require you to play a dual role: parent, who is object of the anger, and advocate, who advises your kid about how to best handle themselves in this situation. When their anger starts to boil, advise your kid on how to deal with *you* by giving them specific suggestions. ("OK, wait. If you keep going like that, I will be forced as a parent to just shut the whole discussion down. Try saying this: 'Mom, I am incredibly frustrated that you won't let me make my point.' Or let's take a break to let things cool down and then get back into it.") This makes you their coach as well as adversary. You may be surprised at how much just this approach can help your kid learn to keep their anger in check.

**Identify it.** If your kid is going to manage their anger, they have to recognize when it starts to build. You can help them recognize their anger if they're not already aware. ("I am *not mad!*") In your initial discussion with them about managing their anger, ask about times they get mad. Have them identify how they can tell if their anger is growing.

O **Body signs**. Anger is a specific kind of aroused state and there are physiological reactions that go along with it. Clenched fists, tension in the body, ears get hot, flushed face, clenched teeth—your kid has their own combination of physical indicators of anger. If they figure out how to recognize them, it will help them (and you) to see an angry outburst coming so something can be done to keep things from getting too intense.

O **Thinking signs**. There are also common thoughts that accompany the build-up of anger, such as blaming, cursing, demonizing, or violent mental images. Have your kid identify the thoughts they have when they get really angry.

O **Provide feedback**. You may find that your kid initially has trouble recognizing when they are becoming angry. Tell them what you have noticed about the times they get really mad. Encourage them to let you be their ally in catching it. See if they will allow you to point out when you think they may be getting really angry. ("You look like you are getting really mad." "It looks like you are about to blow your stack." "We're not in our happy place!") (OK, probably not that last one.)

**Express it.** It is important for your kid to be able to express anger appropriately. This begins by informing other people how you are feeling. Emotions are an important form of social communication and need to be shared so that an attempt can be made to resolve the issue. People with anger problems often jump this step and go right to arguing, verbal attacks, or yelling and screaming. The basic formula for expressing emotions is to say, "I feel ____ because ____."

O  **Prompt them** to identify what they are feeling. ("What are you feeling right now?") The goal is for them to reach the point where they identify what *they* are feeling ("I feel ____") not what the *other person* is ("I feel like you are an idiot.") or what they want to do ("I feel like punching you right in the face."). Make sure that they use emotion words (angry, frustrated, sad, scared, furious, mad as hell) rather than action words ("shove it up your ..."—well, you get the idea).

O  **Find out** what triggered the anger. ("What happened to get you so mad?") It is important that they identify the source of the anger to help you figure out what can be done. ( "I am pissed off because you won't let me go out this weekend." "When you criticize me for my grades, I get so mad!") You might have to prompt them by asking specific questions if they get stuck. ("Exactly what did they/I do?" "What happened right before you got ticked off?") Make a list. Don't interrupt until they are finished. (Is there anything more frustrating than someone interrupting while you are telling them how much you hate them?)

O  **Require them** to use appropriate language when expressing themselves. This can be difficult, but it is an important part of the development of self-control. If they use inappropriate language, immediately impose a break. The conversation will not continue until they have taken a moment to get themselves together (see the Manage it section, below).

**Monitor it.** This is where the body and thinking signs discussed above will come in handy. Your kid will need to track how they are feeling if they are going to be able to use strategies to keep their anger at a manageable level.

○ **Agree to accept feedback from each other** about signs of anger. ("Are you feeling calm enough to continue or do we need to take a break?") If you include yourself in this process, your kid is more likely to buy into the process and to accept your feedback, since it is only fair. Be careful not to drive them crazy by asking too many times. ("Are you angry now?" "Are you angry now?" "Are you angry now?" "*Yeeeeessss!*")

○ **Plan some regular breaks** into your discussions or arguments (about every ten minutes) to check on the anger level.

**Manage it.** This is the heart of anger management: finding strategies for remaining calm or keeping anger at a low to moderate level.

• **Review strategies** that help them physically calm down.

○ The most straightforward strategy is slow, deep breathing. Taking a moment to breathe in to the count of three seconds and out to the count of three seconds, repeated ten times in a row, can be remarkably helpful. A good way for you to introduce the strategy is to claim that you need to use it for yourself. ( "OK, this is starting to get heated. I need to de-stress, so hang on a minute.")

○ Another important strategy is to have more positive and helpful "self" statements when angry. How you talk to yourself about something has a big impact on how things turn out. Your kid will need to have some reassuring, positive, and hopeful statements they use when their anger begins to build, such as "I can do this." "Blowing up will make it worse." "Don't forget to take deep, slow breaths." "If this doesn't work, I'll just try something else." You can help by mirroring useful self statements. ("We can do this." "Hang in there. You're doing fine." "We'll try to work something out.")

○ Relaxation techniques are extremely helpful but can be difficult to get your kid to buy into unless your family already has traditions consistent with this practice. If breathing and self statements aren't enough, you will probably need to consult about their anger with a mental health professional.

O By the way, punching pillows, mattresses, punching bags, etc. have all been found to make anger *worse* rather than better. To develop self-control, you have to use self-control. It is a bad idea to encourage your kid to manage their anger by lashing out, even at inanimate objects.

- **Have an agreement** about taking breaks. Stepping away from the situation is extremely effective. The problem is that many people won't step away or won't honor the need to step away, or the situation doesn't easily allow for taking a break. However, once you and your kid have used this strategy effectively, they will be better able to manage their anger, even when taking a break isn't possible.

  O **Time-out.** The classic, time-tested strategy. Take as many time-outs as you need. Once you have used them successfully, you tend to need them less and less. Here are the components that have to be in place for time-outs to work.

    - Anyone can call it, but you have to call it on yourself ("I need a time-out," not "*You* need a time-out").

    - Everyone has to honor it and move to a separate space during the time-out.

    - A specific time to reconvene is identified. ( "We'll get back together in fifteen minutes.")

    - Everyone must reconvene at the agreed-upon time, no matter what.

  O **Temporary halt.** Sometimes you don't have the time to talk about or finish talking about an issue. Sometimes the issue is so complicated that you need time to figure out what you really think. Sometimes the discussion is so volatile you need to take it in separate blocks of time. If you need to stop for the time being, inform the others that now is not a good time and then find a time when everyone can get together to discuss it. As with the time-out, a commitment to resume talking at the agreed-upon time needs to take priority over just about everything.

- **Acknowledge efforts** to manage anger. Talk to your kid about keeping you informed of their struggles so you can help. Let them know that statements like "This is really hard for me" or "I'm having a really hard time staying calm" can help you be more sensitive to what they are going through. You can also help your kid by reflecting your observations of their efforts back to them: "I can see you are trying to keep from exploding. What can I do to help?" "I appreciate your trying to keep yourself calm while we try to get this resolved."

**Accept it.** Kids will get their way only some of the time, if things are going like they should. Part of anger management is learning to accept that there will be times they won't get satisfaction. This requires kids to keep in mind that how they handle this defeat will affect future outcomes. If they take a short-term view and decide to vent when they don't get what they want, they will feel better—but unfortunately, the other person won't forget, and some may not forgive. Your kid needs to practice how to graciously say "OK" even when they are still mad. Some kids need direct instruction from you about the importance of this as a way to end a battle lost. They need to learn to live to fight another day.

When your teenager is angry, you realize your kid is not a little child any more. You might even find yourself feeling a little fearful of your own kid. Keep in mind that they often don't realize they can now come across as intimidating or threatening. This is all the more reason they need help in learning to be angry in appropriate ways.

# APOLOGIZING

Kids are going to mess up. The great thing about being a kid is that you will be given another chance (and another and another) while also being shown how to fix your mistake and to learn from it.

This chapter explains:

- Why apologizing is an important skill
- How to apologize effectively
- How to make apologies count

Because mistakes are part and parcel of life, an argument can be made that it is important for kids to screw up. Mistakes are the matrix out of which learning and growth arise. When you screw up in the real world though, the consequences can be severe. Insult your boss and you can get fired. Violate the law and you can get arrested. Kids need to know what to do when they mess up.

## WHAT'S A PARENT TO DO?

The art of apologizing is an important skill for your kid to cultivate, especially in close relationships. Apologies demonstrate respect and concern for the feelings (and rights) of others. They show that the relationship is important enough that they want to try to understand and repair any damage done. Apology is the first step in re-establishing trust that has been shaken by a transgression—and it's just the right thing to do.

**Say you're sorry.** Apologies begin with acknowledging that you did something wrong. You have to say it. Let your kid know that voicing regret is extremely important to the person who has been wronged. The simpler the apology, the better. "I'm sorry" works really well.

**Admit responsibility.** Let your kid know that taking responsibility for the ways they screwed up is a fundamental element of a genuine apology. A person with integrity will own up to a mistake instead of throwing someone else under the bus. All it requires is an "I screwed up ... "

**State how you screwed up.** An apology includes not only a recognition that you screwed up but also owning up to *how* you screwed up. This makes it clear to the offended person that you actually get it and, therefore, will avoid repeating the transgression. As a parent, it also provides a point of discussion in case your kid *doesn't* realize how they messed up.

**Be sincere.** An apology needs to be a genuine expression of regret, spoken from the heart. Insincere apologies always ring false and make things worse. (And if your kid can convincingly offer an insincere apology, you have bigger problems.) So, sincere straightforward apologies for the wrong that was actually committed are best: "I'm sorry I took that money." "I'm sorry I forgot to put up the dishes."

But, what if your kid isn't actually sorry for what they did? Having them apologize for something they aren't sorry for doing can be seen as encouraging them to lie—so find something they are sorry for. They are likely to be sorry for how it affected other people and so can provide a kind of secondary apology: sorry for the trouble caused, sorry to disappoint, sorry I upset you, sorry for violating your trust (but I really did have a great time at that party you said I couldn't attend!).

Legitimate secondary apologies do not, however, include things like being sorry they got caught, sorry they didn't get away with it, sorry you had to find out, sorry the police arrested them, etc. If your kid isn't sorry for the original act, start with the secondary apology and expect to put in some time to help them see the error of their ways on that primary transgression.

**Don't blame others.** Regardless of who else was involved or the part played by others, an apology is about taking responsibility for *your* role. There should be no references to the culpability of others when your kid apologizes. Sometimes, a kid has to tell you how everyone else was worse before they can acknowledge their part. Help them make their way to the most relevant issue, which is how *they* screwed up, regardless of anyone else who was involved.

**What they should have done.** This is one of the most important elements from a parenting perspective. This is where you help them learn from their mistakes. Spend some time on this one. Morals, values, ethics, and principles create the foundation for answers to this one.

**Fix it.** An apology should also include some reference to what your kid will do to fix the problem or keep it from happening again. ("I'll be more sensitive to that in the future." "I will work to repair that window." "I won't sneak out at night any more without telling you first.") Then, they need to do it—repair the damage, be more considerate, and don't lie, cheat or steal again. Words help, but it's what they do that matters.

**Give people time to forgive.** It will be important for your teen to realize that it may take a while for the wronged person to accept their apology or get over the transgression—and that some people never will. They need to learn that part of demonstrating they are sincerely sorry for the harm they caused is letting the aggrieved person respond in their own way and in their own time. Trying to get someone to forgive you on your timeline shows you still don't get it. (Hint: Apologies are about the person who was wronged and *their* feelings. Otherwise, apologies wouldn't be necessary.)

**Don't repeat the mistake.** No matter how sincere the apology, repeating the mistake undermines the sincerity of that apology. If you apologize and then do the same thing again, people will conclude that you were simply trying to manipulate them when you apologized. This can be a particular problem for kids (and adults) who have impulse problems. Even when they are trying to stay true, they will end up slipping up in a distracted moment or in response to an overwhelming impulse. These kids need a lot of help in knowing that apologies still matter, whether or not other people understand about impulsiveness.

**What about forgiveness?** Most of the time, when you offer an apology, you are also wanting to be forgiven. You will likely have to help your teen understand that asking for forgiveness can be a bit tricky, because it can lead to the other person questioning the sincerity of the apology; they may think you just want to be forgiven so you can feel better. If the situation warrants a request for forgiveness, it is better to present it as a wish or desire rather than a demand. "I hope that you can find it in your heart to forgive me." "Please accept my sincerest apologies for ... " Notice that these are not *direct* requests for forgiveness (like demanding, "Forgive me!"). Asking indirectly doesn't put pressure on the other person to either offer forgiveness they don't feel or to deny forgiveness and feel even more put upon by the apologist.

Given the importance of apologies for repairing damaged relationships, it is well worth taking some time to help your kids learn how to apologize well.

# ASSERTIVENESS

K ids need to learn how to stand up for themselves. They need to learn how to be assertive.

This chapter explores:

- Assertiveness through actions
- Assertiveness in common situations
- Assertiveness in expressing yourself
- Assertiveness in setting personal boundaries

Assertiveness is the ability to confidently, directly, and respectfully express opinions or needs, as well as to set personal limits on yourself and others and to effectively disagree with others.

Assertiveness is often contrasted with aggression, which is the use of psychological or physical force on others to get your way. At the other end of the spectrum is the contrast between assertiveness and passivity. Passivity involves yielding to the will of someone else, regardless of your own desires or preferences.

There are times when kids need to aggressively pursue important goals or to hold back, even if something is important. They need to be able to choose to respond rather than react. Assertiveness provides just this. It is the means by which kids effectively make their way in the world. While some kids seem to be born assertive, most of them need encouragement and practice. As parents, you are in an ideal position to help them learn how to be assertive, even with you.

# WHAT'S A PARENT TO DO?

Assertiveness is communicated first and foremost through the way your kid moves in and responds to the social world. The basic components are body language (manner of walking, quality of voice, posture, facial expression), personal space, and the language you use.

**Body language.** There has been some interesting research on what criminals look for in selecting potential targets. It's interesting, in part, because these characteristics are the *opposite* of assertive body language—which means you can learn to avoid them. The characteristics predators look for in victims include uncertain or hesitant gait; closed posture (hunched shoulders, head down, hands hidden); halting and quiet voice; and avoiding eye contact while having anxious or shy facial expressions.

You can help your kid learn to be more assertive by encouraging them to be more aware of their body language. If they come into the room to talk to you about something—even if they are about to get in trouble—require them to enter with a purposeful stride, stepping solidly (just short of a march). Have your kid stand tall with shoulders back, head up, and hands out and by their side when talking to you or other people. Help your kid learn how to speak in a clear, controlled, and distinct voice (rather than a tone that is either too soft or too loud and strained). Finally, help them learn to make direct eye contact, with an interested and set facial expression.

**Personal space.** Another basic component of assertiveness is an awareness of your own and the other person's personal space. A general rule in our culture is to keep about three feet between you and the person you are interacting with. (Notice that this is enough room for you to be able to easily avoid someone trying to punch you.) Move in closer and you are at risk of being perceived as being aggressive. Stay farther out and you are likely to be perceived as timid or afraid.

**Self-expression.** Finally, kids need to be able to make two kinds of assertive statements. The first are "I" statements. "I want ____." "I am going to ___." "I feel ___." These are sentences that assert needs, opinions, and desires. The second basic form of self-expression associated with assertiveness is to communicate "No." "I am unwilling to ___." "Stop." "Quit!" "Don't." These statements communicate the establishment of personal, psychological, or physical boundaries.

Most teens need practice developing these basic skills (though they seem to have an instinct for the "no" response). The best approach is to use direct instruction. Talk to them about the ways these characteristics influence how others view and respond to them. Anticipate situations where your kid can use of assertive body language and expressions (distant relatives who are visiting, meeting acquaintance friends of yours, interrupting when you are in the middle of something, etc.). Definitely have them practice on you, especially in a situation where they are in mild trouble.

It is risky to try to teach assertiveness in high-tension or conflict situations, as you will be yelling at your kid for what they did and telling them they are also a failure at being assertive. It is probably best to wait until the situation has been settled and then let them know that you expect them to stand up for themselves, respectfully, even when you are right and they are wrong.

Finally, make sure you don't embarrass them. ("Now, Jimmy, stand up straight and look Mr. Jones in the eye when he talks to you.") Prepare them ahead of time, take them aside, or talk to them about it later. There will be plenty of opportunities for them to work on it. Maintain their dignity whenever possible when you are teaching.

Once your teen has the basic components down, you can also help them practice being assertive in specific situations.

**Making requests.** Asking assertively for something you want or need can be difficult for many kids, due in part to their natural ability to whine and beg. The components of assertiveness that are most relevant here are eye contact, posture, and voice tone.

**Asking for assistance.** Even more difficult is asking for help. Needing something from someone else puts you in a dependent social position. Kids can use practice asking for assistance in a straightforward way to show that they are both comfortable asking and comfortable letting the other person decide whether they will help. Being gracious when their request for help is rejected is also important to practice.

**Correcting or clarifying.** Telling someone that you think they are wrong or what they are saying is incomplete can be awkward. Assertiveness can communicate both respect for the other person as well as respect for your own opinion. It is a useful skill for teens to practice, given the frequency with which they correct or clarify what adults tell them. The only thing they need more practice at is ...

**Disagreeing.** Contradicting someone generates tension. The question is whether it will be productive tension that leads to a resolution or destructive tension that leads to conflict. Voice, facial expression, and personal space are particularly important aspects of assertiveness in this situation.

**Expressing anger.** You can't be human without becoming angry. Anger is a very important emotion for signaling to yourself and to the person you are talking to that you are discussing something that is personally important. Obviously, this situation can easily morph into aggression. "I" statements; neutral, non-threatening posture; calm vocal tone and facial expressions; and respect for personal space are particularly important components to monitor.

**Sharing opinions and observations.** Some kids are hesitant to speak up about their views. They need encouragement and practice to assert themselves in conversations and when they have ideas. Actively solicit their opinions. Talk to them later about the value of their contributions.

**Taking a stand.** Kids will sometimes need to take a stand for something that matters to them. They should believe in something enough to take a personal position. They can use help in learning how to stand their ground without backing down and without becoming aggressive.

**Demanding respect.** How do you assertively demand anything? Respect is a big thing for teens, as it is for most of us. They just don't have a lot of practice insisting on it from others without being aggressive—especially younger teens. You can help them practice politely and assertively asking others to talk to them respectfully. ("Please don't yell at me. I am trying to be respectful in talking to you. I would like for you to show me the same consideration.") When kids say things like this, it can really knock an interaction with an adult off kilter in favor of a kid. It can be kind of fun.

**Setting limits.** Telling someone what you will and will not accept can be tricky for teens. The "I" statements, posture, and vocal tone come in handy here. "I really don't want to do that." "I don't think that is a good idea." "I can't go along with that." This will be an important skill your teens can use in refusing to do things that are against their morals. (Unfortunately, it is also a skill they will sometimes use in dealing with authority, like parents.)

**Changing your mind.** Standing up for yourself includes being able to reconsider your agreements and commitments. While the character issue of commitment and integrity play an important role here, assertiveness is also important to this kind of situation. When your kid changes their mind about something they previously committed to, you can help them be assertive rather than defensive or overly apologetic.

**Responding to jerks.** The most important situation for assertiveness is in dealing with people who harass, bully, or insult you. While there are other components that are important in dealing effectively with jerks, assertiveness provides the foundation for all the other elements. ("Stop doing that to me." "Leave me alone!") Sometimes, assertiveness can end up being enough to end bullying.

As with all learned skills, assertiveness requires practice, practice, practice (and the ability to refine as you go).

# DEFIANCE

S ometimes defiance just leaps out of your kid. This isn't always a bad thing. But purposeful defiance needs to be nipped in the bud.

> This chapter examines:
>
> - Separating defiance from disrespect and argumentativeness
>
> - How to deal with impulsive defiance
>
> - What to do about blatant defiance
>
> - The meaning of repeat offenses

Defiance is the refusal to comply with reasonable parental requests. Remember when your toddler first discovered "No"? Ahh, the *power*. "Want your bottle?" "*No*." "Want your favorite blanky?" "NO." Hahaha. They were so *cute*. Well, there is a renaissance of "No" that gathers like a storm cloud at the dawn of adolescence. And when it breaks, it doesn't seem so cute.

Defiance can occur without disrespect and is different from argumentativeness, although it can be combined with both of these. The most common source of defiance is a teenager's struggle to assert their independence. Early in adolescence, teens are consumed with an overpowering need to decide for themselves where to go, what to wear, who to hang with, and how to spend their time. Unfortunately, they don't have much practice managing this powerful drive or in expressing it in effective ways. Instead, they just bark out a defiant "No! I'm not doing it."

But, defiance also arises from poorly developed conflict resolution skills, a sense of entitlement ("I have a right to ... "), impulsiveness, feeling overly stressed or pressured by you or other areas of their life, moments of inner conflict or turmoil, and from having a long line of people pushing them around. There are also times when teens are defiant because they know exactly what they are doing and consider the defiance worth the cost. Finally (and least likely of all), your kid may really have a legitimate point about the lack of fairness or reasonableness in a situation.

## WHAT'S A PARENT TO DO?

Defiance can be separated into immediate responses and strategic decisions. Examples of immediate defiant responses would include saying "no" to your face or ignoring you when you give them direct instructions. ("Sara, go do the dishes. Sara. SARA! COME BACK HERE!") A variation of this is giving you the correct response ("OK, Dad") and then going on about their business without complying. (This one works really well with busy parents.)

Strategically defiant decisions represent blatant disregard for your instructions or rules. Examples of this include attempts to secretly violate rules (such as sneaking out of the house or using banned technology); doing the opposite of what you tell them; or just ignoring your wishes when making plans or getting things done.

So what do you do in the face of defiance? It's time to snatch a knot in their tail (as Southern mommas would say)—but just a little knot. The first stage is developing strategies for dealing with immediate defiant responses. Then strategies will be presented to deal with strategic defiance.

**Spontaneous defiance.** Impulsive decisions by your teen to refuse to comply require a specific set of strategies:

- **Signal them.** To change their behavior in the future, your kid needs to recognize when there is a problem. You will need to make it clear that they have stepped across a line. This can be done verbally ("Whoa! Back right up there, young lady." "Stop right there." "That is absolutely unacceptable.") or nonverbally (death stare).

- **Briefly identify the problem.** It is useful for your kid to know what they did wrong, just in case they missed the memo. "Behavior like that will not be tolerated in this house." "It is one thing to not want to (do something, talk to me, etc.), but it is another to directly defy me." You can also throw in some guilt induction during this step if you are so inclined. "I can't believe you would disrespect me like that when I suffered through fifty-six hours of labor to bring you into this world and while your father and I work our fingers to the bone to give you the things you need. To think I lived long enough to be treated like this by my own flesh and blood." Feel free to improvise.

- **Do-overs.** This is a good point to rewind the situation and have them try again. "You're going to need to say that another way." You might want to have them redo the interchange several times in a row. "Let's try that a couple of times to make certain you understand what is expected of you." Practice does make perfect, especially when it has the added benefit of seriously annoying them—because that way they get to practice anger management too.

- **Help them out.** It is not unusual for an early teen to have trouble thinking of another way to say "over my dead body." How else could you say it? The intensity of their emotional reaction also blocks their ability to generate alternative statements. It is acceptable for you to help them formulate an appropriate response. "How about this, son: 'Mother, I am very distressed by your insistence that I do the dishes when it is clear that I have more important business on Facebook.'" (OK, this may be a bit sarcastic but you get the idea.) It is acceptable to give them the answers.

- **Don't argue with your kid.** Explain once and only once why what they did was unacceptable. Avoid being drawn into a debate. Some teens mistake parental attempts to help them "understand" as an invitation to try to change their parent's mind. This can easily lead to escalating arguments. Say, "This isn't up for discussion." "This is non-negotiable." "We're done discussing this."

- **If/then**. Make sure your kid knows what they are risking by continuing to be defiant. "If you don't ___ or continue to ___, then (you can hand over your phone right now, consider yourself grounded until you graduate, etc.).

- **Make it worth their while**. Teens need to see the value in responding appropriately. When they disagree the right way, when they express their preferences in a civil manner, or when they express their objections politely, consider shifting your position—at least a little. At the very least, make it look like you are potentially being influenced by how they are approaching you. "You know, when you present it to me like that, it makes me want to reconsider."

- **Acknowledge restraint**. Be sure to recognize the times they comply even though they disagree or don't want to. Acknowledge the effort they are making to behave appropriately. If you change your mind in the future about something, make sure you remember to mention their compliance as part of what influenced you.

- **Support taking responsibility**. This is a kind of counterintuitive recommendation. If they defy you, they at least need to own up to it and accept the consequences for their decisions. Being an adult is not always doing what someone else tells you—it is accepting the consequences for your actions. If they defy you and acknowledge it up front, then combine your disappointment over their lack of compliance with appreciation that they at least demonstrated enough integrity to own up to their choices.

**Strategic Defiance.** Strategic defiance is blatant, intentional (rather than reactive) defiance of your rules and expectations. This kind of defiance will require a more elaborate response.

- **Call a meeting**. Review the areas that have been damaged by their defiance (your trust, their integrity and honesty, your respect, their dependability, and your estimation of their maturity and patience, to name a few). Spend some time talking about how they might have handled it more appropriately and with integrity (for example, talking to you rather than sneaking around or trying to trick you) and the things that might have convinced you to consider giving permission (like trust, integrity, and honesty).

- **Shut down their life** for a period of time until they consistently demonstrate compliance, trustworthiness, and the ability to talk to you directly about something they disagree with. Be as specific as possible about what you will be looking for to relax the grounding.

**Repeated infractions.** Repeated instances of defiance are a sign that there may be something else going on besides normal adolescent striving for independence. You may have a particularly strong-willed kid or one who is more impulsive or more emotionally intense than most, which means it will require a greater number of repetitions for the lesson to stick. They may be under an inordinate amount of stress, or something may be really bugging them. It is worth sitting down (soon, but not when you are addressing an instance of defiance) and checking in with them. You may discover something you can help with. And, of course, you can always consult with a mental health professional to see if there is anything you should be worried about.

# GOAL SETTING

Achieving success in life, whether it's the little things or major life accomplishments, is a learned skill. It will be important for you to help your kid learn how to set their own goals for personal success.

This chapter provides information on:

- Assessing your kid's personal goals
- Breaking down goals into achievable steps
- Preparing for setbacks
- Developing a support system
- How to maintain motivation

## WHAT'S A PARENT TO DO?

**Review their goals.** For your kid to achieve personal goals they have to clarify the goals they want to achieve. This makes a good topic for a family meeting. Make it a family affair where everyone can talk about their goals for the next six months. Take this time to assess progress on current goals, recommit to goals that have been neglected, rearrange priorities, and set new goals. Your child's long-term goals can act as the Holy Grail, helping them weather day-to-day drudgery as they slog toward good grades, lifting heavier weights, moving to the front of the dance line, or whatever their goal might be. Be sure to discuss the connection between goals and the life outcomes that your kid values. It also helps to make the goals behavioral and specific ("I want to make a 3.0 or higher for the semester") rather than general ("I want to make good grades.").

**Identify the specific steps required to accomplish the goal.**
While it is important to have the overall goal in mind to see the big
picture, it turns out that success in achieving goals is most directly
dependent upon identifying the specific steps required to reach the
goal. "I want to be a video game designer" is often followed by
playing video games 24/7 rather than learning about programming,
developing artistic skills, etc. Help your kid break down goals into
the necessary steps. Individual steps can be grouped into milestones;
the steps of consistently doing math homework, seeking help to
truly understand the concepts being taught, and studying—rather
than cramming—for the section test would lead to the milestone of
an improved grade on the test for that section.

**Expect setbacks, challenges, and hassles.** One of the first
places that kids can become demoralized is when they experience
their first setback or failure in pursuit of a goal. They're likely to
feel, "Well, just forget it then!" Make sure you discuss the inevita-
bility of setbacks. Make setbacks and challenges part of the plan
and help your kid figure out how to deal with them. The key is to
characterize them as necessary. Identify possible reasons for the
setback. Revise the plan to account for what they have learned.
Get going again. Learning from your mistakes is a fundamental
element of growth.

**Set up a social support system.** A sure way to fail at pursuing
personal goals is to go it alone. You are in the perfect position to be
part of your kid's support system for pursuing their goals (especially
since you have the transportation, money, and experience to make
things happen). But, of course, support is also provided through
encouragement; they will need someone to vent to about frustration
and someone who believes in them, regardless of setbacks.

Support also includes friends and peers. This is yet another time
to talk about how the company your kid keeps has a significant
influence on their priorities and their resilience in the face of challenges. If their friends think your teen's personal goal is stupid, it
can be hard to hold on through the struggles necessary to achieve

it. When your kid's goals match those of their friends, a natural support system is built in.

**Environment counts.** It turns out that environmental cues have a powerful influence on making progress toward goals. Cues and triggers can work for or against goal pursuit. Having a place that is dedicated to activities associated with a particular goal (like a designated study area) can be an influential part of pursuing goals. That environment is then filled with cues and triggers associated with that goal. If your kid studies in an area normally dedicated to playing video games or sleeping, that environment might automatically trigger them to shift attention to another activity. Pay attention to the potentially supportive—and undermining—aspects of your kid's environment.

**Paint yourself into a corner.** If you have announced to God and everybody that you are going to lose weight, get As, or make an athletic team, it becomes a pretty good incentive to keep working to avoid shame, humiliation, or disappointment. This is not to suggest that you should help your kid out by trying to shame or humiliate them (see Set up a social support system, above). Having your kid make public a commitment about their goals can keep them accountable to someone other than themselves. It is hard to pretend you didn't have something as a goal if you already told other people about it.

**Keep track of progress.** It is easy to overlook progress that occurs in small increments, as most progress does. Help your kid recognize the progress they have made or are making. It helps if there are specific criteria (such as grades, completed homework, weight lost, less time to complete a formerly difficult task, etc.) that you check on a fairly frequent basis, especially at first. Be sure to help them track both overall progress as well as progress on a particular step, in case they are having trouble on that step.

**Reward progress.** It turns out that rewards are much more effective than punishment at a neurological level. Kids are notorious for burning out because the only success they recognize is the ultimate goal (which is another important reason to have specific steps and milestones to celebrate as accomplishments). Help your kid set up a system where they build in rewards for successfully completing steps and milestones. These can be as simple as taking breaks ("I *finally* got that math concept! I'm taking a break.") to tangible rewards such as purchases, to acknowledge and reinforce progress and success.

**Persist.** Stick with the plan. This doesn't mean there won't be fits and starts; it means they need to continue to chase the dream, regardless. It will still be necessary to build in breaks so that exhaustion doesn't play a role in undermining commitment. Many times, pursuing goals that require skill development or making lifestyle changes can reach a point when improvements level out and they are getting no better and no worse. Help your kid anticipate this to avoid their becoming unnecessarily discouraged.

**Don't stop too soon.** Finally, it is important to make sure that your kid doesn't stop tracking the progress of the plan too soon. The biggest jump in success occurs in the early phase of goal pursuit. It is tempting for kids to think they can just play it by ear from that point forward. There are a lot of theories about how long it takes to break habits or create new ones. Think in terms of three months. By three months, complex behavior patterns (like studying, working out, healthy eating, or skill development) have been repeated frequently enough to form a habit pattern and have become integrated into your kid's overall daily routines. By the end of three months, your teen's efforts have replaced less productive habits. They have persisted despite setbacks and have seen enough successes for the goal pursuit to become self-perpetuating.

Learning how to set goals and hang in there to the end is a skill set that can serve them well in almost any area of life. Take the time to help your kid get good at it.

# MANNERS

Requiring your kid to have good manners is crucial to their overall development as a human being. Manners will benefit them throughout their lives.

This chapter deals with:

- The basics of good manners
- Encouraging good manners
- Discouraging rudeness

"Company" is coming—and when they arrive, the issue of your kid's manners often springs forcefully to mind. With all the daily demands on your time, manners training can end up at the bottom of the parenting priority list. But teaching and requiring mannerly behavior from your kids goes beyond the continuation of outdated aristocratic pretensions. Manners require kids to develop restraint, self-control, and consideration for the sensibilities of others, and these qualities have been found to be associated with general success in adulthood. Requiring your kids to behave in a civil, polite way when in public or in the presence of company has long-term benefits they can't appreciate (not to mention giving Uncle Crotchety and Aunt Biddy one less thing to criticize).

## WHAT'S A PARENT TO DO?

While discussions of proper behavior have filled a number of very thick books, there are a few basic forms of etiquette worth cultivating in your kids. These include greetings and leave-taking, general politeness, conversation, table manners, and accepting complements.

**Greetings and leave-taking.** It all begins when someone shows up; you or them. When greeting guests (or anyone, for that matter), start by making eye contact. It also helps to look reasonably pleased to see the person. Most importantly, say some sort of salutation (hello, it's good to see you, thanks for inviting me, wassup, etc.) in a clear voice. When appropriate, make physical contact (shake hands, kiss-kiss, hug-hug, etc.). Leave-taking includes, at minimum, some sort of farewell (good bye, thanks for having me over, take care, etc.). It is surprising how significant these little rituals are in creating a good impression and good will.

**Politeness.** A general tone of politeness is essential in civilized company. Expressing appreciation for the efforts of others on your behalf is fundamentally important (saying "thank you"). Responding to questions from others in a respectful way is also at the core of politeness ("Yes sir/no sir" or, at least, a clearly articulated "yes" or "no" rather than "yeah" or "uh uh"). Letting others go first—through doors, in taking food, or while entering and exiting rooms—is a powerful sign of courtesy and respect. Finally, it is most proper for kids to always help their elders. Since old people move so slowly, this becomes a great opportunity for your kids to practice patience.

**The art of conversation.** Relatives want your kids to tell them all they've been doing *for the last year*. If you don't have one of those talkative kids, there are a few guidelines you can offer (or require) to help your kid survive a conversation without appearing rude. When someone asks them a question, they are required to actually answer. Answers must be given in full sentences with a minimum of six words. A complete answer should contain at least three full sentences. This makes a minimum of eighteen word answers to each question. ("I'm in the ninth grade now. I joined the football team again. We've got a pretty good record.") When you break it down this way, it is harder for your sullen toad of a kid to complain with any conviction.

**Table manners.** Even though you may not require your kids to use table manners with the family, it is crucial that they at least know the basics of proper table manners when they are not eating in the barn you apparently raised them in. This includes knowing how to use (and handle) of any utensils that show up on the table (you know, fork, spoon, knife, asparagus fork, etc.). Elbows are kept off the table; it's difficult but important.

As the meal s-l-o-w-l-y gets under way, your kid will need to demonstrate patience and remember one main rule: no one eats until everyone has been served. Deep breathing accompanied by quietly repeating a mantra can help here. Kids often have difficulty with the concept of reasonable portions. Ask them to think in terms of going back for seconds after everyone has had a shot at the food. When a dish is handed to them, it is polite to take a reasonable portion (or not take any) and then pass the dish on along (rather than parking it next to their plate so they can dig in). Sharing has a significant place at the dinner table. This means teens should take into consideration that there are many people at the table, while the food before you is limited. Don't double up. One strategy that can be a tremendous help in this dance of deprivation is to get some food into your teen before the meal. With the edge off their hunger, it's easier for them to demonstrate proper etiquette at the table.

**Accepting compliments.** A final category of manners worthy of attention is your kid's response to compliments. Instruct them to make eye contact, smile, and say "thank you." Simple, right? (But for some kids, you'd think you asked them to throw their body on a live hand grenade.)

Getting these manners in place is best done ahead of time. *Practice* them when it is just the family. It can put a real damper on a holiday gathering to break into a screaming argument with your kid about how much their manners suck. Practice can be casual when you are in the moment or highly structured, which might include setting aside "manners meals" where everyone has to use their best manners—and might even include enrolling them in classes for etiquette. (The formal classes are a great punishment, by the way, for any rebellion on the part of your teen when practicing as a family.)

During family gatherings, you can help your kid be more successful if they know there is a *time limit* for being on display. Try to group the situations that require manners together and then rescue your kid by sending them off. *Include your kid* when the schedule of events is being generated to make sure the schedule includes personal time for them.

**Reward them.** Talk ahead of time about what you expect. Lavish them with praise and express your pride in them for exhibiting proper behavior. It is important to be proud of them for doing what is right rather than acting grateful, as if they were doing you a favor. Go out of your way to make something happen just for them to reward them for showing such maturity.

**Make them sorry if they don't demonstrate proper etiquette.** Luckily, there is always a lot of cleaning up to do during the holidays. The weeks that follow can be filled with lectures, practice sessions, and assigned reading (from those huge, boring books on manners). Don't forget the value of having them use formal manners in every interaction with every member of the family (especially their siblings) for a specific period of time. ("Excuse me, Johnny. When you have finished with that, I would appreciate it if you would hand it to me.") Any oversights will result in having to repeat the interaction.

The development of manners is a process. Like so much we do as parents, once our kids have achieved one level of competence, we will help them move on by fostering and promoting growth to the next level. Luckily, with this project, practice makes perfect.

# NEGOTIATING

There are many ways for people to get what they want. The most effective, by far, is negotiating. You kid needs to learn this important skill.

This chapter describes:

- What is and isn't negotiable

- Ways to encourage your kid to negotiate effectively

- The steps of effective negotiation your kid needs to learn

Most teens have no idea how to negotiate. They may know how to pressure and annoy people into conceding. They might know how to explode and withdraw when things don't go their way or how to passively (and helplessly) just accept whatever is presented to them. They often figure out how to sneak around limits they disagree with.

Like so many skills that kids need, teens either pick up negotiation skills intuitively or they repeatedly suffer from the lack of those skills. In addition to being useful in increasing the likelihood of getting what they want, research has begun to show that teens who are good at negotiating have higher grade point averages, more healthy dating relationships, and less alcohol use.

## WHAT'S A PARENT TO DO?

**Determine what is negotiable.** Before a negotiation can occur, the issue has to actually be negotiable. Be clear about what is and isn't negotiable. There are certain things that you expect or require your kid to do, whether or not they agree. Morals, manners and not breaking the law are on most parents' non-negotiable list. Even though kids have to do certain things, how they are done or who does them can be negotiable. Areas that are well-suited to negotiations include family responsibilities (chores assignment, helping out), privileges (curfew, activities with friends), and any situations kids perceive as unfair.

**Select the right time and place.** To help your kid learn how to negotiate, you will need to set aside time for it. Pick a time to negotiate when everyone is calm and you can devote thirty minutes or more to negotiate without being rushed or interrupted.

**Show you are open to negotiating.** Many kids just assume their parents won't even listen to them. If there is an existing area of disagreement or conflict, suggest that your kid negotiate with you about it. It can be quite an eye-opener for them to have you bring up something you might consider changing. Continue to be encouraging, even when they are frustrated and not getting what they want. Don't give up just because it is not going smoothly at first. "OK, let's keep at this. If it won't happen right now, we can figure out what will convince me later on."

**Let them begin.** Since you get to do whatever you want (because you are the parent), the only reason you are negotiating is because your kid wants something. So have them begin the negotiations. You may even have to show them how to bring up a source of conflict in a reasonable way (rather than by screaming and railing against the unfairness of the world).

**Compromise.** When you set up this little negotiation, be prepared to give in on something. Your kid needs to have the experience that it is worth their while to negotiate rather than their usual strategy of giving up, ranting ineffectually, or sneaking to avoid detection.

**Give direct instruction.** One of the more useful (and enjoyable) roles you can play in this negotiation is to actually advise your kid about how they can get you to compromise on something. "OK, if you say that, I'm going to say 'No.' Try saying this, instead." This can change the whole tone of the negotiation for the better.

**It ain't over 'til it's over.** Don't stop until you have a negotiated agreement accepted by all parties. This may mean that you have to extend the negotiations over several sessions or, for an important issue, even over several days. Staying with the negotiation helps your kid develop a more long-term view of trying to effect change in the world.

**Regardless, you're the parent.** These negotiations happen because you are allowing them and are not a right to which teens are entitled. Negotiating is a privilege. Negotiations can be ended at any time if your kid steps across the line. Indeed, everything can be shut down until they come to the negotiating table with the right attitude. "We need to stop now because you are about to make things much worse. Let's get together again at (specific time)."

Now that you have some ideas about how to help the process along, here are some of the basic negotiating skills that need fostering in many teens.

**Clearly state what you want to negotiate.** To negotiate, it will be important to know what you want to achieve. Kids are usually very clear, very specific, and very narrow about what they want to negotiate. This can paint them in a corner if the specific, narrowly defined topic won't fly. They may need help recognizing that their goals can be accomplished in other ways, or they can accomplish change a step at a time.

**Listening.** If you are going to negotiate, you have to listen effectively. Teens are terrible at this. They are quick to argue or tune out anything they don't like. There are a couple of basic elements to effective listening. First, don't interrupt, no matter how stupid the other person's view is. Second, summarize what the other person has said. The classic formula is "What I hear you saying is _____. Is that right?" Don't continue without an accurate summary. Third, ask questions of understanding that require the other person to elaborate or clarify a point, as if you are actually interested. Fourth, don't try to counter each and every point as it is being presented. Let people finish presenting their side of things, because interrupting ticks people off. Encourage them take notes if they need to.

**Mutual respect.** Successful negotiations require mutual respect. Respect is demonstrated by making eye contact, assuming an interested posture, and attending to the person speaking. Many teens really *suck* at this. Eye rolling, looks of complete disinterest, and snorts of derision when someone makes a "stupid" point are an adolescent's stock in trade. Your kid will likely need a lot of help with this. Verbal indicators of respect include validating other's position or concerns ("I can see why you would think that.") and addressing others with respect. Needless to say, sarcasm and name-calling are not helpful.

**Know what matters to the other party.** To negotiate successfully, you must know what the other person wants to accomplish. This is a difficult skill to learn. Before you begin to actually negotiate, have your kid identify what is most important to you about the issue under discussion. They often don't have a clue, so you might need to help them out. Don't move forward until they know the two or three things that are important to you about the topic under negotiation.

**Find a win/win solution.** When the concerns of all parties to the negotiation are addressed, you have a victory. Most kids (and many adults) view negotiations as adversarial, a time to try to cheat the other person and get everything you can for yourself. Help them look for a solution where everyone can feel good about the agreement.

**Compromise.** You rarely get everything you want in a negotiation. Help your kid expect to compromise. If they enter into a negotiation with the purpose of having it all their way, it will fail. Help them think in terms of giving up part of what they want in order to get some of what they want.

**Take breaks if tempers flare.** Negotiations will fall apart if people become too angry or frustrated. Teach your kid to know when they need to take breaks to keep their emotions in check.

**Don't give up.** Negotiations are rarely a one-time thing, especially in relationships. It will be important for your kid to learn to make progress toward negotiating for what they ultimately want. Take what success they have and build on it for future negotiations.

**End with a summary.** Make sure everyone agrees on the agreement.

Remember, the idea is to help your kid learn how to truly negotiate. It is not to help them learn how to get the most out of a negotiation at the other person's expense, which is a tactic that may help them succeed in business but will make them fail in personal relationships. Mutual respect, compromise, and persisting when something is important are invaluable life skills that you can teach your kid at home.

# SELF-CONFIDENCE

O ne of the greatest gifts a parent can give a child is a sense of genuine self-confidence.

This chapter discusses:

- Experiences that build real self-confidence
- The importance of (the right kind of) success
- The importance of (the right kind of) failure
- Self-confidence as arising from a moral core

You can see it in their eyes. You can hear it in their voice. The hesitancy, the anxiety, the fear that keeps them from putting themselves out there, taking that risk for something they really want, or overcoming an obstacle. Most parents are faced with the challenge of helping their kid develop self-confidence or recover from a blow to it.

Kids benefit from the general belief in their capacity to effectively accomplish goals, complete tasks, and adapt to challenges. While self-confidence isn't necessary for accomplishments (because luck, natural ability, arrogance, fear, habit, ambition, interest, survival, love, and guilt can also drive success), confidence underlies a stable, legitimate sense of self-regard and respect. Self-confidence also fosters a true sense of independence and an expectation that good things will come from working toward personal goals. Self-confidence shows in a kid.

# WHAT'S A PARENT TO DO?

**Success.** Nothing makes a teen feel self-confident like succeeding, if the success is genuine and based on actual accomplishments. Make sure there is some area in your kid's life where they experience success.

**Accurate, balanced feedback.** If all your kid gets is the message that they are great and able to do anything, they are heading for a fall. If all they hear is what else needs improvement, they will have trouble rising up. Self-confidence comes from a clear recognition of strengths and weaknesses. Comment on their strengths and their progress. Provide constructive criticism, but only if you have provided specific, genuine praise first. Avoid shaming at all costs. ("At this rate, you'll never amount to anything!") Shame wounds deeply and never helps.

**Encouraging risk-taking.** Appropriate risk-taking feeds self-confidence in the pursuit of goals. When a risk pays off, a teen's self-confidence increases. Encourage your teens to challenge themselves. Find experiences that stretch their abilities and give them a nudge. Following a dream always involves a risk (as well as hard work, if they expect to succeed).

**Real accomplishments.** Self-confidence must be based on actually accomplishing something. Reaching goals that require effort and persistence help kids feel more self-confident. Arrange for your kid to make real accomplishments. Don't let them quit before they have completed a task or sufficiently mastered a skill.

**Meeting and overcoming challenges.** Few goals worth pursuing are achieved without having to overcome obstacles along the way. As kids meet and conquer challenges, their self-confidence grows. You can help them out by talking about failure and why it is important. Don't let them shrink from challenges. Help them think through ways they can deal with setbacks and obstacles as well as outright failures.

**Commitment to something larger.** Your teen will need to have a broader perspective on life to be truly self-confident. A kid whose self-confidence is based on success in a single area of life is likely to be disappointed when their life expands in adulthood. Devote some time to their spiritual development. Help them understand that a meaningful life can take infinite forms but always requires productive work.

**Responsibility.** It is difficult to be self-confident if someone is always taking care of things for you. The confidence part is based on knowing you can do things for yourself. Problem-solve *with* them, not *for* them. Ask their opinion (as though you think their views are relevant). Require them to be personally responsible for their decisions and actions.

**Real skills.** Self-confident kids don't have to know how to do everything well, but they do need to be able to do at least a couple of things very well. Being able to say, "At least I'm good at ____" can help protect a bruised ego when success eludes them in the pursuit of other goals. Point out your kid's strengths. Get them involved in activities that require persistence and the development of skills.

**Failure.** Failure is a crucial part of learning rather than a sign of impossibility, inadequacy, or inability. It is one of the most important kinds of feedback on the road to success. Self-confident kids need to be able to take something meaningful from failures to adjust and adapt in the future. Communicate a sense of optimism and confidence. Let them know that you are certain they will be able to overcome adversity. Stand with them; show solidarity. Express pride when they take the risk to fail. While self-confidence is about independence, that doesn't mean being alone. Let your kid know you are with them and stand behind them, even if you can't (or won't) do something for them.

**Attributing failure to lack of effort.** If your kid thinks they failed because they didn't try hard enough, the solution is in their power. If, on the other hand, your kid thinks failure was because of luck or that they just didn't have the natural ability or because someone else kept them from succeeding, get ready for the possibility that your kid will sit down in the road (and whine). Analyze lack of success in terms of what they might have done differently. But be careful not to attribute acts of God to effort, because that creates a whole different set of problems. If your kid really couldn't do anything about it, *that* needs to be acknowledged too. Sometimes, stuff happens. And not everyone is an Olympic athlete.

**Strong values system.** Morals hold us accountable. They provide the scaffolding that supports and guides our actions. Honesty, integrity, kindness, courage, persistence, generosity, responsibility, and honor are important virtues; talk often about them. Have a personal value system be one of the sources of self-confidence for your kid. ("At least I stand by my principles!")

It's possible for teens to feel self-confident about things that conflict with your family values. People with some of the highest scores on self-esteem measures are imprisoned criminals. Remind your kids that self-confidence is about the belief that you can accomplish something, not the belief that you are the greatest thing since sliced bread. Real effort, real accomplishments, and real values that guide your actions are worth cultivating in your kid.

# SELF-CONTROL

S elf-control is a crucial element of emotional and psychological maturity—and it can be taught.

This chapter discusses:

- The importance of self-control

- Strategies for encouraging it

- How to balance self-control with spontaneity

Self-control is beginning to get increased attention these days because it is one of the strongest predictors of every kind of success during late adolescence and adulthood. Unfortunately, self-control is a pain (like most things that don't fit the motto "If it feels good, do it"). Teens today have to cope with the speed of change, instantaneous access to information, global competitiveness, a consumer economy, planned obsolescence, the new "new" thing, and money (more and more money); none of these encourage kids to delay their responses or think, plan, and act with deliberation.

Self-control requires a number of skills. First, kids need a reason to exert self-control. Ideally, the motivation will arise out of some long-term goal that requires sustained effort or the realization that self-control is a characteristic of a good, moral, decent, and mature person. Self-control can also be derived from more negative processes, like fear of punishment (either human or divine) and a desire to avoid shame, embarrassment, and humiliation. Once there is a reason for self-control, kids need to be able to recognize when to use it. Next, they need to have strategies for inhibiting their urges, temptations, and impulses. Finally, they will need to be able to catch themselves before their self-control begins to slip.

## WHAT'S A PARENT TO DO?

**Stories of self-control.** Indirect communication is an easy (and sneaky) way to expose your kids to information, strategies, and morals. Look for opportunities to tell stories that show the benefits of self-control and the costs of not using self-control. Think about Ghandi, yourself when you were younger, and any self-destructive celebutantes as well as fictional characters and favorite myths/legends/fairy tales to find examples of good and bad self-control.

**Morals and values.** In most situations, using morals to guide your behavior runs counter to being impulsive and reacting to immediate desires or urges. Morals provide a framework that is already in place before your kid is faced with a choice of how to act. Define being an adult as having self-control. Look for casual opportunities to comment on it. Point out people who show this quality and why it makes their life better for it. Talk about why self-control is important—it enables people to make effective decision, keeps them on track to attaining goals and accomplishing difficult tasks, and keeps them from being a slave to their desires and emotions and suffering the damage these can cause to themself and others.

**Opportunities for self-control.** If your kid is going to develop greater self-control, you will need to make sure they have the chance to use it. Don't keep all temptation away, but don't give them free rein, either. Provide them with some room to develop this important ability.

**The cookie jar.** Self-control is developed through practice. You may not have realized how many ways self-control training can be slipped into everyday situations. The key component is to require your teen to delay gratification, meaning they must wait for things rather than get them the instant they want them. The cookies are right there in the jar, just waiting to be eaten. And they are sooooo delicious. They could take just one and no one would be the wiser.

But they are not allowed to take one whenever they wish. Waiting takes self-control.

A good example of hidden self-control training is the use of manners. Waiting for everyone to get their food before beginning the meal (with kids being served first, so they have to wait longer); giving thanks before a meal; remaining at the table until everyone has finished; letting others go first through a door; and most other forms of polite behavior—including having to sit through adult religious services—all build self-control. Taking turns is another example. Activities like taking turns during video games or watching TV shows, letting others speak during an argument or discussion, and sharing possessions (rather than everyone having their own) are all excellent opportunities for developing self-control.

Surprisingly, developing self-control in one area influences the development of self-control in other areas. In one study, things like squeezing a hand grip strength developer as long as possible, twice a day, or giving up sweets for two weeks (Lent, anyone?) resulted in significant improvements in self-control in another, unrelated area.

Make sure your kids are well-mannered, not just because it makes it more pleasant for everyone else, but because it helps them build self-control. Make them wait. Require them to share. Have them defer to their elders. Expect them to be gracious. When you have confiscated some possession as punishment, leave it in plain sight so they have to exert self-control to leave it be. If you put it away, you're creating an "out of sight, out of mind" situation instead of an opportunity to learn self-control. If they do give in to temptation, they should have to see the possession tossed—that's right, the cell phone, video game system, mp3 player, gone! Lacking self-control will cost them in life. Then they must start all over again to earn another one.

**Give direct instruction.** "You will need to wait and be patient." "Wait your turn." "Your little brother gets to watch his show first." Help them see where they need to exert self-control. Then help them learn how to change their focus from the immediate to the longer term. "It will only be a couple more minutes and we'll get started." "Find something else to occupy your time until your sister is finished." Teens will need help shifting their focus off the desired object or activity. The more they focus, the more likely they are to override self-control and go for it. Help them focus on long-term goals or benefits (such as getting to play the game at all, being able to finish dinner and leave rather than have extra time added on for being rude, etc.). Encourage them to distract or preoccupy themselves until the right time arrives or until the desire drifts away.

**Know their limits.** Keep a close eye on your teen's level of frustration when using self-control. You want them to be successful. Try to determine how long they can maintain self-control and go just a little bit past. As their self-control improves, gradually increase their frustration. "After we finish here, we will do something they would like to do." "Hang on for fifteen (or thirty or sixty) more minutes."

**Praise, praise, praise.** Notice when they use self-control. Mention how pleased you are with their maturity (because self-control equals maturity). Provide some form of reinforcement for having self-control to make it worth their while, such as admiration or special access to valued possessions (perhaps video game playing time) or activities like hanging with friends. Note: be sure not to overdo rewards. They can end up undermining the internalization of self-control. Small to moderate rewards are best.

**Long-term goals.** Working toward a long-term goal requires self-control and simultaneously promotes the development of self-control. Require your kid to form important goals, such as saving for a vehicle, demonstrating responsibility for a set amount of time to earn (or earn back) a desired possession, etc.

**Advice for peers.** Consider asking your teen what they would recommend for a peer in a situation similar to the one in which they find themself. See what suggestions they would make to a movie character faced with the need for self-control. Take advantage of opportunities on the news or in daily life to talk with your kid about someone faced with a dilemma regarding self-control versus impulsiveness. Thinking for someone else gives teens some distance from the immediate pull of impulse. They are much more likely to think in terms of a long-term outcome when it's not their own temptation.

**Feed them carbs.** Some very interesting research has indicated that using self-control depletes brain cells of energy, which then makes people much more impulsive. You can counteract this effect by having your kid carb up, ideally with complex carbs like unprocessed sugars, oats, and whole grains. Keep emergency supplies of granola bars. When your kid is faced with the need for self-control, cram one in their mouth.

**Spontaneity.** While self-control is an important quality for success, there is also a place for impulsive and spontaneous actions. Spontaneity might underlie other important qualities like kindness, generosity, and self-sacrifice. If you ignore the allure of impulsive, emotion-driven actions, you might miss the opportunity to help your kid have fun and be creative. Conversations about self-control should be balanced with conversation about how to be spontaneous while avoiding being reckless, cruel or harmful to others, destructive, or dangerous. It is important to stop and smell the roses too.

While you will be swimming upstream as you try to help your kid develop greater self-control, the stakes are so high and the skill is so important for success in life that it will be worth the effort.

# SHYNESS

S hyness in teens is more common that many people think. Many kids will be too shy to let you know how much their shyness interferes with their life.

This chapter covers:

- Making sure your kid wants your help

- Making a simple plan

- The importance of body language

- The basics of conversation

- A few tricks to social interactions

There are kids in this world who are reserved and socially cautious. These gentle, kind, and considerate kids are often sensitive, anxious, and insecure. Many of them were just born this way. Some have encountered life circumstances that leave them feeling socially inadequate or without the skills to relate easily to their peers.

Being shy can leave a teen lonely and hopeless about ever feeling really included. Most of these kids would like for things to be different, but they don't know what to do.

## WHAT'S A PARENT TO DO?

**Have a talk.** It is always useful to start helping your kid by making sure they want to be helped. Find out if they would like to try to do something about their cautiousness. Have them tell you about the situations that are particularly difficult for them. Get them to describe how they would like to act (and have others act toward them) instead. This will give you an idea of what you are working toward.

**Validate their strengths.** Start off by talking about what you *don't* want them to change about themselves, which may include aspects of their shyness and cautiousness. Being shy also involves being sensitive to other people's feelings and considerate of their time and priorities. Shy people are often generous, kind, and self-sacrificing. Be sure to let them know how important these qualities are to you and to people in general. It is also worthwhile to talk about the costs of being overly gregarious (needing to be the "life of the party") and being overly focused on yourself. You will be working on finding a balance they are comfortable with.

**Personal plan.** Tackling any problem is best begun by making a plan. Help them identify what they want to change. Making a list is really good for this kind of task. Once you have the list, pick out one thing to work on rather than trying to work on all of them at once. Try something that is only a little bit challenging. Making small changes can yield big results.

Have your kid identify a couple of peers who are good at what you picked to work on. Your kid will need to stalk them (so to speak). Have your kid pay attention to how their peer does it. Have them practice with you. After reviewing the remaining suggestions below, put a plan into play. Once. Have them come back and evaluate how it went. Work out any bugs and then try the plan again and again whenever possible (and appropriate). Then move on to the next thing on the list and repeat the process. It won't take long for things to begin to change.

**Taking your time.** Make sure your kid respects their own personal limits. Don't let them start until they are sure they are ready. This means they should work their way up to meaningful conversations rather than just trying to jump right in. They will need to build connections with people rather than just trying to start up a friendship from nothing. It will be important for them to begin to develop a base of information on people they talk to, which will allow them to refer to things they know from previous conversations. One component of relating better to people is to be "discovered." This will develop out of your kid initiating conversations with people as well as the revelation of some skill or talent (more on this below).

**Nonverbal communication.** A huge difficulty that shy, cautious teens have in relating to other people is how they come across to others kids. Sometimes, making a few adjustments in this is all it takes for things to change. The basics are: make eye contact, smile, have an interested expression on your face (not a goofy one), look around, and walk confidently (with shoulders up and an open stance).

It will be important for your kid to demonstrate that they are open to being approached. Teach them that something as simple (and easy) as saying "Hey" can make all the difference in people beginning to notice you. Even the nonverbal "'Sup" head nod can help. You don't have to be friends with people, you just have to make eye contact and acknowledge them before you move on. No pressure. No need (yet) to have a conversation. In a group, your kid can indicate interest simply by listening intently, nodding in agreement, and laughing in appropriate places. No words need be exchanged.

**Reading other people.** It is also helpful if your kid knows at least the rudimentary signs demonstrated by other people who are interested in or open to interacting with them. Some shy, cautious kids don't recognize when someone is interested in including them in the conversation. If someone makes eye contact, odds are they are open to interacting.

An even stronger sign is if they give your kid differential attention. When someone is talking, do they seem to direct their remarks to your kid? Have your kid pay attention and report back. People may already be trying to include them.

Finally, your kid may actually be getting social invitations and not realizing it. Do people ask them questions or solicit their opinions about things? Do they actually invite them to join in? Make sure they aren't missing this clear sign of inclusion.

**Conversation skills.** An important aspect of successful social interaction is being able to participate in a conversation. Shy, cautious kids can freeze up at this point. Have them give some thought to things they can comment on relating to shared experiences. These would include things about school, classes, what they did over the weekend, work, summer, school breaks, or general personal experiences. Your kid will also benefit from some skill at asking questions. Two simple aspects of questioning others are a) finding out what someone is interested in (remind them to listen carefully and remember it for later questions) and b) asking for more detail about something they are talking about. People like it when you find them interesting.

Sharing personal information is another conversational skill that shy cautious kids tend to avoid. It doesn't have to be a deeply personal issue. It is just an opinion, preference, interest, or experience. Kids might think they need to find a way to make a big impression, but it is better (and more natural) for them to just become a quiet presence. (See Taking your time, above.)

Finally, don't forget to let your kid know how influential compliments are in getting people to notice you. Make sure the compliments are genuine and low-key. ("Hey, awesome skateboard!") The same is true for kindness, generosity, and encouragement. These are an unexpected pleasure for the people who receive them. They will remember—and if they are a jerk about it, your kid knows not to waste any more time on them.

**Escape clauses.** A final skill for overcoming hesitancy and avoidance of social interactions is to have strategies for exiting a situation when your kid becomes uncomfortable in some way that doesn't consist of turning and breaking into a run. An exit strategy will be useful when the conversation lags, when your kid runs out of things to say, or if they become too anxious. It's good to have some exit lines. "Catch you later," "I gotta get going," "See you 'round, man/dude/girl," and "Later" are all tried-and-true examples.

Natural reasons to leave might include having somewhere to go (a previous engagement, something "remembered," etc.), tasks that need attending to (bathroom, food, drink, a purchase) or some kind of time limitation. ("Man, I didn't realize the time. I gotta go. My extremely hot girlfriend is waiting on me.") Nevertheless, make sure your kid knows they don't have to explain themselves. It's okay (and actually better and less potentially awkward) to just say they have to get going.

**Self-talk.** What your teens say to themselves about their efforts to be more social will have a powerful effect on how things turn out. It will be important to help them recognize when they are talking themselves down. They will need to develop some self-encouraging phrases and statements to use if things don't go as well as they would have liked. It is also crucial that they encourage themselves when things go well (as opposed to treating their success as an accident).

**Personal skill.** One of the best solutions to feeling inadequate and socially isolated is to develop a personal skill. A skill will naturally draw attention to your kid and, in many cases, will provide a natural social group of people with shared interests and regular contact. They might pursue more traditional, structured, school-based activities like sports or clubs. There are also activities like body building, martial arts, triathlons, boating, off-road biking, mudding, Frisbee, gymnastics, dance, cheer, hunting, target shooting, hang gliding, flying, parachuting and base- jumping.

If those are a bit too conventional for your kid, there is always the development of unique, "cool" skills like magic, juggling, hacky sack, cards (games and tricks), palm reading/fortune telling, animal training, origami, string figures, parkour (as long as you have good medical insurance), or learning to play the harmonica or unusual musical instruments (didgeridoo, concertina). Think of skills that require little or no equipment. Unique skills can be kept secret until your kid feels competent enough to reveal them. Knowing they have a skill can have a very powerful effect on your teens' feelings about themselves and on the ways other people see them.

**Superficial fixes.** There is a place for makeovers in this process. Do what you can to help your kid look the part of a cool kid. Hair, clothing, shoes, even piercings (God forbid) can have an impact. Find someone who has a sense of teen style (adult or kid) and see what they suggest.

**Recognizing success.** Involving you in the process of becoming less socially shy and cautious is important in a number of ways. First, you get to encourage and support them. They aren't in this alone. More importantly, you are going to notice and highlight their successes, including every tiny little improvement and positive change.

As always, your role as confidante, encourager, and a resource for ideas (and finances) can make a huge difference in your kid's development. Many shy, cautious kids can, with encouragement and a little shove, become more engaged with their peers and satisfied with how they handle themselves in social situations. If anxiety or lack of confidence is so intense your kid can't make use of these strategies, it is probably time to consult with a mental health professional for some additional ideas.

# SUICIDE WARNING SIGNS

If your kid mentions suicide or being dead, take it seriously and address it directly.

> This chapter covers:
>
> • Basic suicide prevention
>
> • When to wonder and when to worry
>
> • What to do if you are worried

Every time a suicide makes national news, therapists get nervous. Suicide is one of those behaviors with a contagion effect; the inhibitions of a suicidal kid can be weakened by hearing about others who have followed through with killing themselves.

This is a terrifying subject for parents; no one gets over the death of their child, especially by suicide. But parents are often unclear about what they should be looking for and when to take seriously the possibility that their child is feeling bad enough to consider killing themselves.

## WHAT'S A PARENT TO DO?

**Know your child.** The best preventive strategy is to know enough about your child to notice when they are having trouble. Keep up with what is going on in important life domains (their friendships, school, social sphere, personal accomplishments and disappointments, etc.). Be nosy but without being intrusive; in other words, don't get caught.

**Build a foundation.** Meaningful work, real accomplishments, satisfying relationships, physical activity, fun, a healthy diet, time spent in nature, sunshine, facing and surmounting challenges, social support, spiritual growth, and keeping a perspective on life's possibilities on the other side of tragedy—these are important elements of a satisfying, balanced life. See what's missing from your kid's life. See what you can do to facilitate these experiences and activities.

**Provide perspective.** Difficulties in life can sometimes overshadow everything else. One benefit of getting old is that you develop a sense of perspective, whether you want to or not. You might as well use what you have learned to help your kid appreciate the amazing possibilities that life presents us, even following devastating loss and disappointment. You've been through it. You've seen others go through it. Hope, spiritual enlightenment, optimism, and courage and persistence in face of adversity brighten our lives and help us prevail and grow emotionally. Pass this information along. Don't underestimate the power of storytelling to transmit these messages.

**Know the signs.** Knowing what to look for is the first line of defense against your kid following through with suicidal thoughts or plans. There are a number of factors associated with kids who have attempted suicide. Here is a system that can help you know how serious the risk might be. It arranges the symptoms into three categories: Worrisome, At Risk, and Danger.

## WORRISOME SIGNS

Worrisome signs represent normal teenage experiences that are also associated with adolescent suicide attempts. Think about each of these as another brick in a bag weighing them down. Some kids are in better shape than others, but even strong kids can end up with more bricks than they can carry.

It will be important to work with your kid to address these factors. Get whatever resources your family needs to resolve the problems, so they don't pile up. Worrisome factors include:

○ Major loss (especially social rejection or the break-up of important dating relationship), humiliation, or blows to self-confidence

○ Recent arrest or other embarrassing failure experience

○ Being the target of bullying or harassment

○ Reactive aggression (This is a curious characteristic. Some kids are relatively peaceable but react aggressively if someone provokes them. This is worrisome because these kids can also be at risk for reacting to despair in the moment by considering suicide.)

○ A drop in grades and academic interest

○ Alcohol or drug abuse

○ Feeling stuck or trapped

○ Dramatic mood changes

○ Sleeplessness

○ Social withdrawal or isolation

○ Loss of interest in things

○ Being stressed-out by the need to achieve (overachievers)

## AT-RISK SIGNS

At-risk signs are factors that can so easily overwhelm or demoralize a kid that they might consider suicide as a way to resolve the situation. When these factors are present, it is important to monitor your kid's emotional state on an ongoing basis. Working with a mental health professional is strongly recommended. Even if you are not meeting with them on a regular basis, you will have someone to call when you have questions or if your parent radar is going off. At-risk factors include:

○ Previous suicide attempts

○ Previous suicidal thoughts

O Prior psychiatric hospitalization

O Persistent bullying and harassment by peers

O Diagnosed with depression, bipolar disorder, or schizophrenia

O Family history of suicide

O Dangerous, reckless, or very-high-risk behavior

O Talking about or writing about being hopeless, worthless, the meaninglessness of life, etc.

O Increased energy and mood following a period of profound depression (because they may be suicidal but didn't have the energy to do anything about it, until now)

O Running away from home or ongoing intense family conflict

O Acting out and rebelling, especially if it is uncharacteristic

## DANGER SIGNS

When danger signs are present, teens are seriously considering suicide. Put your kid under strict twenty-four hour watch (which includes sitting up with them while they sleep) until you meet with a mental health professional or take a trip to the emergency room for an evaluation. Danger signs include:

O Talking, writing, or drawing about suicide, wanting to sleep forever, or death and dying

O Acting as if they will be leaving or won't be around for long, or actually saying good byes

O Giving away or throwing away favorite possessions

O Idealizing or romanticizing death as a solution to problems

O Joking about suicide

O Lots of worrisome and at-risk signs

**If you wonder, ask.** There is no evidence that asking a kid whether they are suicidal or have been thinking about death or dying "puts it in their head." Having the opportunity to talk about it is almost always experienced as a relief by the suicidal teen. Don't beat around the bush. Get everything out in the open so you can help them do something about it.

**If you worry, consult.** Don't try to figure out something this serious by yourself. Consult with a mental health professional. You may be worried about nothing, or you may have headed off a disaster. It can be the best money you ever spend.

**What to do if you discover your kid is suicidal.** If you believe your teen is seriously considering suicide, it's time for immediate action.

- *Don't pass it off as a stage.* If they mean it, it's serious. If you think they don't mean it, your response could make it serious. Dismissing or minimizing suicidal talk might force your kid to *prove* they are serious. Taking immediate action will keep them safe, show them that you take this seriously, and encourage them to only talk about suicide when they mean it.

- Immediately put them under twenty-four hour watch (including bathroom and sleeping).

- Take them to the emergency department of your local hospital or schedule an appointment with a mental health professional who has been informed of your concerns.

- Remove all lethal weapons (especially firearms) from the house, permanently.

- Lock up any dangerous over-the-counter or prescription medications.

- Be supportive, understanding, patient, and non-critical for now. Don't try to talk them out of it by minimizing their feelings ( "Everyone feels like that") or by telling them how they think or feel. ("You don't really mean that!")

- Don't try to give them false or shallow hope (avoid saying "Everything will work out OK" if you can't guarantee it).

- Emphasize that you will go through this with them, and they won't have to deal with this alone.

- Be the voice of hope through experience (by sharing personal stories of despair where things worked out OK) while validating their pain and suffering in the moment.

- Be clear about what would happen to the people who care about them if they died. Provide graphic descriptions of how difficult it would be to go on and the years of grieving you would go through. It's true. Having them see you cry just thinking about it can help.

The vast majority of kids who wonder if life is worth living or who are thinking of suicide do not attempt suicide. All kids who attempt suicide have wondered whether life is worth living or have decided to attempt suicide. If you have any inkling that your kid may be wondering whether living is worth the trouble, get to a therapist. Better safe than devastated.

# LIFESTYLE ISSUES

# DIET

Food is the fuel our bodies run on. What kids eat not only affects their weight and energy but can influence their thinking, their health, and their physical development.

This chapter covers:

- Learning about healthy eating

- Evaluating your kids eating habits

- Encouraging healthy eating

- Making nutrition a family thing

Most teenagers' eating habits are very, very bad. Seventy-five percent of teens eat four or more times a day. Thirty-three percent of teens are overweight. Eighteen percent are obese. Only 6 percent of teens eat the recommended daily amount of vegetables. Only 24 percent eat the recommended amount of fruit.

The majority of teens are deficient in the amount of calcium and iron needed to meet the demands of their growing bodies. Sodas, energy drinks, highly processed snack food (junk), and high-fat and high-sugar convenience meals are the norm. The top three sources of calories for kids and teens are desserts, pizza, and sodas. Parents are faced with the task of helping their kids develop healthy eating habits while being inundated with relatively affordable, readily available, highly marketed unhealthy food choices.

# WHAT'S A PARENT TO DO?

**Educate yourself.** You will need to know something about the amounts of carbohydrates, fats, and protein experts recommend for your kid's daily nutrition. The US Department of Agriculture has a useful booklet that provides the basics on calories, healthy eating, and a balanced diet.

It is also helpful to have a general idea about daily servings of grains, fruits, vegetables, proteins, and dairy recommended for optimal health. You should also know if your kid's weight is unhealthy. There are online websites that can be used to determine whether your teen is underweight, healthy, overweight, or obese.

**Track your kid's eating habits.** Keep an informal diary for a week to see what your kid is eating and when. You may discover that you don't have anything to worry about—or it may be worse than you realized. What you discover about your kid's diet will provide the basis for making changes in your family diet to improve everyone's eating habits.

**Nutrition talk.** If your kid is going to eat a healthy diet, they need to know something about nutritional health. Have a conversation about the importance of a healthy diet. Talk about how your family can have more healthy eating patterns. Find out your kid's thoughts about their eating habits. The majority of teens report an interest in having a more healthy diet.

Give some thought and some discussion to what gets in the way of healthy eating (see below). Make these talks part of an ongoing conversation about nutrition. The key will be to make some initial healthy changes then gradually keep adding to the plan.

**Vitamins and minerals.** It is always helpful to make sure your kid is getting the basic nutrients to take the pressure off having perfectly balanced meals. Make sure your teen gets a multivitamin every day. Find out what the experts are saying about important supplements. For example, teens need 1300 mg. of calcium a day (which is the equivalent of four, eight-ounce glasses of milk). The typical teen gets the equivalent of about one and a half glasses a day. Most kids also don't get the recommended amounts of vitamins D and C, iron, and Omega-3 fatty acids. Supplementing your kid's diet with these vitamins and minerals can have important benefits for adolescent health and development.

**Healthy meals.** If you want your teen to eat a healthy diet, it will help to plan healthy meals. As a rule, the more processed the food, the less healthy it is. A healthy breakfast is crucial. A light dinner, three or more hours before bedtime, is desirable. You can easily spend hours a day reviewing the information available on healthy meals and recipes, but most parents don't have this kind of time (or dedication). For the less ambitious, the government provides a good way to think about food groups to include in every meal. (You can find references to these resources on the website for this book.)

**Stock healthy snacks.** Your kid is going to snack. Rather than trying to discourage it, stock up on healthy, tasty snack foods. Fruits, fresh vegetables and dip, whole grain snack bars, popcorn, pretzels, nuts, and frozen yogurt are tasty and also provide nutrition. Make a list to post on your refrigerator and take to the grocery store.

**Eliminate or limit empty-calorie foods.** Get rid of junk food that's in your pantry—that includes chips, candy bars, cookies, and anything that can be bought in a vending machine, even non-whole-grain breakfast cereals. Don't buy sodas and sugary drinks for your home. If you don't want (or can't bear) to eliminate these unhealthy foods from your family diet, find ways to limit them. Buy only enough to last until the day after grocery shopping day (and make a rule that you can't buy them in between). Don't keep any junk food in the house, so you have to make a special trip to buy some (and make a rule that you can't just pick junk food up on the way home). Have *lots* of healthy snack alternatives including ...

**Healthy drinks.** Water. Lots of water. No sugary drinks–and especially no energy drinks. The options range from fruit juice, milk products, and smoothies to, of course, water. Good luck making much headway on this one.

**Stock easy and pre-fixed foods.** Teens often follow the path of least resistance when it comes to deciding what to eat. If they have to exert too much effort to prepare foods, they will start searching for an easier alternative (like fast food). Give some thought to having healthy, easy-to-fix meal options in the fridge (such as lean lunch meat, lean grilled meats, the ingredients for protein shakes or smoothies, and salad ingredients, including low-fat salad dressings). Get your kids into the habit of eating a balanced meal with meats, vegetables, grains, and dairy (rather than a lot of just one thing, like a bag of chips). Unfortunately, this will require you to plan ahead (in your spare time).

**Limit drive-bys.** The majority of fast food is full of bad fats, processed carbs, and few essential nutrients. It is best to limit your teen's fast-food runs. (The typical fast-food purchase for teens is soda and fries.) Make fast food the exception rather than the rule.

**Teach them to cook.** Most teens don't know how to cook even simple meals. Have them help you in the kitchen. Assign your kid a night when they have to prepare the family meal. They are much more likely to put a healthy meal together (rather than scrounging for junk or fast food) when they know their way around a kitchen.

**Monitor school meals.** There is a lot of unhealthy eating that can occur during the school day. Keep an eye on their food consumption when they are at school (or on summer days).

**Eat family dinners.** Have family meals. You will think more seriously about the components of the meal and the food you eat will be healthier if you know everyone will be sitting down together. You have more direct influence over what your kid eats when you're eating with them at the family table. Food consumption is different (based more on actual hunger) when eaten at the table rather than in front of the television or other screens. In addition, when kids are with friends instead of family members at meal times, the consumption of unhealthy foods is much more likely. And one more thing: there are a number of psychological and social development benefits that are associated with regular family meals.

**Tie healthy eating to healthy living.** Depriving your kid of food by eliminating it or limiting calories can often lead to greater cravings and gorging when they get the chance to eat. Frequent fast-food eating—while generally unhealthy in its balance of proteins, fats and carbs—does not automatically lead to obesity. It is that diet combined with other unhealthy lifestyle choices. Consider requiring your kid to trade off healthy eating and regular exercise for access to junk food.

A real understanding of nutritional health in teens can be overwhelming for non-experts. If you have any concerns or are especially interested in improving your family's dietary health, contact a licensed dietician. They know all about the range of issues related to diet and healthy lifestyles.

# EXERCISE

## Part 1:
### Exercise Basics

Exercise does more than just promote good health. It is also associated with a wide range of emotional and psychological benefits.

> This chapter outlines many of the benefits including:
>
> - The importance of exercise
>
> - How to get your kid to exercise
>
> - Types of exercise to consider for your kid (and your family)
>
> - How to make sure your kid does not overdo it
>
> - How to make exercise fun

Having physically active teens is the Holy Grail of parenting. Exercise is the cure for almost everything: anger, conflict, depression, low self-confidence, video game addiction, lack of energy, lack of motivation, poor health, high blood pressure, and obesity. While younger children get an average of three hours of exercise a day, this drops to forty-nine minutes a day by age fifteen (and down to thirty-five minutes a day on the weekends).

Teens who exercise have been found to be less likely to smoke, drink, use drugs (other than marijuana), engage in premarital sex, miss school, and get brain cancer (!), heart disease, and osteoporosis in adulthood. Teens who regularly engage in moderate to strenuous exercise feel better about themselves, have more energy, sleep better, get better grades, are more likely to wear seat belts, and are more likely to get As in science and math, complete household chores (!), and have summer jobs outside of the home. Exercise during adolescence counteracts the effects of the recently discovered "fat gene."

## WHAT'S A PARENT TO DO?

**Talk exercise to them.** Talk about the importance of health and physical activity. Talk about why exercise is important, both now and for their future. Talk about what you are going to do as a family to stay active and get enough exercise. Talk to them about the new day that is dawning, a day where they will know the satisfaction of pushing their body to the limits of endurance; a day where they will fall, exhausted, into the comfort of their bed at night; a day where you will make their lives a living hell if they don't get out and do something physical *every day!*

**Make an exercise plan.** Be specific about what you expect from your kids regarding being physically active. Have them identify where exercise will fit into their day. Make specific plans for physical activities with the family every two to three weeks (see ideas below). Make it clear how they will make up missed daily activity by adding time on the weekend. Be sure to meet back on a regular basis (weekly, monthly) to monitor progress and celebrate improvements in physique, stamina, and health.

**Medical exam.** Before you embark on this grand adventure, have a medical professional make sure your kid doesn't have any limiting health issues. And don't forget to have yourself checked out, since you are likely to be right in the middle of this exercise thing too.

**Healthy diet.** Staying healthy includes getting the right amounts of vitamins, nutrients, and calories for energy. Now is as good a time as any to have your kid (read "your family") begin to eat a healthy diet.

**Body Mass Index.** The most common measure of physical health is the Body Mass Index (BMI). This calculation compares your kid's weight to their height. (BMI calculators are easy to locate on the internet.) While this measure isn't perfect, because it underrates thin kids and overrates muscular and taller kids, it can give you a starting place to talk with your kid about their general physical health. The BMI can become a goal for overweight kids (either maintaining a particular BMI or getting their BMI under a specific number).

**Misery loves company.** A very effective way to promote regular exercise by your kid is to exercise with them. It is more difficult for them to argue they are being singled out when you are complaining about exercise right next to them. A mutual dislike for exercise can bring the family together—it can be like a common enemy. And you get to model enthusiasm and excitement about the many benefits of becoming more physically fit!

**One hour a day.** Health benefits for teens begin at a minimum one hour a day of moderate exercise. This would also translate into seven hours a week, if scheduling or interests make daily exercise difficult.

**Passive to active ratio.** Kids who are particularly activity-resistant may need extra incentive to get up and get moving. Consider making them earn passive activities like video game play and TV watching through exercise. Think in terms of a ratio of passive activities to physical activity (for example, two or three hours of video game play for every hour of exercise). No exercise, no access to media.

**Make it fun.** Do everything you can to try to find fun or meaningful ways to exercise. (See the next chapter for ideas.)

**Throw them out.** If you send kids out of the house (and ban them from going to someone else's house), they are likely to get exercise, even if it is just walking around looking for something to do.

**Jump-start exercise.** If your family is not physically active or has become increasingly sedentary, consider planning a fun, physically active trip (like surfing, canoeing, hiking, water or snow skiing, etc.). This can either give you a goal to work toward for workouts leading up to the trip or can be the beginning of a healthier lifestyle to continue after you return.

**Get a dog.** Sometimes, extreme measures are called for. Researchers have reported that people with dogs get more exercise. This is presumably because people are more likely to walk the dog than they are to walk themselves. Maybe it is also from playing with the dog. If you already have a dog, it's about time it earned its keep. Send your kid out behind the dog for walks. (If you have a fat dog, you might have solved two problems—although there are stories of lazy dogs lying down and refusing to walk another step.)

**Trainer.** It is always important to consult with experts to make sure you are addressing all the important aspects of a situation. Athletic trainers can keep kids on track and continue to move them forward in their workouts. They can also reduce the likelihood of pushing too hard. Kids who have limited experience with physical activity can easily become demoralized or just plain frustrated when working toward a goal (especially if it involves slimming down). They don't know about the motivational and physical ups and downs of getting into shape. Having someone who will guide and encourage them can be a great help. Almost every workout facility has trainers on staff.

**Active lifestyle.** The ultimate goal is to encourage your kid to make physical activity and exercise a part of their daily life. The benefits of regular, moderate exercise have been demonstrated across every phase of the lifespan.

There isn't any one way your kid needs to be active. The important thing is for kids to be active. Think of activities they can do and enjoy for the rest of their lives.

# EXERCISE

## Part 2:
### Getting Teens Up and Going

For your teenager to get the benefits of exercise, they will have to *do* something. Happily, there is a range of possibilities for getting them up and going.

This chapter covers:

- Matching exercise to your kid's level of physical fitness

- Fun (and unusual) ways to exercise

## WHAT'S A PARENT TO DO?

To begin, your kid will need to learn how to monitor their body to make sure they don't overdo things. Depending on how active your kid has been, they may need to start slowly and work their way up to more strenuous activity. One way to assess whether they are pushing themselves too far is by keeping track of their heart rate. To do this, you need to ...

**Measure the pulse.** Heart rate is an important indication of whether your kid's exercise routine is mild, moderate, or intense. It will be important for them to monitor their pulse while exercising. (Information is provided on the Reference page of the book website to learn how to do this.) Start by having your kid determine their target heart rate for exercising. (Information on measuring target heart rate is available on the Reference page of the book website.) Moderate exercise for teens is generally accomplished by maintaining a heart rate between 120 and 140 beats per minute. This will be an important measure of whether your kid is pushing themselves beyond a safe limit. The other general principle for exercising safely is to ...

**Stop when it hurts.** Pain is your body's way of telling you something is wrong. The old adage that you should "push through the pain" is a formula for injury. If your kid experiences pain while exercising, they need to drop way back or stop until the pain passes. If the pain persists, it is time for a visit to your personal medical professional. Keeping your kid physically active is (ideally) going to be a long-term, ongoing part of their life. You don't have to rush it. It is miserable enough to have to actually exercise; being in physical pain the whole time or suffering a major injury makes motivation dramatically worse.

**Basics.** There are two main components of exercise: strength training and aerobics. Both are important for development and ongoing health. Muscle building can be as simple as pushups, crunches, and isometrics (which are activities that involve tensing muscles against resistance) or as complicated as the fancy machines you find in upscale gyms. Aerobics are activities you engage in for an extended time at moderate intensity levels (such as walking, jogging, biking, running, etc.). Many activities combine both of these components of exercise.

## EXERCISE IDEAS

Exercise doesn't have to be boring or tedious. There are a wide range of activities that can be fun, interesting, and character-building while still getting their blood pumping.

**Organized sports.** Football, basketball, baseball, softball, soccer, tennis, competitive swimming, martial arts, hockey, cheer, rugby, wrestling, volleyball, gymnastics, and dance all count. If your kid develops a natural interest or a willingness to participate in these sports, you're set.

**Home workouts.** Physical activity doesn't have to be high-tech or expensive. Strength training can be done with a set of dumb bells (or plastic gallon milk jugs). There are plenty of sites that provide information on easy home strength training exercises for teens. For an aerobic workout, just have them start moving. Any activity that brings their heart rate into the moderate range will do.

**Fitness gyms.** It seems like there is a gym or fitness salon within ten miles in every direction. They provide a structured, social environment to keep active and get fit. (It also makes it easy to drop your kid off while you go sit and have coffee and a pastry.)

**Video workouts.** Video workout programs are popular, probably because they can be used in the privacy of your own home. Consider the kind of kid you have when choosing a program. There are some extreme workout programs for kids who are interested in sculpting their bodies, and there are also more encouraging, progressive workouts for less ambitious kids.

**Virtual exercise.** Don't forget about the new (and somewhat disturbing) world of electronic exercise. These are referred to, unfortunately, as "exergames." These games mimic the players arm or whole body motion. There is a range of programs that have players engage in virtual exercise, competitive sports like tennis or dance, and even perform in virtual bands. They're video games, yes, but they result in lots of movement.

**Tricking them.** You can always resort to engaging your kids in exercise hidden within a potentially enjoyable activity. Go hiking. Spend the day on the river, at the lake, or in other places where they will accidentally swim. Take a biking tour or head out to the water park on a hot day.

**Extreme sports.** There are sports that say "I'm a rebel." (And "My parents have good health insurance.") Things like skateboarding, rollerblading, rock climbing, ultimate Frisbee, mixed martial arts, and parkour (a quaint little activity that involves kids jumping back and forth between ledges, balconies and roof tops, running up walls, and generally risking plummeting to their death or incurring severe brain damage). Hey, whatever it takes to get them exercising, right? What could go wrong?

**Unique activities.** You can also draw kids into exercise by coming up with something unusual. Paintball is an intense activity that will have your kid drenched in sweat from running, rolling, and getting splattered with paint. The equipping costs are steep but some kids really take to it. That means you won't have to talk them into participating.

The same is true for airsoft sports. Airsoft is a modern version of a pellet gun that uses little plastic pellets. Kids who have a fascination with guns or the military will be all into it.

If you have never tried fencing, you may not realize that swordplay wears you out! You have to maintain a semi-squatting position and constantly shift your feet back and forth as you fence. Fencing also provides a rather unusual talent that your kid can reveal on special occasions (or if ever attacked by a brigand).

In many cities, there are groups of folks who are into medieval combat and gather at local parks or open fields to hit each other with swords, maces, axes, and other ancient weapons made of plastic pipes and foam. Then there are games like badminton and Ping Pong. Both take relatively little in the way of equipment and both require a surprising amount of exertion, especially when you get some good competition going.

**Event training.** Having some kind of goal your kid is working toward can help keep them focused and dedicated. Sign them up for a distance running event. It can be a charity run, or a marathon or half-marathon. You might also let an athletic child train for something more ambitious, like a triathlon (that is where you swim, bike and run).

**Cool talents.** You can encourage your kid to learn something they can display in a social setting to gain some attention. They might be interested in learning to do cartwheels, back flips or the like (rather than taking gymnastics in general). There is also a kind of game called hacky sack that involves juggling a small bean bag with your feet. Kids can do it by themselves or with other kids. It is very active, requires a lot of practice which you can do just about anywhere, and it will get a lot of props (that's cool kid lingo for compliments and admiration) from their peers.

The benefits of regular physical activity are both immediate and long-term. Unfortunately, modern lives revolve around sedentary activities. It takes specific effort to incorporate exercise into daily life. Helping your kid develop a commitment to being physically active and staying fit is one of the important contributions you can make to the quality of the rest of their life.

# PLAY

A ll work and no play ... Teens need time to play. Play is an important source of joy, pleasure, satisfaction, fascination, happiness, interest, and curiosity. Play time builds skills and provides a way to explore learning without pressure. It is also a way for teens to learn about their physical abilities and the opportunities afforded by the world around them.

This chapter discusses:

- What play is (and isn't)

- How to encourage your kid to play

- How to get out of the way so your kid can play

During play, teenagers practice taking (controlled) risks. Play is an important mechanism to release pent-up frustrations and other negative emotions. It is a chance to try on new roles and test social boundaries. While playing, teens learn about cooperation, conflict resolution, and relating to others.

Kids use more sophisticated language when playing than they do when interacting with adults. Play allows teens to examine new ideas, test out theories, and pretend. It also turns out that play (in the form of recreation) is related to all kinds of positive mental health outcomes. When teens are playing, they learn without realizing it, which can be useful for a parent to keep in mind.

# WHAT'S A PARENT TO DO?

First, make sure you can recognize play when you see it.

**Play doesn't have a purpose.** If you try to get your kid to play the "right" way, you are defeating the purpose. Providing meaningful experiences for your kid and requiring them to engage in productive activities is something else altogether. You aren't supposed to know what they will get out of playing. Play is for fun. If you set kids loose, they can stumble upon things about themselves and interests that enlighten and enliven the rest of their lives.

**Play doesn't have rules.** If something has rules and directions, if someone programmed it, or if it has predetermined steps, it isn't free play. That doesn't mean the activity isn't important or useful or valuable or fun—but it isn't free play. Think of setting your kid loose at a stream or in the woods as the model; they'll find lots of things to do with no clear indication of what they are supposed to do (other than play).

**Play has many forms.** Your kid might need help realizing how many different ways there are to play. There are physically demanding activities, socially oriented activities, intellectual stimulating activities, artistic and creative activities, and activities that challenge them.

○ Physical play. There is a whole range of play that is about your teens experimenting and pushing themselves physically. This would include spontaneous jumping and frolicking, skateboarding, pickup sports, and exploring the environment. (It does not include structured sports, trained dance, or purposeful and goal-directed exploration.)

○ Object play. Play can involve examining objects and putting them to new uses. Playing with objects includes taking things apart, putting things together (especially in new and impractical arrangements), repairing (without instructions), building, and destroying. It is not being taught how things work or engaging in a predesigned building project.

○ Fantasy play. Play can also take the form of pretending and role play. Fantasy play would include acting out imagined situations and scenarios (with or without other people), playing dress up, using make up, donning bizarre clothing, playing paintball or airsoft weapon sports, or using gangsta rap posturing.

○ Social play. The play we are most familiar with is when kids play together. This form of play does require some (very minimal) structure. Your kid will need to be able to know (and be able to signal) what is and isn't play. Fighting, bossing, and violating others personal boundaries is not play. Playmates have to know how to trade off and play fairly; one person can't be in charge all the time. Teens must to be able to recognize when they cross a line (like when they get too rough or hurt someone's feelings) and make up for it. Finally, they must not repeatedly violate these general rules. Social play includes rough and tumble activities like wrestling, jostling, boxing, and tackling. It also includes spontaneous group celebrations such as birthdays, unexpected demonstrations of skills, sporting events, concerts, and cooperative activities that combine other forms of play.

○ Creative play. Finally, play can also be a part of coming up with something completely new and different. Creative play is seen in artistic efforts like drawing, painting, music, dance, and storytelling, and in imaginative thinking—such as considering how impossible situations might exist. Creative play might involve thinking about completely unusual ways to put things together. Creativity can be part of a very structured, guided, and highly skilled process—but creative play is spontaneous and unstructured.

Playful moods can be very fragile. It doesn't take much to inadvertently shut a playful mood down. Here are some pointers for encouraging and validating playfulness in your kid.

**Be playful.** Lead the way. Cut loose. Have fun. Be spontaneous. Follow your impulse. Your kid will learn by example. (Note: All of these suggestions assume you are a reasonably psychologically healthy individual, so that your spontaneity and impulsiveness is positive and joyful rather than negative and destructive.)

**Encourage it.** Teens will seek out opportunities to play when they have the chance. All it usually requires is letting them off the leash. Don't forget to put play on the list of required productive activities (along with excellent grades, high standardized test scores, athletic prowess, high-ranking social status among their peers, and curing cancer). Whatever you do, lend moral support and encouragement for the importance of playing.

**Require it.** Some kids actually need permission to play. High-achieving kids, naturally serious kids, depressed or anxious kids, and kids who have experienced some kind of trauma can have trouble making time to play. Give them a little nudge. ("Close those damned books and go do something fun!")

**Make it easy.** You may need to help your kid learn (or re-learn) how to play. In our urban, modern neighborhoods, teens often feel that recreation requires some kind of parental support (like video game systems, sports equipment, or electronic devices). Turn off the electronics and send them out (or drop them off) to play.

**Structure the environment, not your kid.** If you are worried about issues of safety or the potential for trouble-making, put your teens in the right environment rather than putting limits on them. Look for settings where only a determined kid will get hurt or in trouble (and you will already know if you have one of those kids). It is a *real* bummer to have your mother continually saying "Come back over here so I can see you, Johnny. Get away from that. It's dangerous." That means it will be important to ...

**Help them find a playground.** Playing is much more likely in an environment where there is lots of random, interesting stuff. Nature is the quintessential rule-less playground, especially if your kid is stuck there with no electronics. There are sticks and rocks and bushes and trees and water and bugs and hidden places that are completely open to exploration or imaginative uses. Consider tossing your kid out in the middle of nature as a way of encouraging them to play. But don't assume that nature is the only setting for fun. Lots of odd, interesting, and curious stuff can be found in places like grandma's attic or a garage workshop. (Actually, pretty much any place old people have been accumulating things holds the potential for play.)

**Encourage risk-taking.** Play is seriously limited by fear: fear of embarrassment, fear of screwing up, and fear of doing it wrong. Teens might also feel anxiety over not knowing exactly what they should do, insecurity about their skills, and nervousness about breaking something. Your kid may need permission to be careless and worry-free. If your kid is stuck in a narrow view of fun, consider organizing a family activity that introduces them (and the rest of the family) to something new and different.

**Purchase, produce, or borrow a playmate.** Playing is easier with someone who knows how to play. Find someone (or something) that comes with a natural sense of playfulness. Think dogs. Think cute, cuddly, baby animals. Think young children. Put them together with your kid. (Babysitting doesn't count. "Go play with your little brother while we go to Chicago for the weekend. Be sure to have fun.") Some kids are more playful than others. Try to find one of those kids for your kid to play with.

**Let play happen.** It is important that you don't try to help your kid play. There is no right way. Don't step in if you think something isn't going quite right. ("Now you boys know better than to ... ") Hovering, anxious, "helpful," or sternly critical observers will drive a stake directly through the heart of play.

**Be enthusiastic.** Enjoy your kid's frolicking. Laugh and be entertained (from a distance). Take your cue from your kid and revel in their fun. Be happy for them. They can feed off your enjoyment.

**Monitor but from a distance.** Don't stick your nose in. For younger teens, be careful how closely you watch; your kid may become self-conscious. If they glance over at you, avert your eyes. For older teens, monitor by having regular check-ins—every hour or so, text or call, or wander around to see what they are up to without making it obvious.

**Remove stress.** Kids don't play when they are stressed. They don't play when they are pressured. Pay close attention to the amount of stress your teen is feeling. See what you can do to create a stress-free zone. (See the chapters on Stress Management for ideas.)

**Set some limits.** All play and no work makes Jack useless to himself and others. Play and recreation is supposed to be an element of life, not the essence of life. It turns out that humans get bored and lose a sense of purpose if they don't have responsibilities or struggle to accomplish things. They also won't be able to support themselves. Play is valuable as a break from the everyday pace of life, but it should not be the central activity of living. Make sure your kid has activities that are difficult and require them to work hard. ("Get off that skateboard, get in here and do your homework! And don't give me that look!")

Play opens up the possibility for spontaneous discoveries and realizations. It provides an opportunity to discover real interests and abilities. Play is the place that serendipity can enter your kid's life. There are no down sides to authentic free play.

With the emphasis on competitiveness and academic success that has come to pervade our culture, playing has become synonymous with laziness or irresponsibility. It turns out that play is an important part of a balanced, happy life. Make sure there is a healthy dose of play time in your teen's life.

# SELF-EXPRESSION

Ridiculous clothing, embarrassing hair styles, piercing something— adolescence is defined by teen attempts to distinguish themselves from "old people." It is important to give your teens some room to express themselves—within limits.

This chapter explores:

- Resolving differences in personal taste
- Responding to a desire for more permanent change, like piercings and tattoos

Adolescence is all about becoming your own person. That means trying on possible ways of being, looking, and becoming. It is a time of searching for your own style, and establishing (or changing) who you are. It is about looking the part (of the person you are trying on at the moment). Adolescence is about distinguishing yourself from the crowd you are simultaneously trying to imitate.

But, most of all, teens are determined to distinguish themselves from their parents and other authority figures. Clothes, hair styles, musical preferences, and body art (like piercings and tattoos) are the arenas where teens and parents can end up battling for supremacy. Guess who is going to win? (Hint: It's not you.)

Many teens are happy to pursue these expressions of individuality without pushing their parents past the breaking point. For those parents, these teen twists and variations are not significant enough to generate much real conflict. But there are still plenty of teens left over whose interests and style preferences are hard for a parent to stomach.

Your challenge, as a parent, is figuring out how to shape their decisions while respecting the need to experiment.

## WHAT'S A PARENT TO DO?

**Personal tastes.** Clothes, hair styles, and music are forms of personal expression that teens can easily shift and change. You have lived long enough to see how fickle fashion tastes are. The fact that they may change their style, sometimes overnight, doesn't make these forms of self-expression any less important to your teen. It just means that the newest styles aren't likely to last and so are worth some tolerance on your part. When it comes to these areas of personal taste, there are a few things you can to do address your kid's preferences.

**The outer limits.** Begin by deciding the absolute most you can tolerate in their style of clothes, hairstyles, and music. Notice the use of the phrase "absolute most you can tolerate." If your kid stays within that range, you can stop here and count yourself lucky. For many parents, there is a gap somewhere between what they can accept and what their kid prefers. If that difference is too great, you risk losing touch with your kid altogether. You can actually drive them out from under your influence by taking a hard line on clothes, hair or music. (Tattoos and piercings will be discussed below.) Do your best to give teens as much room as possible for self-expression in these areas.

Nevertheless, some things are going to be non-negotiable. Clothing that is too extreme, promotes violence, or is dramatically sexually suggestive; music that is prejudicial, sexist, profane, vulgar, or degrading; personal styles that are permanent (such as piercings and tattoos) fall into this category.

Specify to your kid all areas that are completely unacceptable. Consequences for crossing those lines need to be clearly identified. If they violate your rules, toss the offending clothes, music, or piercing and redo the offending hair styles. Seriously consider paying for tattoo removal. (At the very least, do everything you can to convince your kid that you *would* surgically remove tattoos that were not approved by you—and that you'll have the tattoo artist arrested, to boot.)

**Talk it out.** Once you have established what you can tolerate, tell them. If they agree or don't put up much of a fuss, then you're done. If not, it is time for a conversation. Have them explain why that particular form of self-expression is so important to them. "I just don't get why you want to show your butt crack." "What do you think others will think of you when you (wear something like that/have that music playing/look like that)?" Really listen to their answers. This is more than a conversation about clothing or music—it is about your kid wanting to be taken seriously and to be accepted for who they are.

You can disagree without automatically forcing compliance. Talk about your concerns. (Talk, not lecture, rant or cry). Require your kid to demonstrate that their basic character and morals are not being threatened by these radical styles. Make them convince you that they are not limiting their future prospects for employment or relationships by that kind of self-expression. You can also respond by clearly stating that it is *your* problem that they have to deal with. "It is just too much for me. You will have to wait until you are on your own to do that."

**Give a little.** Look for any way you can to let them try out their style of the moment. This is a sign of respect for their opinion and an indication that you are willing to give them some room to be themselves (or be one of themselves). This is especially important if the style isn't permanent.

**Maintain a balance.** If you are going to give a little, then they will need to give a little. One potentially useful compromise is having them strike a balance. They can pursue a form of self-expression that is particularly odious to you as long as they explore other forms that are more in the direction of your tastes. Each particular form of fashion, hairstyle, and music has a range of expression within that style. Look for something you both can live with—or require your kid to have a range of interests rather than exclusive pursue only one form of self-expression. For example ...

**Dress for success.** Appearances matter—otherwise, they wouldn't be so all-fired set on self-expression. Appearance also reflects on the people you are with. By identifying (or even creating) zones where certain behaviors and forms of self-expression are required of your kid, you help them learn to appreciate the sensibilities of people other than peers. Make sure there are times they have to dress up. Have situations or circumstances where they are not allowed to play music that may offend others. This is not the same as not allowing it at all. They need to at least know how to act in polite society.

**Dress for the occasion.** Having an outlet for self-expression can help siphon off some of the rebellious energy of adolescents. Kids can also define themselves into a corner as others respond to their particular forms of self-expression. Consider allowing them to dress differently for different situations. Require them to dress in socially appropriate (that is, adult-sanctioned) ways for particular events or situations (such as religious practices, grandma's house, or when they are out with you). Allow for more personal forms of self-expression in other situations like social outing with peers, parties, down time in their room, etc. This is about the ongoing challenge everyone faces of having an individual style while also being sensitive to the demands of civil society.

**Permanent changes.** You know, it is one thing to screw up in ways that only a few people know about. It is another to have your mistakes permanently branded onto your body. This is particularly true for piercings and tattoos. These more permanent forms of self-expression have become widely accepted and increasingly common. Piercings are the more broadly accepted form of self-expression. The less extreme forms (ear lobes, ear cartilage, lip, nose, etc.) are only semi-permanent in that the piercings in the skin will close if you stop wearing the ornament. Some of the more extreme forms (tongue piercings, piercings of other body parts) are also primarily semi-permanent. However, piercings that stretch the skin in a distorted way (like ear lobe plugs) are permanent. And, of course, tattoos are also permanent forms of self-expression.

- **Piercings**. Dangling objects from holes in your skin is a form of ornamentation that has been around forever. Your challenge will be how to deal with your teen's potential interest in this form of self-expression. Unlike in the '60s and '70s, piercings do not reliably indicate anything about sexual preference or sexual experience. They have evolved into a form of decoration and style. To begin with, it is important to set some parameters about piercings regarding the possibility of infections. There are some areas that are particularly susceptible to infection (belly button, tongue, nose, private body parts). You also need to inform your kid of any limits on the number and scope of piercings they can have. Other than ear lobe piercings, kids frequently grow tired of the maintenance required for more exotic holes in their skin. (Keep this in mind should you decide to have a trial run with your kid.)

- **Tattoos**. The rise in popularity of tattoos is a rather interesting phenomenon. An initial tattoo is almost universally a form of celebrating or honoring some significant event (a change in status like breaking up with someone, graduation, death of a loved one, a rite of passage, development of a personal realization or philosophy, etc.). The ordeal kids must endure to acquire the tattoo creates its own rite of passage. Here's the thing, though. It is widely reported that people don't have just one tattoo. People tend to have either no tattoos or multiple tattoos. This can be a problem given the idiot ideas teens have about what would make a good tattoo.

What can you do if your kid has developed a hankering for a tattoo? Start by reviewing the law. Legally, they can't get a tattoo or piercing without your permission. In most states, it is a misdemeanor to tattoo a minor unless they are at least sixteen and covering an existing tattoo—and even then, they must have parental permission.

Body piercing on someone under eighteen years old requires the consent of a parent or legal guardian, and they must be present for the event. If someone pretends to be a parent or legal guardian, it is also a misdemeanor in many states.

It can be illuminating to do an internet search for the many ways that these procedures can go wrong. Look up pictures of tattoos on old people. Find stories of people who regret getting tattoos and piercings. Be sure to explore the medical procedure required to remove a tattoo, including the cost. This should be what your child faces if they decide to go against your wishes regarding tattoos.

The desire for unique self-expression is particularly important during adolescence. If your kid has the right values, if they are well behaved, and if they have their priorities in place, a case can be made to justify letting them decide about personal tastes. Permanent changes present a more challenging issue. If you are opposed to specific forms of bodily self-expression, engage them in a real dialogue about their desire to permanently adorn themselves. Find ways to support their personal tastes in non-permanent ways, and hope this is just a phase.

# SLEEP

Teenagers do not get enough sleep, and it is causing all kinds of problems.

This chapter looks at:

- The problems of inadequate sleep

- Indications your kid has sleep-related problems

- Things that affect sleep

- The importance of routine for a good night's sleep

Sleep deprivation in adolescents is associated with depression, anxiety, behavioral problems, drug use, problems at school, poor grades, and low life satisfaction. Guess what constitutes sleep deprivation? Anything less than nine hours of sleep—*less than nine hours of sleep*. Whatever time your kid goes to sleep to arise at six a.m. (and then 6:15 and then 6:30 and then 6:45 until it's *"Get your butt out of bed right now or you are going to be late again!"*) it is rare to find a kid who gets a full seven hours of sleep, let alone nine.

There is fascinating information that has come to light on the role of sleep (and dreaming) in repairing and rejuvenating the body and consolidating intellectual (and even physical) learning that occurred during the day. Sleep interruption has been shown to have direct effects on learning and retention of information as well as the consolidation of physical skills. Sleep deprivation is no small issue for teens.

But, as most parents know, addressing this issue isn't so straightforward. There is a lot going on in your kids' lives that push productive time into the late night. And anyway, teens don't want to go to bed!

# WHAT'S A PARENT TO DO?

If you're going to consider adjusting your teen's sleep habits, first you have to ask yourself a few questions.

**Is it important?** This may seem like a set up, but with all the things kids try to cram into their days, it is difficult to get them to bed early enough to get adequate sleep. This fight may not be worth it. You may not care much about it. You may not want your kid to trade off keeping up with schoolwork just so they can get a good night's sleep.

On the other hand, while there may have to be some compromises, it is likely that you can find ways to increase sleep time by problem-solving with your kid. If they are sacrificing sleep for legitimate reasons, it can be useful to schedule a time to pay off what has been called a sleep debt. The body usually requires a two-for-one trade-off: one night of limited sleep requires two days of extended sleep to restore a balance. You may even want to experiment by evaluating any differences in mood and grades when your kid gets a full night's sleep, compared to their usual amount.

**Is it a problem?** Your kid is not likely to be getting nine hours of sleep (since the average is something like 6.5 hours). But are they really sleep-deprived? Here are some of the indications that a teen is sleep deprived:

- Tired all the time
- Difficult to get up in the morning
- Staying up into the night (until midnight or one a.m.) on a regular basis
- Irritable upon waking
- Sleeping in class
- Napping frequently
- Falling asleep when they stop moving

○ Walking around with hollow eyes, a shuffling gait, inability to speak in complete sentences, a nasty temper, and a tendency to snap at you

**What does your kid think?** Talk to your kid about the importance of sleep. Find out if they are feeling any of the effects of insufficient sleep. Talk about what can be done to improve the amount and quality of their sleep. Think in terms of balance in their life. Consider dedicating certain nights as "early bed-time" nights.

**How good is your kid's sleep hygiene?** There are a number of things that affect the quality of your kid's sleep.

○ Avoiding caffeine and large meals within two to four hours of bedtime. You may be surprised how much caffeine your kid is consuming, especially if they are powering down those supercharged "energy" drinks.

○ Doing something relaxing before bedtime. There should be a transition time between being awake and being asleep. It is important to actually plan that time into the bedtime routine.

○ Creating a calming sleep environment that is free from distractions. Too much stimulation keeps the brain engaged. Keep distractions to a minimum at bedtime.

○ Exercising during the day contributes to a good night's sleep (but not within two hours of bedtime). Your brain can be ready for sleep while your body is still wired.

○ Soaking in a warm bath before bed goes a long way toward creating a calm mood leading up to bedtime. And warm milk might help. And a cookie. (OK, the cookie isn't exactly necessary. They are just tasty.)

**What is your kid's sleep routine?** A good night's sleep begins with a regular bedtime routine. Here are a few of the more important components.

○ Have a regular schedule. Teens should go to bed at a set time and wake up at a set time, every single day. Keep the body on a schedule.

○ Create a chill-out period leading up to actual bed time. Remember when your kid was young and had bedtime rituals? A routine is equally important during adolescence (although it is less likely to include reading "Goodnight Moon"). In the hour leading up to bedtime, things should begin to settle down. This hour is a time to give some thought to preparing for the next day. This is a good time for parents to stop by their kid's bedroom to check in and say "goodnight," even though they are teenagers. That visit can kind of be a signal that it's time to settle in for sleep. Encourage your teen to do quiet, passive, and non-physical things each night during the hour before bed. They can listen to music (but not death metal) or read books, magazines, comics, or whatever. They can pray or write in a journal. (No video gaming, though, and don't start any arguments.)

○ Have a warm beverage. Herbal tea (nothing caffeinated) and warm milk can become part of a routine associated with the transition to sleep.

**Are electronics contributing to sleep deprivation?** Texting, Facebook, cell phones, video/computer games, and television/movies show up again and again as the culprits responsible for sleep deprivation. Kids can be sleeping blissfully when a text comes through from a friend up at two a.m. Late night is sometimes the only time left for teens to update their social media page, catch up on what has been happening with friends during the night, or have some time to work on leveling up on video games. It will be important to set limits on these kinds of interruptions.

**One more thing.** Push back the starting time for high school. OK, here is my little soap box about schools and sleep. The sleep/wake cycle shifts during adolescence to eight a.m. wake/eleven p.m. sleep. Another component of addressing teens' need for sleep would be scheduling high school start times to be in sync with this biological reality. There are arguments for why this doesn't happen. Just saying.

# STRESS

## Part 1:
### Temporary Stress

Stress is a part of life, for kids and adults alike. If there's too little stress, personal growth tends to slow. If there's too much stress, personal growth is derailed. Teens need to know how to recognize when they are overly stressed and what to do about it.

> This chapter's first section covers:
>
> - How to make a quick stress assessment
>
> - Strategies for dealing with temporary or immediate stress

A certain amount of stress is a natural part of relationships. ("Does she or doesn't she like me?" "Why didn't you text me right back?") Stress is also a natural element of any involvement in activities ("The gig is *tonight!*") and making your way in the world. ("Hey, *watch it,* jerk!) This kind of common, everyday stress is something we all learn to deal with.

But now and again, everything seems to happen at once to teens: a burgeoning romance (with all of the uncertainty and longing), simultaneous tests in four different classes, conflict among friends, a break-up during semester finals, parents on a rampage about grades when Call of Duty Black Ops has just been released. Kids can use some guidance in learning to cope with this kind of immediate, situational stress.

## WHAT'S A PARENT TO DO?

Ask yourself whether your teen has a normal load of stress or stress that's reaching an unhealthy level.

**Quick assessment.** To start with, kids need to be able to recognize when they are stressed. While everyone feels stress in their own way, there are some common signs. Help your kid recognize how they show stress (see list, below). The more things they check off, the greater the likelihood they are stressing out. Once you know what to look for you can help your kid become more aware of when they are stressing out.

Stress shows up as physical symptoms like:

O headaches

O upset stomach or butterflies

O tense and uptight body sensations (hands tremble, shoulders or neck tight, etc.)

O sleep problems (too much or too little)

O appetite problems (too much or too little)

O low energy or motivation

O rapid heart beat

O sweating

O clenched jaw

Stress also shows up as emotions and can make your teen feel:

O irritable and quick to anger (especially when interrupted)

O easily frustrated

O continuously anxious or worried

O sad or down

○ negative about most things

○ tearful "for no reason"

○ unable to truly enjoy things

Stress can be revealed in certain behaviors, such as:

○ difficulty concentrating or remembering

○ letting things slide

○ nervous habits (biting fingernails, pulling at hair, biting lip, etc.)

○ talking about feeling overwhelmed, stressed or freaking out

○ running out of time to get everything done

○ withdrawing from people

○ escape behavior (avoidance, distraction, procrastination, etc.)

○ perfectionism

Situational or temporary stress usually causes emotional arousal and physical tension (anxiety, frustration, exhaustion). Teens can benefit from learning ways to tone down the emotional upset and relax. There are a number of strategies that can help them do just that.

**Chill.** Relaxation is a great strategy for dealing with situational stress. This can range from taking a moment for slow, deep breaths, to full-body progressive relaxation techniques. But anything that lowers muscle tension will do—suggest they read, daydream, nap, go for a drive, or get a massage. You can arrange these activities or actually do them together (for whatever is stressing you).

**Exercise.** Exercise is another healthy way to relieve stress. It transforms physical tension and emotional arousal into a productive, physical activity. Take a walk with your kids. Go to the gym. Do calisthenics. It is surprising how much physical movement can clear the head and reduce stress.

**Take a break.** Working straight through, especially when stressed, makes you less productive rather than more. Have your kid stop and step away. Encourage them take a moment to do something unrelated. Even a five minutes break every hour can make a difference. An occasional "mental health" day off may even be justified.

**Distraction.** Kids can also manage short-term, situational stress by doing things to take their mind off the stressor. Watching videos, playing video games, listening to music, pursuing a hobby, and getting into an argument with parents are among the number of ways kids can distract themselves. You can help by either making suggestions or by understanding the need to get some relief from their stress (except by arguing with you. That one requires some punishment to distract them from their stress).

**Savor.** Psychologist Fred Bryant has been studying ways people fully enjoy the moment, which he refers to as "savoring." Savoring can be a very effective de-stressor.

- **Marvel at nature**. Get outside or bring the outside in. Open the windows. Lay down in the grass. Walk in the brisk cold. Watch clouds. Stargaze. It's naturally calming.

- **Bask in relationships**. Talk to friends. Hang out with people you love. Spend some time with fun people.

- **Luxuriate**. Indulge your sense of touch (taking a warm bath, snuggling in a blanket); smell (enjoying the scents of aroma candles, citrus fruit, flowers, pine, fresh-baked bread); sight (watching candles or a prism in the sunlight); sound (listening to music that soothes you, running water, or the call of birds); and taste (munching on chocolate or other foods with a high fat content).

- **Give thanks**. Count your blessings. Pray. Stop and reflect on five positive things that happened that day. Recall joyous moments and revel in the memory.

**Anticipation.** There are some situational stressors that you can predict: simultaneous projects due in multiple classes, semester exams, holidays. An important stress management strategy for predictable, situational stressors is to plan for ways to minimize the stressful aspects. Any school requirement your teen can do in advance of the due date—not the night before it's due—will help relieve stress.

**Social support.** All it takes is one supportive relationship to significantly reduce the effects of stress. For your kid, that can be you. The most direct support is providing comfort and encouragement. Making sure they have food and drink; walk by and just put your hand on their shoulder occasionally; offer to be a sounding board for their frustration. These little acts can go a long way toward helping relieve your teen's immediate stress. Parents can also provide more tangible kinds of support during a stressful time by helping with detail work (gathering things they might need, helping do the clerical—not content—work on school assignments) and temporarily relieving them of their usual responsibilities like taking care of their chores. It is surprising how much of a difference just your willingness to pitch in makes (even if there isn't much you can do).

**Constructive venting.** Situational stress can result in the building up of intense emotions. You can help your kid find a way to constructively express this frustration—sometimes called "venting." This strategy can be helpful when it is controlled and constructive. Screaming and foot-stomping can help. Encourage them to write a long list of the ways in which their life sucks and then conduct a ritual burning of the paper (ideally not in the middle of the living room floor). Let them play the drums or have a Metal music sing-along. Lashing out physically, even at benign, inanimate (and innocent) objects like pillows or mattresses is actually a bad idea. Being allowed to cuss at you so they can feel better is a *very* bad idea. These behaviors actually promote poor self-control, right at the time kids need to practice it the most. They also lead to the additional stress of being punished for disrespectful and inappropriate behavior.

**Run away.** Finally, stress can also be managed by taking off. Most kids initially cope with situational stress by distraction, avoidance, or escape. Getting as far away as possible from the stressor—either mentally or physically—is really effective but only when the escape is temporary (such as taking a time-out). Running away can be a problematic strategy if they don't eventually come back and finish the task or deal with the situation that caused the stress.

These stress-management strategies can go a long way in dissipating the stress your kid experiences in specific situations or for limited periods of time.

# STRESS

## Part 2:
### Chronic Stress

Not all stress is temporary and manageable, however. Continual or chronic stress can cause all kinds of problems if it isn't addressed.

This part of the chapter looks at:

- Accurately identifying chronic stressors

- Ways to cope with lifestyle stressors

- Strategies to cope with environmental stressors

- Strategies for coping with relationship stressors

- Strategies for changing thinking patterns that lead to stress

There is a long list of chronic and persistent circumstances that stress kids out: the death of someone close, parental separation or divorce, family conflict, chronic physical or mental illness in themselves or a family member, financial hardship, changes in school or residence, loss of friendships, ending a long-term relationship, harassment or bullying, dating relationships marked by conflict, extremely difficult academic subjects, learning disabilities, conflict with a teacher, time-consuming competitive sports or extracurricular activities, friends with personal problems—or, worse, a combination of any of these.

# WHAT'S A PARENT TO DO?

Coping with this kind of chronic stress requires a more complex combination of managing emotions, remaining productive, reassessing priorities, and, sometimes, learning how to accept the "slings and arrows of outrageous fortune."

**Quick assessment.** If kids are going to do something about stress, they have to be able to recognize when they have it. As with situational stress, a good place to start is doing a quick stress assessment. (See the previous chapter on Temporary Stress for more detail.)

**Identifying stressors.** Stress originates from things kids impose on themselves, from unavoidable things that just happen to them, and from demands put on them by others (like you). Take some time to talk with your kid about all the things that stress them out. Go through all the major categories: school, friends, parents, family, relationships, loss, daily frustrations and hassles, perceived (or actual) failures and inadequacies, the feeling of being pulled in several directions at once, over-scheduling, and sleep deprivation. What you find will guide you in using the stress management strategies discussed below.

**Lifestyle Strategies.** Kids who are experiencing ongoing stress need to pay attention to their general physical health. Stress translates directly into a strain on the body. As you work with your teens to develop strategies to address sources of stress, it will be important to include elements of a healthy lifestyle into their daily routines.

○ **Regular (at least annual) physical exams**. If they haven't had a checkup recently, schedule one. You want a medical doctor to keep an eye on their physical health.

○ **Exercise**. At least twenty minutes a day (and it should be sixty minutes a day) of moderate exercise—after consultation with a physician, of course.

○ **Sleep**. Nine hours of sleep a night. I know, I know. Read the chapter on sleep and teens for suggestions.

○ **Diet**. Healthy snacks. Complex carbohydrates. Foods from the major food groups (fruits, vegetables, grains, lean meat, dairy, and dessert) in the right proportions. Limit empty calories like soft drinks and processed foods. Minimize sugars and stimulants (high fructose corn syrup, sugary drinks and foods, caffeine drinks, energy drinks, quick energy pills, etc.). Know your kid's nutritional requirements. Include a daily multi-vitamin to fill in any nutritional holes.

○ **Fun**. Pleasure. Joy. Comfort. Satisfaction. At least a little, every day. If this isn't happening, make it a priority to find healthy, productive sources of fun for your kid.

○ **Routines**. Have a regular schedule for sleep, eating, waking, and accomplishing tasks of daily living like chores and homework. Constantly changing routines are a major source of confusion and anxiety—in other words, stress.

**Emotion-focused strategies.** Strategies that manage emotions are the backbone of dealing with situational stress (see above). They are also important in managing the emotional arousal that accompanies ongoing, chronic stress. Kids need experience using these strategies when stressed. Include them as a part of their everyday life.

**Action strategies.** When kids are experiencing chronic stress, they need clear strategies to avoid feeling isolated, helpless, and powerless. It is important to make sure they aren't just stomping out fires as they flare up. Teens need a fire control plan. You can help your kid learn how to change stressful aspects of their environment and to develop the personal coping skills that equip them for lifelong stress management.

**Environment-focused strategies.** When the source of your kid's stress is their environment or the people they are around, there are several strategies that can help them cope:

○ **Social support**. When stress is chronic, the support of parents, family, friends, and professionals (clergy, therapist, etc.) is an important coping resource. The people who love your teen can provide direct assistance, garner resources, provide information, and comfort and support them. Help your kid learn when and how to seek out the help and support of others.

○ **Be the change**. The attitude kids have toward a situation or relationship has a significant effect on how it turns out. Help your kid see the potential benefits of a situation—the glass half full. Encourage them to be proactive rather than reactive.

○ **Negotiation and compromise**. If it always has to be their way, they are going to find themselves chronically stressed. You can help them learn how to be more flexible and cooperative.

○ **Change the relationship to the stressor**. Sometimes, it is better for kids to distance themselves from the people or things that are stressful. They might need help recognizing that some people actually add stress to their life, and some situations are more stressful than others. Limiting time with people who create drama or circumstances that generate stress is an important skill you can teach your kids. It may also be an important boundary that you need to set for them.

○ **Simplify**. There is a point at which the benefit you derive from involvement in multiple activities is outweighed by the stress of having too much to do. Your kid may need to shorten their list of commitments and activities. You can help by encouraging them to limit the number of activities they attempt (or, again, setting some limits for them).

○ **Acceptance**. Finally, kids have to learn to accept that some things can't be changed. They will need help in figuring out how to change what they can and learn to live with what must be borne. You can help by providing perspective, translating spiritual and faith beliefs into practice, and focusing on aspects of the situation they *can* do something about.

**Coping skills.** The heart of coping with chronic stress is the use of personal coping skills. Kids can't readily minimize or eliminate stress if they don't have the necessary tools. Here are some of the most important skills kids can use to reduce ongoing stress.

One set of strategies focuses on managing stress that arises from interactions with other people.

- **Maintaining personal boundaries**. Some of us are lucky enough to have kids who will just keep striving or giving or working without any real consideration for themselves or their limitations. But just because your kid is capable of doing something well doesn't mean it is right for them (or respectful of the limitations of their time, energy or emotion). This may require you to rein in their enthusiasm while also helping them learn to recognize how to put personal restraint into the equation. Help them learn how to say "no" (to someone other than you).

- **Conflict resolution**. Unresolved conflict can float below the surface of relationships, leaving people tense and frustrated. Kids will need your help to learn how to successfully resolve conflicts. You can start with the relationship most likely to have conflict: their relationship with you. See the chapter on Negotiating for some suggestions.

- **Assertiveness**. Being able to stand up for yourself can do a lot to eliminate ongoing stress. Kids often need help knowing how to stand their ground in an appropriate and productive way (rather than just caving in or trying to crush the other person). You are the perfect person with whom they can practice appropriate assertiveness. Suggestions for helping your kid with this can be found in the Assertiveness chapter.

- **Bowing out gracefully**. Kids regularly change their mind about or misjudge the amount of commitment various tasks they undertake will require. Continuing to participate in something they've lost interest in when they want to devote themselves to other activities is stressful. You can help them learn how to exit gracefully and with consideration for others involved.

Another set of strategies focuses on developing some of the personal cognitive skills that are important for managing ongoing stress.

- **Self-awareness**. Sometimes chronic stress occurs because kids are not able to recognize their own needs and frustrations. You can help your kid by prompting them to check on their feelings or what has been on their mind. Talking it out with them can lead to the discovery of important issues that require some attention.

- **Goal-setting**. Ambition is good. Extreme ambition can be debilitating. Kids need to learn how to set achievable goals. Setting goals includes finding a balance among multiple goals. It is worthwhile to take time, now and again, to go over your kid's goals in the various areas of their life (academic, social, work/money, fun, family, etc.). You can find some suggestions in the Goal Setting chapter.

- **Decision-making**. Kids are used to being told what to do. While this is the most efficient way for parents to manage the household, it doesn't give kids much experience in how to make decisions. It is very stressful to get stuck every time a choice has to be made because you don't know how to weigh alternatives. Help your kid go through the process of considering the different alternatives and making the choices that seem right.

- **Problem-solving**. Chronic stress can also occur when a problem goes unresolved. Kids (and more than a few adults) often approach problems using the time-honored strategy of sweeping things under the carpet. Teens can use help in learning how to approach resolving a problem so that it doesn't drag on and on.

- **Time management**. Chronically stressed kids almost always have time-management problems. They either don't know how to manage their time or they are so overscheduled that there isn't enough time in the day to fit everything in. Sit down with them to look over their to-do list. Prioritize the items. Be practical about how much can be accomplished. Begin the process of weeding out some of the commitments. Make sure there are breaks and periods of down time for recovery. (You should not consider time scheduled with friends to be frivolous and expendable. For most kids, it is high on the list of revitalizing activities.)

Coping with stress is a fluid process that requires many different kinds of strategies. You shouldn't expect to tackle all of them at once. Kids are supposed to develop these strategies over time; one of the ways they learn is by over-extending themselves, only to be overwhelmed. You can help them by tracking their stress, helping them recognize it, and having suggestions for things they can to do effectively manage the stress that will be a regular companion throughout their lives.

# MOTIVATION ISSUES

# APATHY

**M**otivating teens can be really challenging. There are some basic strategies that can help with a teen who doesn't seem interested in much.

This chapter reviews:

- Reasons for teen apathy

- Ways to try to turn their apathy around

- Three important things to do with an apathetic teen

People mean a lot of things when they talk about motivating kids. They might be talking about an apathetic kid with no passion for anything, or they (especially parents) might mean their kid isn't motivated to do what *they* want them to do. Maybe their kid is lazy with a generally lackadaisical attitude about things that require effort. Maybe a teen is not very ambitious (fine with earning Cs, content to be second string, etc.). Kids may be motivated by the wrong things (like those damnable video games) or their priorities may be in the wrong place (working as many hours as possible for money, improving their long-board tricks, etc.). They may also have reached a point where actual effort is required to succeed after a history of easy success.

It ain't easy to get this turned around. But it can be done.

There are a lot of reasons kids become apathetic. They may be low-energy kids. They may be out of shape or overweight. Some kids are afraid to take risks. Kids can become apathetic when they don't have anything meaningful to do. They can get stuck in a routine of boredom (with its close equivalent, playing the same video game over and over) or they can come to rely on others to come up with their entertainment. Some kids will shut down after a series of frustrations or failure.

# WHAT'S A PARENT TO DO?

**Get to know your kid.** If you are going to get them motivated, you will need to know what they care about. What is their favorite movie? What kind of music do they listen to? Where would they go on a trip if money was no object? What do your kid's friends like to do? What do they plan on doing after high school? You are going to need this information when you start trying to plan possible activities.

**Foster areas of personal interest.** Motivation works best when the interest comes from inside your kid. *Everyone* has personal interests. It is just harder to identify them in some people. Keep your eyes open for any signs of interest in a topic, task, or issue. The idea is to start exposing them to experiences they *might* find interesting. If they know you are on the hunt and are going to make them do something, you may find them working with you to figure out what is worth trying.

**Expand on existing interests.** No task or activity is too insignificant or ridiculous. Start where their interests lie. Show that you have an interest. Ask a lot of questions. Look for qualities that can generalize to other tasks or can translate into potential adult employment.

**Break the mold.** Introduce some fun into a teen's life. See if there is something they want to do but thought you would say "no" to. Find a way to make it happen. If they don't have any ideas, arrange an adventure. Do something unexpected. Try to shake up their ho-hum, predictable life. You never know when you might stumble on something that will spark their interest. Do they like graphic novels (those modern day comic books)? Find the dates of a Comic or Anime Convention. Take them to hear a local band that plays their kind of music. Arrange for a flying lesson. Try to find something that will challenge them. Think outside the box. Have fun with it.

**Try teamwork.** Consider working together on a project. Ideally, it will be something that doesn't have to be done perfectly or quickly. You can carry the enthusiasm and motivation until your kid catches the wave.

**Require them to develop a skill.** You are trying to find a way to have your kid engage in an enjoyable task that challenges them, something that requires effort and persistence to develop real-world competence. Look for activities that lead to acquiring information, developing a skill, or gaining experience. Watching TV or playing video games doesn't count.

**Ignore their crappy attitude.** Your kid may be pessimistic about things turning out well. They may be jaded and cynical about joy and enthusiasm. They may even have a secret desire they keep locked away for fear that someone will think they aren't cool. Don't let their attitude turn you away from your mission. Don't let their huffing and puffing discourage you.

You might be surprised to find that just getting your kid moving toward pursuing any interest tends to expand the range of their interests, generating enthusiasm for many other areas of their life.

One last thing: remember that not all motivation is purely psychological. Of all the things mentioned, these three suggestions may have the biggest impact.

- **Require daily exercise**. Being active and eating well results in more physical and mental energy, good health, and a better mood. Get your kid up and doing something active. That alone may open them up to recognizing and actively pursuing natural interests.

- **Schedule a physical**. Sometimes a psychological problem is actually an undiagnosed medical issue. Before you decide that your kid is a slug, make sure they aren't suffering from anemia, thyroid disease, or any of a number of potential medical conditions.

- **Rule out depression**. Apathy has a lot in common with depression; lack of interest in things, no energy, isolation. The difference is that depression also includes sadness, worthlessness or guilt, fatigue, anxiety or nervousness, changes in eating and sleeping habits (either too much or too little), tearfulness, and thoughts of death or suicide. If you think the culprit may be depression, be sure to consult with a mental health professional.

# LACK OF MOTIVATION

**W**hen parents talk about an unmotivated teen, they often mean a kid who doesn't care about what their parents want them to care about (rather than having *no* interests, like apathetic kids). The challenge here is redirecting a teen's actions.

This chapter covers:

- Twelve strategies for motivating your kid

- When to admit defeat

If your kid is not apathetic but just unmotivated, there are some strategies that will help increase your kid's motivation to do something they don't like, don't consider important, or won't make the time for.

## WHAT'S A PARENT TO DO?

If you want to get your kid moving, you need a plan of action.

**Structure.** Start by clarifying expectations, elaborating the benefits of fulfilling these expectations, and identifying the costs of not meeting the standards you set. Be clear and specific about what you expect from them in the area under discussion (things like maintaining a particular GPA, participating in an extracurricular activity, getting a job, exercising, finding a hobby, etc.). Establish the minimum expectations for time spent by setting a number hours per week they must work on this project; designating a start time ("You have two weeks to pick something; otherwise, I'll pick something for you.") and what will happen if they back out or get themselves removed from the activity (fired from the job, dropped from a sports team, or falling below the expected GPA).

Structure helps with problems your kid may have with organization, initiation, self-discipline, and persistence. You are going to provide an external incentive, since they don't have an intrinsic interest in the task or activity. This is sometimes referred to as "lighting a fire under" them.

**Goals.** Be sure to set reasonable expectations. If you set the bar too high, your teen will have failure to add to a lack of motivation. It is best to have what are called "process goals" rather than "performance goals." Expecting them to put in effort and develop some skills from involvement in the task or activity. Don't start out expecting them to make first team at a sport, earn straight As in school, or master an extremely difficult rollerblade trick. (Remember, we are talking about a kid who is not already achieving. The expectations would likely be more ambitious for a kid who is already motivated.) Some teens will need to have early success, so how you define success will be crucial to this experience.

**Choice.** Even though you are imposing these expectations on your kid (granted, for their own good), you are still meddling in their life. Give your kid as much choice as possible within that framework. Keep them involved in the process from beginning to end. Other than your broadly defined expectations, make everything negotiable. If you are requiring them to study, let them set the time and the location. If they must play a sport, let them pick the sport (and be open-minded; skateboarding can fit the criteria when you require competition).

Have them set their own goals in the tasks you are requiring them to perform. When you give kids a say in something that involves them, even when they are being required to do it, they will feel more ownership. Every little bit helps. Collaboration helps kids learn how to articulate their preferences and desires, assert their opinions, negotiate, and effectively resolve disagreements, even when they are frustrated.

**Trade-off.** If your kid is fulfilling expectations you have for them because it is important to you, find a way to make an equitable trade in supporting another area that is important to them. If you are requiring them to make better grades, make sure they also get to spend time at things that really interest them. It's like saying, "I know you are doing this because I am making you do it, so I'll make sure you have time for things that matter to you, too." Trade-offs reduce some of the resentment about being put through a living hell by The Man; that way, their life is just *mostly* a living hell.

**Relevance.** Your kid may not realize why you are trying to ruin their life by making them actually commit to something and work to accomplish it. Be sure to help them understand the relevance of this horrible intrusion into their freedom of choice to be a vegetable at your expense (though it is probably best to edit out the sarcasm). Relevance helps kids get the big picture and to see how their daily life is linked to their future.

**Encouragement.** Enthusiasm is contagious. If you have a kid who is unmotivated, they will need a lot of encouragement and support. Act like you are curious. Be interested. Be positive (but not annoyingly chipper). Your interest in and optimism about what they are doing (but not how *you* would do it) can serve as a substitute for their lack of interest, confidence, or optimism. Encouragement helps kids see the potential fun and value of an activity.

**Companionship.** Misery loves company. Some kids develop interests because of the interests of their peers. Look for team- or group-based activities for your kid. If their friends are involved in something, see what you can do to get your kid involved too. You may have to be their miserable company if you can't find anyone else to do your dirty work for you. Companionship helps kids have an alternative motive for continued participation when things get frustrating or difficult.

**Supervision.** Since your kid is not intrinsically motivated to engage in the task or activity, it will be important for you to keep an eye on their efforts. Stay as far in the background as possible. Monitor from a distance, stepping in only when things stall or your kid tries to back out. Supervision helps you be a resource when things get difficult as well as an external motivator for your kid to keep at it.

**Expertise.** It is important to encourage your kid to develop real skills. Being good at something is motivating. Consider requiring them to excel in something: a grade of A in a specific subject, athletic skill (though not necessarily excellence) in a sport, mastery of a musical instrument, greater responsibility at work, knowledge about mechanical repairs, etc. Self-confidence is built, in part, on the presence of real skills and competence in one area of your life.

**Acknowledgment.** It will be important for your kid to know that you recognize their sacrifice for something you consider important for them (but that they didn't want to do). Mention how much you appreciate their efforts. Don't require them to act excited, even when they begin to be successful. *You* can be excited, but just leave it at that. This means you should not say things like, "See, I knew you could do it!" or "You know you like this." Be glad they are taking it seriously, even though it wasn't their choice, by saying, "I am very proud of you for really trying, even though it wasn't something you were interested in."

**Rewards.** The best kind of reinforcement for a teen trying hard is your pride, admiration, and appreciation of their efforts (rather than focusing on whether they "won"). If you use traditional reinforcers like money or concrete compensation for their efforts, you are likely to undermine any natural interest your kid might develop in the activity or task. One exception can be recognizing a period of particular difficulty by providing some special celebration or gift (a desired meal, video game, equipment for some other area of interest, etc.).

**Punishment.** Using punishment as a motivator for unmotivated kids is risky. Ideally, you will want to motivate by structuring their time, encouraging them, and supervising their efforts. Save punishment for direct defiance, when they refuse to do the task or activity at all. Notice that this punishment is because they are defying you, not because of the quality of their efforts at the task. More to the point, make other enjoyable activities dependent upon your kid doing the required task or activity. As a parent, you need to make decisions about what will prepare your teens to be self-sufficient adults. This is one of these things. They don't have to like it. They don't have to agree. They *do* have to mind you.

**Surrender.** Know when to stop. Identify the criteria for when your kid can stop trying (when they have obtained a specified level of expertise, finished the season, participated for a specific period of time, etc.). Sometimes, the activity is just not a good fit, or you might have a kid who is extremely resistant. Your teens can't be good at everything. Some things are just not interesting. Make sure you require your kid to pursue a task or activity long enough to get past the learning "plateau" (the period between developing basic skills and developing competence at the task). For many adolescent skills, this will require six to twelve months of persistent, repetitious practice.

Make sure you express your admiration and gratitude that they were willing to give it a try. Then, let them move on to some other activity.

**Quick Summary:** Set the parameters for what you expect from your kid. Make sure there is as much room as possible for personalizing the activity or task. Stay close and connected so that you can transmit interest and enthusiasm until they find their own intrinsic interest (if they ever do).

# RELIGION AND SPIRITUALITY ISSUES

# RELIGION AND
# SPIRITUALITY

Religion and faith begin to decline right at the time teens are making many life-changing decisions. This apparent falling away from the faith is a source of great concern and stress for many parents.

This chapter presents:

- Interesting—and surprising—information about teens and religion

- A long list of things parents can to do encourage the continued religious development of their teen

Religion, and the spirituality it reflects, is crucial for everyday concerns and quality of life issues. Religion is soulful. It is a source of moral clarity. Religion is a fundamental source of hope and healing in the aftermath of the inexplicable horrors and suffering in the world. It provides perspective and an ultimate guide to living a good life.

American teenagers arc a generally religious bunch who are open to (and even interested in) involvement in the faith of their parents. Surprised? In 2005, Christian Smith and Melinda Denton conducted one of the most comprehensive examinations to date on the religious and spiritual lives of teens. The results of their work can be found in the book *Soul Searching*. The book is not only technical and academic by presenting the scientifically relevant details of their massive study but also provides a wonderful consideration of the implications of their findings. It is a remarkably informative study. (Visit the References page of the book website for more information.)

First, here is the summary of findings that have implications for parents. Eighty-four percent of teens characterize themselves as religious. They participate in their parents' religious observances and report that religion is important in their lives. Teens have a conventional view of religion (read this as "they seem to be content to believe what their parents believe"). They are not a bunch of atheistic heathens dancing naked around a bonfire making sacrifices to Satan. The vast majority of teens are happy to accept the religion in which they were raised.

Very few kids in the study were interested in trying to develop their own, personal spiritual path outside of religion. Let me quote this next one: "(T)he evidence clearly shows that the single most important social influence on the religious and spiritual lives of adolescents is their parents" (p. 261). We'll talk more on how to take advantage of that later.

When teens have more religious people in their lives, have access to more religious activities and programs, and are challenged (asked and questioned about, not confronted) by others about their spiritual and religious beliefs, they are more religious and spiritual. What's the conclusion of these research findings? "(R)eligious faith and practice themselves exert significant positive, direct, and indirect influences on the lives of teenagers, helping to foster healthier, more engaged adolescents who live more constructive and promising lives" (p. 263).

Despite the importance of religion in their lives, teens have almost no real ability to talk about how religion and spirituality influence their lives and moral decision-making. Teens have come to see religion as mostly about feeling good and being happy, secure, and at peace rather than as a source of solace and a guide to living right. Telling right from wrong becomes murky with this kind of moral system. Teens have little connection with the larger adult issues of life like the choices and sacrifices that would help inform their faith beliefs.

Your kids are going to need your help being (or remaining) a person of faith.

# WHAT'S A PARENT TO DO?

**Model it.** What you do matters. The role (or lack) of faith beliefs and spirituality in your life will be evident. Tend to your own spiritual needs. Act according to the tenets of your beliefs. Make religion a part of your life, so that it becomes part of theirs.

**Practice what you preach.** Find a faith community to join with your family. People rarely live in close proximity to relatives these days. Your faith community can serve as an extended family. But, more importantly from a spiritual perspective, deep faith requires practice and sacrifice. Get up and go to religious services.

**Church/temple/synagogue/mosque for teens.** Find a place where your kids feel comfortable to practice your faith beliefs. Actively involve them in selecting where your family will attend. Find a place they like and then stick with it. If you don't particularly like the congregation, suck it up until your kids are out of the house and then find a place for yourself.

**Respect your teen's lack of religion.** If your kid rejects religion (or, more likely, the particular religion or church they are attending), be respectful of their doubts or outright rejection. Make them go anyway, but try to find a more compatible congregation (see above). Seriously consider some kind of reasonable trade-off. Since they will be going to the religious service against their will, you can demonstrate your appreciation for this sacrifice by matching their time commitment with something important to them. You might consider something like allowing a later curfew one night, for example, or participation in some activity you previously disapproved of (as long as it's not illegal, inordinately dangerous, or immoral). The idea is to provide them with something that concretely recognizes the weekly sacrifice they are making.

**Be a religious family.** Attending religious services just because they are good for you is not enough. You must actually have faith outside of religious services. There is something about religion itself that is good for teens (and also for you). It's not just the moral stricture, not just the threat of everlasting damnation (in some faiths), and not the promise of heaven (in some beliefs). Being religious provides a cornerstone of personal and family beliefs, values, and actions. Religion is about something more than money or success or pleasure or suffering or joy or possessions or beauty. It is about grace and soul; that which is beyond words. Your kids will need this perspective in the years ahead.

**Talk in terms of faith.** Faith beliefs should be present in how you talk about choices and decisions, success and failure, sacrifice and generosity, morals and exuberance, and life and death. Be familiar with your faith beliefs. Refer to religious Scriptures.

**Teach the tenets.** Read Scripture together. Teach your kid what it means to be a faith-full person. They should be able to summarize important concepts. They should have a favorite Scripture or two.

**Discuss faith with your teens.** In the research mentioned earlier, teens were found to be frighteningly clueless about their own religious beliefs. They attend religious services but haven't really thought about their religion. Talk *with* (not at) your kid about the basics of your faith. Ask them probing questions. Challenge them about what it means to be a believer and to have faith. Don't give the answers right away.

**Make faith relevant.** If you are not careful, faith beliefs become a Sunday (or Saturday) kind of thing—or something just for old people. Apply faith to everyday situations. Find ways to translate faith beliefs into guidance for daily action. Talk about how their religion affects their everyday lives. Your kid will need to know what their faith has to say about all aspects of their lives. Make sure you make the connections clear for them.

**Scripture as motto.** Have your kid identify one or two Scriptures to use as guides to life. Have a family Scripture as motto and put it on the fridge—or have everyone's Scripture painted as a border on the family room or printed on a tee-shirt or impressed in a wrist band or printed on a necklace charm. Refer to it often.

**Encourage questioning.** Thinking teens will have doubts. (Thinking teens are such a pain!) Encourage questions about their faith. Have discussions. Talk about a crisis of faith you may have experienced. (But be thoughtful about how much you reveal. Suggestions about talking about your past can be found in the Talking about Your Past chapters.) Consult with theological experts together. You don't have to know the answers. It is important to encourage teens to wrestle with their doubts while you are with them.

**Toss moral relativism.** There is a right and wrong. There is truth (though, granted, it is hard to nail down and has different facets). Every opinion is not equally valid. Take the time to help your kid draw the line—which means having a line yourself. Religion is well-suited for this task.

**Dig deep.** If your family just does religion superficially, it will leave your kid wanting. They will get the idea they can pick and choose whatever is convenient. What are the real implications of one's faith beliefs? Dive into the meaty and hard-to-accept aspects of your religion. Part of the fundamental value of faith beliefs is they hold you accountable to a higher purpose and authority. Faith helps people get around the tendency for self-deception.

**Practice tolerance.** Every major religion promotes tolerance. Your kid is going to need this in the global economy. Others are entitled to their own spiritual beliefs. Telling someone that, unfortunately, they are going to hell is rude and rarely works as an effective means of turning them around. Deep conviction and profound faith–in every major religious tradition–lead to a stronger sense of love and compassion for others. If you don't feel that, you have more work to do. If your kids don't feel it, you have more work to do.

**Develop a faith community.** You want your kid surrounded by the right kind of people (which, in part, means a deeply moral community). Faith communities have people like that built right in. But attending on Sunday won't be enough. Get involved. Get to know people in your church or synagogue or mosque or temple. Participate in the small-group activities. Have your kid become actively involved in the youth programs. Drag Grandma and Grandpa to the activities for elders.

**Faith throughout the week.** Faith ain't just for the formal religious service. Remember to reference religious beliefs and concepts throughout the week. Incorporate thanksgiving to the Creator at meals, and remember to be thankful for other blessings received. Have a family devotional (for example, ten minutes right before everyone goes to bed) devoted to spiritual reflection.

**Starting an avalanche.** Sometimes all it takes is a little nudge. Start small. Begin praying at meal time. Ask your kid what they have to be grateful for. Place your hands on your kid and briefly pray that they be blessed and find the right path in life.

**Assume buy-in from your kid.** Don't listen to your kid when they say they don't care about faith or religion. Know that your kid wants (and needs) spirituality and faith to be part of their life. Use their rejection as a signal to increase the messages. Challenge them. Require them to go through the motions out of respect. Just ignore their protests and keep plugging away. (You also might want to pray for guidance and the salvation of their immortal soul where they can hear you, just to make a point.)

**Telling stories of faith.** Use stories from your faith tradition to teach and entertain. Learn the stories, or read them as a family. These tales will become a deeply personal and treasured tradition for your kids.

Religious practice and a focus on spiritual issues naturally decline during adolescence, only to resurge in young adulthood. The experiences kids have leading up to this period are an important influence on their return to a life of more consistent religious practices. When you raise your kids to be people of deep faith, you have provided them with a source of comfort and joy as well as a sanctuary when they are confronted with the many ills of life.

# SIBLING ISSUES

# SIBLINGS
# WATCHING SIBLINGS

**M**any people do not have the financial resources to stay home with their kids, hire someone to watch them, or pay for daycare or camps to fill those hours when you are at work. That leaves you with the task of determining whether your kids can stay home alone.

This chapter examines:

- How old is old enough to stay home alone

- Ways to prepare your teen to watch their siblings

- Rules for when kids are home alone

- The consequences they will suffer for causing trouble

- Ways to monitor from a distance

## WHAT'S A PARENT TO DO?

**Age and independence.** The age at which it is safe to entrust a teen with the responsibility of watching siblings is not straightforward. Apparently, there is no specified legal age in many states after which children may be left home alone. Depending on local laws, parents may be criminally liable if they knowingly expose or fail to protect a child under the age of eighteen from neglect (as well as abuse) that results in physical injury or that adversely affects their health or welfare. In general, physical neglect is a failure to meet the basic needs for a child's physical development, such as supervision. So where does that leave you when making decisions about having one of your kid watch the other kids?

From a developmental perspective, kids begin to demonstrate higher order cognitive processing around the age of twelve. At this age (ages eleven to thirteen), parents can reasonably leave their kids unsupervised for three to four hours in a familiar environment like the home. Younger teens (thirteen to sixteen years old) can reasonably be left unsupervised for periods of six to eight hours—although overnight is chancy, at best. Many older teens (age seventeen and above) are capable of managing many of the issues (and emergencies) that might arise if they are left unsupervised for a full day and night, although it depends on the experience and maturity of the particular kid. In all these instances, it is important to consider your teen's emotional and intellectual maturity (see Teen leader qualities, reviewed below) as well as educating them on basic safety issues and how to deal with various potential emergencies (see Safety and emergencies, below).

The age differences between the lead teen and their siblings will also make a difference. There probably should be at least two years difference between the teen in charge and their next younger sibling to minimize the likelihood of a successful uprising. If the age difference is smaller, your kids need to get along particularly well. Kids who are six or younger should not be left in the daily care of a teen under the age of sixteen.

Finally, you will be asking for trouble if the ratio of siblings to teen leader is greater than two siblings to one teen leader. In many of these instances, age and independence factors can be addressed by making adjustments in supervision, monitoring, and length of time kids are left alone.

**Teen leader qualities.** There are several qualities that make for a good teen in charge. These include keeping their cool and the ability to set limits on others. Teens who are responsible, decisive, patient, caring, and empathic are the best sitters. (What wouldn't a kid with these qualities be able to do?)

**Training.** Make sure your teen knows what they are doing before you leave them in charge. There are good manuals developed for babysitters published by organizations like the Red Cross. More importantly, have your teen complete a babysitting course; these are often offered by the organizations like the Red Cross. Your kid will get an education about all the important things to consider when caring for kids.

**Set the ground rules.** Time for a family meeting. Make sure everyone is clear about who is in charge when you are gone. The other kids need to know that the teen in charge speaks with your authority. (See the Magistrate, not potentate section below.) Be clear about expectations regarding tasks, rules, and safety. Clarify the role of the teen leader in setting agendas and giving directions. Be sure to review the limits of the teen leader's authority (no grounding, spanking, pummeling for their own good, requirements to wait on them hand and foot, etc.). Especially important will be clarifying that discipline will be meted out by *you*. Let the teen leader know that if they take things into their own hands, they likewise will suffer.

**Safety and emergencies.** Everyone should be clear about safety rules. Topics to be addressed should include fire, water, weaponry, practicing mixed martial arts or World Wrestling Federation moves, answering the door and phone, and injuries (as well as changing status on their social network site to "Party at my house, parents at work").

**Start small.** It is important that kids be required to practice being in charge (and being accountable) before they are endowed with this awesome responsibility. That means both the teen *and* their potential minions need practice in their roles. Structure brief stretches of time where your teen is responsible for watching their siblings while you are present and occupied with other tasks (allowing the teen to be what is sometimes known as a Mother's Helper, though it is probably best to refrain from using this label). Use this as a time to watch and make suggestions—then build on this. Put teens in charge while you run errands. This will give them practice and give you an idea about whether off-duty police officers will be required to keep the peace.

**Rewards.** Teen leadership is a responsibility and a burden. It really is a job. While the teen leader should be satisfied with the pride they feel in the trust you have in them and with the satisfaction that comes from a job well done, you will probably need to sweeten the deal to make it worth their while. They should expect that performing this job well will bring benefits. The most straightforward way is to pay them (the average baby sitter rate). But, since the problem of finances may be the reason you need your teen to babysit in the first place, you can provide the special privileges that come to a responsible and competent teenager instead of cash.

Don't forget about rewarding the siblings. Putting up with a bossy teen in charge is annoying. If they didn't push things and make extra trouble, think about small treats or something that accumulates with days of peace and cooperation. Help them see the tangible value of making this system work.

**Consequences.** There must be effective consequences for kids who disobey your instructions and, especially, for those who directly defy the teen in charge. If kids do not follow appropriate direction or outright refuse to do what they should, decide on what the teen in charge will do (call you, leave it and wait for you to get home, pin a sibling to the floor if they try to run away, etc.). You should be the provider of suffering and misery for misbehavior, *not* the teen in charge—no matter how much they beg. Punishments can be meted out when you return home. Remember that child misbehavior puts the family finances at risk if you have to come home early from work or arrange to send them to camp.

Punishments should reflect the seriousness of their inability to function when you are at work. Consequences for violating the safety rules should be more serious than other kinds of misbehavior or rule violations, because those violations threaten both family finances *and* their wellbeing. Remember, you have all evening to make them suffer. If you can't generate effective or satisfying consequences, consider consulting with a mental health professional for suggestions.

Ultimately, the consequence may be implementing some form of oppressive supervision or monitoring, like having to sit in your office all day or having a backup sitter they would hate. Consider having them "pay" for this extra expense (out of their allowance, by working at extra tasks around the house, etc.). They may also have to spend time in a structured summer program or camp.

**Magistrate, not potentate.** Power corrupts. Putting teens in charge with absolute authority will lead to tyranny and possibly bloodshed. A job description can help minimize the confusion on the part of the teen in charge. The teen leader is a low-level functionary—not the lord or lady of the manner. The teen's job is to monitor, remind, and transmit direct instructions from the royals as well as report to the person with real authority (you). The teen's job is *not* to make sure siblings do their chores, have the right attitude toward a (minor, bureaucratic) official, or demonstrate the highest moral character.

Teen leaders are not to ad lib. They are not to decide that your parenting rules need a little tweaking. If you have a teen who has a tendency toward despotism (being a bossy know-it-all, morally self-righteous, short-fuse, etc.), ongoing adjustment and training will be required.

**Remote monitoring.** Regardless of the length of time you leave your kids under teen leadership, it is important to monitor progress across the day. This means that the teen leader is responsible for checking in with you to report on how things are going. You will also want to have contact with the minions for an alternative view. Don't forget about the wonders of technology. You can make use of readily available, computer-based cameras that allow you to check in or to keep a window open in the corner of your computer screen for ongoing monitoring.

By putting a teen in charge, you are transferring some of the burden of parenting onto their shoulders. They actually get the crappy parts (monitoring and structuring kids) without any of the good parts (love, affection, and the joy of parenting). Make sure they can handle this. Make sure they are given the tools and the structure to be successful. Make sure the risk is worth it. Make sure your teens benefit from being mature enough to handle this responsibility.

# SIBLING CONFLICT

Siblings squabble; that's natural. At some point, though, either the conflict is too frequent or it becomes just too annoying to tolerate.

This chapter provides suggestions for:

- Basics of parental intervention
- A two-phase punishment structure

"Mooooommmmm! Robby's bugging me!"

"*He's lying.* He won't let me watch my *show!*"

"*Stop it! Ouch! Quit it! Let go!*"

"No! *Ow! Ow!* Mom! Ow!"

(Laughter followed by muffled screaming.)

"Mom! *Mooommm!* Robby hit me!"

"*He wouldn't leave me alone!*"

There is nothing like the harmonious strains of brotherly and sisterly love. You would think that dire threats would serve to motivate your kids to quit bugging each other, wouldn't you? Well, you would be wrong! Jealousy, competitiveness, personality, personal space, developmental differences, hormones, and limited resources (of things like bathrooms, hot water, only one gaming system, only one big TV, etc.) all work against your efforts to maintain a serene and cooperative family environment.

# WHAT'S A PARENT TO DO?

**Make the trouble maker(s) come to you, even if you have to go get them.** As soon as the yelling starts, call your kids to you. Having to trudge to where you are (or follow you back to where you came from) can serve to discourage frivolous complaints. If you disrupt the whole situation around which the conflict is raging, the participants are punished before you even start.

**Parents are judge and jury.** When someone has been wronged, parents are the only ones authorized to deal with it. You are the *only* one who can mete out punishment. Conflicts will escalate because the kid being wronged tries to punish the troublemaker. In some cases, they think nothing will be done by you about it. This is because the most common parent response to arguing children is to holler from the other room for the troublemaker to stop. ("Anita, leave your sister alone!") This is a very unsatisfying response to the wronged kid. It is as though the criminal gets off with just a slap on the wrist (while flashing a huge, gloating grin). This tempts your kids to take things into their own hands. They need incentives for letting you deal with the problem.

**Criminals must be punished.** The first incentive will be that troublemaking results in consequences. Punishment discourages repetition of the wrongdoing. It also legitimizes your authority and engenders confidence in the family judicial system.

**Vigilante justice is not tolerated.** The second incentive is that kids who take matters into their own hands will be treated to the same punishment as the troublemaker. The troublemaker is punished for making trouble, but the vigilante is punished for not letting you deal with it.

**Phase One Punishment.** Once you need to punish them, be creative. Try to think of something that is satisfying to you. For sibling conflict, consider long lectures on the importance of close sibling relationships mixed in with stories from your childhood about how your siblings did/did not do the right thing and how great/bad the relationship is now. Read long passages relevant to sibling relationships, love, consideration for others, compassion, etc. from the Bible or other religious texts while commenting on the applicability to real life. Try to use a monotone voice to make it as miserably boring as possible. Do this for at least fifteen minutes, or longer, if you can stand it.

**Phase Two Punishment.** Once they have been bored to death, make the troublemaker (and the vigilante, if applicable) give up something significant in the moment (time on the video game, access to electronics, etc.) and/or make them stay with you while you are doing something unpleasant (chores, watching a TV show they hate, or sitting together to listen to your favorite music while you hold their hand). The old-fashioned "time-out" can be quite effective all the way through adolescence. It is surprising how excruciating sitting quietly for thirty minutes, sixty minutes, or two hours can be to someone who—just a few minutes before—was busy fighting for the opportunity to do something else. (As a bonus, older teens are deeply insulted by being treated like a child. It's great!) Besides, you need to save the big guns like grounding and confiscating essential luxury items (cell phones or electronic devices) for major infractions. These suggestions are for typical transgressions, ones that do not involve dangerous weapons, serious assaults, anything requiring medical attention, or destruction of major property. If more serious offenses are occurring, it is time to consult with a mental health professional.

**Both parties need to learn a lesson.** Check with the aggrieved to see if they are satisfied with the punishment. Look for ways that they might be more considerate, aware, or generous toward their annoying sibling (even if the situation doesn't absolutely require them to be). You might also remind them that the shoe may be on the other foot in the future, so going for that pound of flesh might not be the best long-term strategy. The troublemaker could probably use some strategizing about how to handle the situation differently next time.

You might also problem-solve with them about how they could come to you in the future so you can help them get a fair shot at the missed opportunity *before* they get into trouble. This reinforces planning and self-restraint as well as greater self-awareness of frustration, jealousy, and other emotions. Don't forget about requiring them to role-play the appropriate role, to gain insight into the issue.

**Don't worry if you can't figure out who is guilty every time.** You may be surprised how much easier it is to figure out what is really happening when you get your kids to actually involve you in the process before everyone is screaming and crying. Even so, you don't have to be able to sort every situation out with certainty. These steps are remarkably effective in eliminating much of the conflict. Once you commit to being involved with each conflict, by the second or third repetition, the truth begins to shine through.

Like other situations where discipline is needed, remember to make sibling conflict a learning opportunity for your kids. They should benefit while, at the same time, suffering for interrupting you.

# TECHNOLOGY ISSUES

# CELL PHONES

Cell phones have changed the essence of parenting. While they make it possible to be linked to your child at all times, it is important to establish some boundaries, to keep phones in the category of beneficial technology.

This chapter provides suggestions for:

- Cell phone etiquette
- Establishing rules for cell phone use
- Minimizing the ways cell phones can lead to trouble

Watching kids with their cell phones brings to mind those sci-fi shows about some horrifying, technological future in which machine parts have been grafted onto humans so that you can't tell where one ends and the other begins. A study by C&R research in 2008 found that 26 percent of eight- to eleven-year-olds had their own cell phones, up from 7 percent in 2003. During that same time span, cell phone "ownership" for kids twelve to fourteen went from 21 percent to 58 percent. (Uh, what "ownership" really means is that parents bought the damn thing for the kid. Kids just *think* they own it.)

Consequently, if you're a teen and you don't have a cell phone, you are *soooo* out of the loop. And, like every "got to have" item (remember when it was just a certain pair of tennis shoes?), every advancement in cell phone design, function, and technology leads to a desperate bid by teens to be in on the latest upgrade. Digital music storage, surfing the internet, texting, photographing, video recording—teens hardly ever use a cell phone for talking any more.

It turns out the primary reason for kids having cell phones is parents are buying these things as a way to keep tabs on them. Well, if you are going to provide this luxury, it is only reasonable to establish some expectations that go along with it (in addition to elaborating the consequences for messing with your rules).

## WHAT'S A PARENT TO DO?

**Establish cell phone etiquette.** Etiquette is an old fashioned word for being polite. Unless your teens are expecting an important call, proper manners for phone usage require you to excuse yourself to check a call (or other signals like texts or email). This also means that the person texting will have to wait for an answer until the current, real-life interaction is finished. In addition, there are some situations where cell phone use is rude or inappropriate. This includes public settings (movies, theater, church); some family gatherings (dinner, restaurants, family movie time, any time with the grandparents); times when they are being helped or served (checkout lines, fast-food lines, bank tellers); and finally, times when they should be developing their abilities to concentrate, stay focused, and learn (during homework, in classrooms, at sports practice, during music lessons or practice, etc.).

**Limit their time.** If you check the call log of your kid's phone, you might be shocked at how late into the night (or early morning) they are receiving or sending calls and texts, even during the week. That attitude your kid has in the morning might not be because they are a surly teenager—it may be due to sleep deprivation. Establish "cell phone hours" and enforce them.

**Cap the apps.** Applications and service packages enable the phone to text, store, and play music, create pictures and movies, and surf the internet. While many of these are fun, there is no real need for your teen to have all these bells and whistles. Think carefully about what services and extras your kid really needs. It is useful to minimize their expectation that a full and meaningful life can only be had if you have all the possible options on some electronic gadgets. If they complain, take the phone away and give them a book to read.

**Lost or broken phone agreements.** What happens if the cell phone falls in the toilet (a remarkably common accident, as it turns out) or it gets lost or broken? This is one of those opportunities to teach responsibility and the real cost of luxuries. Even if you get replacement insurance on the phone, there are lessons to be learned. Consider having them pay for the replacement. You might provide a very inexpensive phone until a set time has passed to restore your trust in their ability to "handle this responsibility."

**No sexting.** You've read about it and the dark rumor of it has haunted your nightmares: the use of the video/photography function of the cell phone to send sexually explicit images to friends and acquaintances. Before you even get to the long list of problems with this new little pastime, it is important to know that sexting is pornography. It's child pornography if the subject is younger than eighteen years old. Sexting is a felony in many states, even if juveniles take the images of themselves. If convicted, the person possessing the pornographic image might have to register as a sex offender for the remainder of their life. Further, access to the internet provides the opportunity to download questionable or pornographic material directly to a cell phone—and the ability to upload privately shared images so they're available to everyone with internet access.

The safest decision is to just block all internet access on your kid's phone. They aren't some high powered executive that needs to constantly be in touch with the office. In many phones, blocking the internet will also block picture mail. Problem averted.

To monitor and enforce these expectations, a few conditions will need to be put in place before you hand the phone over to your teen (or before you are willing to continue making it available). They must hand it over any time you ask. This allows you to check phone use, texts, pictures, and videos to ensure they are respecting your rules. It also provides an opportunity to check their contact list. Who do you know, and who don't you know that your child has been communicating with?

When you check, if all is as it should be, you can breathe a little easier. Part of the lesson here is that people earn trust by demonstrating trustworthiness. Back off (but not without random spot checks) and give them the space they have earned.

If your kids don't like giving you access to their cell phones or if they violate your rules, turn the phone off. If they apologize and recommit themselves to your rules, all can be forgiven. If they violate your rules again, think creatively. You might be able to have the phone service limited to set times of day or only to allow access to your phone number. You can replace their phone with an ugly, technologically antiquated phone that they'll have to use until they have reestablished trust. Or you can take a hammer and smash the phone into a million pieces and be done with it. Your call.

# TEXTING

f teens have a cell phone, then they are texting. Texting presents unique opportunities with commensurate problems that require clear and specific rules of use.

> This chapter covers:
>
> • Texting etiquette
>
> • No-texting zones

Texting is, hands down, the greatest advancement in communication for adolescent boys—ever. Conversations are conducted in brief, poorly constructed, grammatically incorrect sentence fragments. There is plenty of time to formulate a reasonable, yet cool, response. No more loooonnng, excruciating silences while "talking" on the phone, directly, to their current squeeze. No more bumbling attempts to express some vaguely experienced and poorly understood emotion. Monosyllabic answers are expected in texting—and even these can be abbreviated! (*Abbreviated monosyllables!* The recession has hit even the English language! "Great deal, folks. We're slashing letters. "OK" has been cut by 50 percent. K?")

Text responses are limited to 160 characters. And texters can be doing several things at once during the conversation without people yelling about how they're not paying attention. Insensitivity, shallowness, superficiality, or lack of emotion can be blamed on the medium. As stated, texting is a godsend.

Texting has turned out to be pretty useful for girls too. They can keep in constant contact with a large, extended social network simultaneously. The insecurity of waiting for someone to get back to them has been cut to seconds, at most. They can have conversations with a guy that actually seems meaningful and reciprocal. Text conversations feel much more genuine and lead to fewer uncertainties about his interest ("Why is he just standing there staring at me?" "Is there something wrong with me?").

However, with all these benefits comes a set of challenges for cognitive development, personal growth, and legal liability. Texting can be one more area where teens don't have to learn how to delay gratification. Phones are with them 24/7. They can become slaves to the technology or, worse, to the texter on the other end of the signal. Rather than setting limits for themselves in a relationship, your kid is being trained to respond whenever someone else places a demand on them. ("Wassup?" "I have to text back or they will think I don't like them.")

## WHAT'S A PARENT TO DO?

**Face-to-face people get priority.** It is just good manners to give undivided attention to the person who is standing before you, engaged in conversation. Continually looking down to read and reply to texts is rude ("I'm *talking* here! Put that damn phone *down!*"). It's insulting (when it becomes obvious that you are not as important as the texting partner) and leads kids to become insensitive to their obligations as a social partner and member of civil society. ("I'm listening, K?!")

Texting provides an ideal situation for them to work on self-restraint. It also provides an opportunity to teach them the polite way to excuse themselves from a situation for something important. ("Excuse me, I really must take this. I'll be right back.") This, by definition, does not include every random electronic blip that someone has forwarded to their phone.

**Establish no-text zones.** The immediacy of texting can create a virtual obsession with checking and responding. Creating no-text zones will help teens develop the ability to focus their attention and to put electronic things out of their minds for a while. No-text zones might include meals, performances, conversations, check-out lines, classrooms—and cars they're driving (see below).

**Educate your child about the dangers of leaving a written record.** When kids are talking directly to a friend or on the phone, the sound waves dissipate into the void—but digital information is a permanent record. Many kids have begun to learn this lesson with their social networking pages (e.g., Myspace, Facebook) and emails. Many of them still have to be reminded of this regarding text messages. Saying you are going to kill someone when you are mad is very different when you speak it to a friend in the context of an ironic conversation than when you have written it in a text and now it's being forwarded to a potentially endless list of "friends."

**No texting while driving.** Hard to enforce, important to try. Research shows that texting while driving is as dangerous as drunk driving. It's also against the law. That often means a hefty fine plus court costs, plus more serious repercussions if your teen actually causes an accident while texting and driving. Since texts have a time stamp, you can check to see if texting occurred while they were also driving to their destination.

**Check your child's texts regularly.** This one is complicated in that, on the one hand, texting is like private conversations (something you would normally not have access to, as a parent) and it is important for teens to have some degree of privacy. On the other hand, the implications of what may be written can affect the whole family. It is also worth mentioning how often parents have discovered serious issues in texts—alcohol or drug use, risk-taking behavior, illegal acts, and worse—that might otherwise have gone unnoticed.

The policy for texting should be similar to that for maintaining a social networking page (like your teen's Facebook page). While they are under your roof and accessing luxuries you pay for, you have access. Violations lead to restricted use or the elimination of texting for a specified period of time. With that being said, don't nitpick. If you check now and then and there isn't anything serious, overlook minor infractions of language or opinions you might not otherwise know about. Try to remember what would have happened if your parents had listened in on what you and your friends talked about when you were a teenager.

# SOCIAL MEDIA

## Part 1:
### Introduction for Parents

E ighty percent of teens have a social media account (like Facebook). The social network is the place your kid is increasingly likely to hang out, possibly for hours at a time.

This chapter looks at:

- What social media is

- What you need to know about it

- Talking to your kid about your concerns

- General suggestions regarding oversight of your teen's online presence

- Giving your teen a social media readiness test

In the old days, kids had to meet up in the neighborhood. Families knew each other. Then the mall became the new neighborhood, but kids had to be able to get there, so parents were still in the loop. Cyberspace is the neighborhood for the 21$^{st}$-century teen. Your kid can get into just as much or more mischief online in their bedroom as they could out on the streets.

Because of social media, the conversation has changed:

"Hey, Dad! I'm going to hang out with John."

"OK. Wait. Who is John?"

"He's a kid I just met."

"Where did you meet him?"

"I friended him the other day."

"Where do you know him?"

"I told you. We met online. He's a friend of Mark's."

"Where does he live?"

"I don't know."

"Does he go to your school?"

"No."

"How old is he?"

"*Dad!* You worry too much. He's just this guy Mark knows."

"Wait! Who's Mark?" OK, so you've lost control of your kid's participation in internet social media. It is moving too fast, and your kid has too much time (and too many peer consultants) to help them keep up with all the new opportunities.

## WHAT'S A PARENT TO DO?

While you may not be able to know all the intricacies of every new opportunity for your kid to socialize online, there are ways you can try to rein in the beast. To start with, you will need to know what you are dealing with.

**What is social media?** Social media are all the ways your kid can interact with other people electronically. There are broadly four main categories (in addition to texting, which was discussed in the previous chapter).

First, there are social networking sites where kids maintain a list of friends and post ongoing information about their lives including written comments and pictures. Facebook, Myspace, Friendster, and Xanga fall into this category. Then there are video- or photo-sharing sites where participants upload images to share, such as YouTube, Vimeo, Flickr, and Photobucket.

Your teen could be writing a blog, which is sort of like—and sometimes exactly like—an online diary. This would include microblogs like Twitter, where kids send a list of people short descriptions of whatever is on their mind, instantly. Finally, there are chat rooms where people communicate through text or webcam with anyone who happens to be logged on (with the worst examples being 4chan and Chatroulette).

You cannot afford to turn your kid loose on the internet, and you need a degree in information technology to be able to responsibly monitor your kid's social media accounts. Unfortunately, you will be sorry (and potentially devastated) if you don't address it.

Here is an attempt to make social media somewhat manageable. There will references to books and web sites where you can get more complete information.

**Educate yourself.** You need to know something about these social media sites and how they work if you are going to help your kids—so inform yourself. Information on Facebook, blogs, and YouTube can be found on the References page located on this book's website. Just ban your kids from chat rooms and be done with it. (You'll see why when you check out the sites mentioned earlier.)

**Have the talk.** Talking to your kid about all the issues involved in social media use is more important than any control you can set in place, although having rules and monitoring will keep your teen accountable. Here are some ideas.

- **Don't exaggerate the dangers**. Online predators are not lurking around every cyber corner. If you try to scare your kid with this, they will stop listening to you. The real issue is about keeping private matters private, to stay reasonably safe. You wouldn't leave the car door unlocked in the mall parking lot with your cell phone and laptop in the front seat. In fact, you wouldn't leave those items in full view, even in a locked car. You never know who is passing by.

- **Teaching about privacy**. Your kid needs to keep personal information personal. Since you have reviewed all the ways that personal information can be revealed (by reading the sites listed above), you can talk comprehensively to your kid about what that actually means.

- **Teaching about trust**. "But they seemed like such a nice person." It is important to help your kid learn how to trust (but verify). Talk to them about how you can tell whether someone is trustworthy by looking at what they think is OK, how they treat other people, and their past behavior. Be careful, though, because this discussion can too easily slide into "don't trust anyone" (which is as unhelpful as automatically trusting everyone). The point is to recognize that trust should be earned and demonstrated, not just granted. It is important for them to go slowly when deciding to give someone access to the more protected (and private) areas of their internet life.

- **Complete transparency as a family rule**. Your kids have to keep you informed about what is going on. They need to let you know when someone is giving them a hard time online. You have to know every way they have a personal presence on the internet. You must have direct access to anything they are posting online.

- **Friendship**. Being a friend takes more than just being on someone's friends list. It is not humanly possible to have 200 friends. Who are your teen's real friends? What does it take to become a real friend? What is the problem with having random people as friends (who also have access to information on your kid's site)?

- **Permanance**. Anything posted on the internet is *permanent*. Anything you post can be forwarded, printed, or copied to anyone else, at any time. The implications can be small (someone reads what you say about them) or large, if your teen inadvertently reveals personal identity information like a birth date or Social Security number.

- **Sexual communications**. Have a *long* talk again about some things being private (rather than for public consumption or as entertainment for others). Unfortunately, the use of sex and sexuality to sell everything these days will make this a difficult point to make. Take some time to talk about how youthful indiscretions can come back to haunt them. It is one thing to have personal experiences (and make private mistakes). It is another to display your mistakes for all the world to (potentially) see.

- **Personal trust and good judgment**. Finally, you should talk to your kid about how their use of social media affects your own trust in them and the quality of their judgment. How responsibly they manage their social media presence will be linked to all kinds of other privileges.

**Put monitors and filters on your computers (and cell phones).** You should have programs on your computer that filter out undesirable sites. You should consider having a keystroke monitor as a backup and checking it regularly. Many of these products can alert you to potentially problematic activity occurring on your computer and on your kid's social networking sites. An article that will get you started can be found on the References page located on this book's website.

**Keep computers in common areas.** Your kid doesn't need a computer in their room, even if you think, "My kid is too young to get into much trouble online." Or "She is too innocent." Or "I trust my kid." Keeping the computer where you can see it will save you *so* many potential problems. Don't be one of those parents who shows up in a therapist's office having to deal with the effects of their kid wandering onto something disturbing (or destructive) on the internet.

**No one needs a webcam.** But now cameras are on almost every electronic device. Know how they are being used by your kid. Consider disabling webcams. Ban online video communication.

**Monitor it like you would the local and national news.** Make it obvious that you are tracking everything. They need to think that everything they communicate on the site will be read by you—because it will (at least initially). Have a password protected internet monitoring program running on your teen's computer. Have a keystroke monitor on your home computer.

**Send your kid messages through the media.** Post things on your kid's social media site to remind them you are keeping an eye on things. This may seem like when your mom listened in on your phone calls using the other phone (for those who had landlines). But things are different now. You were only talking to one person. Getting people's phone numbers was a huge deal. We are in a whole different universe now with social media.

**No account before they're thirteen years old.** First, those are the official rules of almost all social networking sites. But really, kids younger than thirteen just aren't socially mature enough to handle an online presence. They will potentially be interacting with people ranging in ages from thirteen to adulthood. Social pressure, combined with the lack of adequate relationship skills, might encourage young teens to try to mimic how others relate online rather than developing their own voice. They are susceptible to *all sorts* of influences.

**Predators are not as prevalent as you think.** The vast majority of kids who have contact with a sexually interested adult know they are talking to an adult who has been explicit in what he (99 percent are male) is after. The biggest threats social media presents to your kids is being socialized by a bunch of other idiot kids (and some questionable adults) and setting themselves up for a lot of useless and avoidable drama and emotional upset among peers. The issues are the same ones you are already trying to help your kid successfully make their way through: setting the right priorities, sexual decision-making, alcohol and drug use, and being a person of good character.

**The best predictor of online trouble is your own kid.** With appropriate education, limits, and monitoring most kids can handle social networking sites just fine. If you are having trouble with your kid in other areas, you probably will also have trouble with them regarding the internet.

**Real friends.** In the world of social media, the kid with the most friends wins. This approach to friendships focuses on the appearance of having friends while not bothering with actual friendships. Even if settings are set at private, there is a problem if they have 2,000 friends. Consider reviewing who is on their access list every six to twelve months to weed a few people out (like tossing out old clothes from the closet).

**Make them earn it.** Your kid doesn't have a *right* to a social media account. They should earn the privilege. It shouldn't be just because they ask or because they are now thirteen years old. One way is to have them demonstrate they are capable of handling it responsibly, like ...

**Test their readiness.** How do you know if your teen is ready to have access to a personal social media account? Here's a little test you can use. (Make sure you go over these with your kid if you are going to use them as criteria for having their own site. They need to know what will be on the test.)

These items are divided into two categories: novice and expert.

**Novice.** Your kid will need to demonstrate certain skills and abilities so that you can be reasonably sure they can handle having a social networking account. Once these items are checked off, your kid will have earned their Novice status, which allows them to have a social media account that you closely monitor (every five to seven days).

- **Six straight months of appropriate general internet use.** One way to know if your kid has sufficient self-control and compliance with rules is to observe how they follow rules. They should not try to trick, sneak, or bypass the general family rules for using the internet. The clock begins again every time there is a violation. (If they keep violating the rules, it may be time to consult with a mental health professional to see what the problem is.)

- **Knows the social network account rules**. No, seriously. If they can't tell you the rules (see the Ground Rules chapter) by heart, they should not be allowed to have a personal account.

- **Texts responsibly**. Since you have put some rules in place regarding texting, you can get an idea about their ability to delay responding and having some self-control regarding social media. They should be able to let texts go unanswered (or even checked). Texts should be appropriate and well-considered (in the language used and information shared). Texting is an ideal test run for a social media account. No social media account until they can handle texting appropriately.

- **Remains trustworthy**. They keep their word in most areas of their life. (All kids will be tempted to lie to avoid punishment. The problem is when they keep lying—because they have to or even when they don't have to.) Your teens should be responsible in other life areas. If you can't trust them in more obvious areas, you won't be able to trust them on a social media site.

- **Owns up to violations and mistakes**. Your kid is not supposed to be perfect. They are going to screw up or be tempted to try to get around rules. However, they are supposed to take responsibility for their actions. This means that when they screw up–whether on purpose or accidentally–they admit it. If they can't even acknowledge when you have caught them, you can't rely on them using social media responsibly.

**Expert.** Once your kid has successfully achieved Novice status, they must also demonstrate at least these additional qualities to gain relatively unsupervised access to a personal social network account. Once Expert status is achieved, you can continue to monitor them by being included on the access list and occasional checking.

- **Six months as a Novice** with no slip ups on the social networking use policy (see below).

- **Resists social pressure.** Can your kid turn down offers to do things that are wrong? Have they actually done that?

- **Assertive.** Can your kid tell people to shut up (preferably not you)? Do they make up their own mind about an issue? Can they express disagreements with you directly and openly, or do they just kind of give in (or just clam up and stew)?

- **Self-control.** Can they hold their tongue when mad? Do they know how to express their anger appropriately? Or do they pop off at the mouth when they are upset?

- **Media savvy.** Can your kid identify how commercials and advertisers try to influence them? Can they tell the difference between a need and a want? Do they question something that is too good to be true?

- **Talks to you about problems (optional).** Does your kid tell you about things other kids have done wrong or that your kid disapproves of? Will they tell you about difficulties they are having?

Once they are seventeen years old, just let it go. If they don't get it by now, you have lost the battle. *Everyone* has their own social media account by this age, so you might as well give up and just hope for the best.

There are some websites and books you might find helpful located on the References page of this book's website.

# SOCIAL MEDIA

## Part 2:
### Ground Rules

Once you have decided to let your kid have their own social media account (and you have some idea what is involved), you need to clarify what you consider the appropriate and what will happen (misery and suffering) if your expectations are disappointed.

This chapter covers:

- Setting up the initial account

- Establishing age limitations

- Rules for maintaining a social media account

- Punishment for the misuse of the account

## WHAT'S A PARENT TO DO?

**Setting up the social network account.** Review with your kid what is and is not acceptable on their account. In a number of these categories, the social media account can be customized to conform to your rules. Other requirements will be revealed to you as you monitor the site. (Connect Safely has an excellent guide for parents, with everything you need to know about Facebook and setting up an account. Their web site is listed on the References page of this book's website.)

Here are some of the topics to address.

- **Personal information**. All identifying information can be taken from the main page and misused by people, including your teen's name, town, school, birthday, and home address. Decide what details are acceptable. For example, sites can be customized to display the birth day but not the birth year. More information is worse in this case.

- **Acceptable words and messages**. Review what your child considers appropriate language to use on their site and what they should do when others use inappropriate language.

- **Pictures (and tagging).** Establish a policy on acceptable and unacceptable pictures your teen can include on their site and what kind of pictures of your kid can appear in on other people's sites.

- **Private and public information**. What information is going to be public and what is going to be private? Each site has a range of settings for limiting access to information, including providing access only to specific people.

- **Who can be friends** (and how many friends they can have). Do they actually know the person? Can anyone be included as a friend? Which kinds of friends will have access to personal information? What are the geographic borders for possible friends—same county, same state, same country, same continent?

- **Online bullying or arguments**. What do you expect your kid to do when someone is cyberbullying them? What do you expect of your kid when it comes to bullying or harassing others online?

- **What not to say**. Your kid needs to consider what can happen to the information they post online in any format (on a social media site, in an email, etc.). Find out what your kid thinks. You may be horrified at what they consider acceptable, which should lead to a useful and rather lengthy conversation to clarify what you feel is appropriate. What are the limits you expect your kid to observe?

- **Receiving or sending sexual or aggressive messages**. What is the difference between a joke and sexual harassment (especially for younger teenage boys)?

- **Tracking your kid's location**. Some social media sites have a function that reads your kid's cell phone GPS signal and posts their location automatically on the site. You will probably want to have your kid disable that.

**No cell phone internet access until sixteen years old.** Think about how the average teenager looks for ways to gross each other out. Now think about the internet. Your teen does not need internet access through their cell phones or mobile cellular technology (like mp3 devices). Don't provide it. They are going to *scream* about this rule. "Everyone else has it!" "My life will be over!" "I'll never talk to you again!" Whatever! If you decide that your child *must* have the internet to update their status on their social networking account while walking around in the mall, be sure to use an accountability software program (like Covenant Eyes or X3 watch) that gives you information on what they have been accessing. Check it regularly.

**Parents have every password.** Do not allow your teen access to the internet without having the passwords for every one of their personal sites. Period. On the other hand, make sure you only review their account when they are with you. Doing so will demonstrate your respect for them and their privacy. They know when you are looking and have the opportunity to respond to any questions you have. They can benefit from the spontaneous look of horror on your face at what you have seen.

**No unknown friends.** You should know your kid's friends, online or otherwise. If you don't know them, your teen can't hang out with them (in person or online). You'll be able to check out their friends through your position as a "friend" on your kid's account, which gives you privileges to visit other friends' sites. Raise any concerns with your kid.

**Parents are a "friend" on every account.** And be included in the customized access to every level of information on the site.

**Conduct regular site reviews.** For kids under fifteen or who are in the Novice stage of social media use, make the effort to review their sites every five to seven days. For fifteen- to sixteen-year-olds (or those in the Expert stage), review their sites every month or so. By age seventeen, your kid can either use social media responsibly and intelligently or it is too late; time to let go. Don't forget to mention how their appropriate use of the internet and social networking sites was a factor when you give them privileges or allow them more freedom. It is important for your kid to hear directly from you when they are behaving responsibly and to know that they have earned your trust because of their responsible behavior in several life domains.

**Limit time spent managing the account.** Some kids can become obsessed with updating a site and monitoring friends' sites. When they first open an account (as a Novice), you will probably have to set some limits on the frequency with which they review, update, and post on their site. Anything more than three times a day and your kid is beginning to turn their lives into a reality show with ongoing commentary and artificial drama.

**No chat rooms.** Letting kids go into chat rooms is asking for trouble. There is no need for chat rooms if they have a social media account. Social media sites can track every kind of interaction a kid has (while developing a personal marketing plan for each and every user), which makes it easier for you to track what they are doing. Chat rooms don't give you that option.

**Limit (or eliminate) automatic geo-location.** If your kid has a cell phone, they can be tracked. If they have a wired electronic device, they can be tracked. With everything linked these days, the GPS signal on your kid's electronic devices can be sent to social media sites to update their location automatically—so be sure that function is disabled on the social media site. There are also programs that allow people to see who is in their general vicinity (known as geo-social networking). This can be done on any device has the wireless access activated (including Bluetooth devices). There are also apps for this such as Foursquare and Gowalla. The only person who should be able to track your kid is you.

**No online video communicating except with strict supervision.** Parents are confronted with more problems from video communication technology than from the internet itself. Teens do not need a camera to be connected to the social world, and that connection can lead to impulsive trouble. Video communication encourages them to think about their lives as something to be documented rather than something to be lived. Create very strict rules for the use of visual communication and images.

**Truth or Dare (or jail).** Be clear about your expectations regarding sexually explicit images. This should include both the transmitting of sexually explicit or pornographic images that they dig up on the internet as well as of sexually explicit images of themselves or their peers (including naked butts). In some states, anyone possessing or transmitting sexually explicit images of minors (even if minor teens take and transmit these images themselves) is guilty of child pornography. Conviction for child porn might mean having to register as a sex offender forever.

**Consequences.** Social networking accounts are a luxury. Most of your teen's friends will have one, but your kid doesn't *need* to have one. If they are not using their account responsibly, you have important issues to address, including good judgment, self-discipline, and respecting your rules (and the obligations they have when you provide them with a luxury). Identify the consequences if your kid violates your social media rules, and be sure to review these consequences before implementing them, so your kid isn't surprised when they go into effect.

Some possible consequences that might work include:

## First violation:

- **One month probation** with reduction to next lower level of social media use (Expert to Novice, or Novice to None).

- **Supervised social media use** (they can only use it when you are sitting next to them) for the first seven days of probation. This consequence is just to make sure they know how they are supposed to use their account correctly. You can even make suggestions for responses to messages or posting status updates. It will be a fun, bonding experience you both will enjoy!

- **Daily talks for seven straight days** about the importance of integrity, morals, self-discipline, what things were like when you were a child, and all the aspirations you have for them in the areas of career, personal life satisfaction, and relationships. Focus on how the decisions they make and actions they show as an adolescent will have a powerful impact on how they turn out as adults. Make sure each talk lasts at least twenty minutes, but feel free to go on as long as you want. Don't worry if you have to repeat yourself. Repetition makes for excellent retention.

- **Return them to their previous level** of access if they make it through the month without any further violations.

- **If the violation is with chat rooms**, online video communication, or sexting, then shut down all access to internet and texting for a month. Replace their cell phone with one that has no camera. Get a knowledgeable computer technician to disable the camera function on their computer.

## Second violation:

- **Lock them out** of their account by changing the password.

- **Drop them down** to pre-Novice level for three months and then allow them to jump back up to their previous level of access (Novice or Expert).

## Third violation in twelve months:

- **Close their account** by changing the password. Contact the service provider to explore your options for removing all personal content from the internet. (It won't be easy.)

- **Lock out internet use** from your house

- **Cancel texting and internet access** to your kid's phone

- **Consult with a mental health professional.** You need to find out more about what is going on.

**Just in case.** If you think your kid may have created a ghost account to get around your monitoring, there are several ways this can come to light. There are alert services (or functions in various sites) that can send you emails if certain words or phrases are used. In addition, your kid's closest friends will have the ghost account on their friend list. Finally, your kid is going to forget to log off eventually. All the strategies for ferreting out hidden accounts your kid may have constructed is beyond the scope of this column, but most internet consultants can assist should you become concerned and need to do some investigating. This level of deception may also require consulting with a mental health professional, to explore how far the problem goes.

**Helpful websites.** Connect Safely and Common Sense Media are two good sites that address internet and social media issues. You will find links to these sites on the References page of this book's website.

Most kids will handle social media accounts responsibly once you clarify what you expect of them. Many teens will try to push the boundaries but will respond to your initial consequences by falling back into line. Have ongoing conversations with your kid about the good and bad possibilities of social media. Establish clear expectations (with consequences). Monitor social media use from an increasing distance. These strategies will get both of you successfully through adolescence.

# VIDEO GAMING

## Part 1:
### Parent's Overview

Like cell phones and texting, video gaming has become an integral part of daily activity for many teens. This is neither inherently bad nor good, but there are things you need to consider.

This chapter looks at:

- Different video game genres
- The problems, the benefits, and the signs of trouble

Arguments are ongoing within the professional community about whether video game play is good or bad for kids. Some scientists believe video games are unequivocally bad. Others are emphatic in their views that research has not proven the negative effects of video games. Links to articles on these topics can be found on the References page of this book's website. Parents are faced (yet again) with a war of the experts and their conflicting opinions.

### WHAT'S A PARENT TO DO?

Here's a quick review of the kinds of behaviors teens regularly observe in video games:

- kindness
- cooperation

- collaboration
- competition
- self-sacrifice
- coordinated team goal-setting
- repetitive and boring essential tasks
- lying
- cheating
- stealing
- property destruction
- violence in every form (including sexual violence)
- lack of real world consequences (they can just replay the level)
- glorification of criminal and immoral behavior
- lawlessness
- objectification of the human body (both male and female)
- simplification of social relationships
- self-centered decision-making
- cursing
- name-calling
- leadership through insults and shaming
- emotional venting and explosive anger
- risk-taking without natural consequences
- threats or violence in response to confrontation
- resolving problems or disagreements using brute force
- complete, often immediate, recovery from crippling or lethal wounds

- environments where the rules and norms of civilized society don't apply

**Video game genres.** Understanding the potential influence of video games will require a quick review of different kinds of games. Problems and benefits will differ, depending on the genre of the video game. Video games can be categorized as Shooter, Action Adventure Role Playing, Sports, Construction Management/Strategy, Vehicle simulation and Exercise/Skill Development. (Note: Classifying video games is not an exact science, but these categories will serve the purposes of this discussion.)

Video games that are most strongly associated with negative effects are, obviously, Shooter games (such as Halo, Call of Duty, and Gears of War). These games require the player to direct characters to shoot, maim, and kill opponents, often from a distance. Game action is viewed through the eyes of the character (or from just behind the character) to give the player the feeling of being really there.

Action Adventure Role Playing games (like Final Fantasy, Star Wars, and RuneScape) involve fighting and killing, but they follow a storyline that requires characters to explore their environment, gather items, and solve puzzles. The violence in these games is often designed to be less realistic and violence is not the central focus of the game play.

The most benign video games (from the perspective of violence and dehumanization of participants) would be games based on Sports, Construction Management/Strategy, Vehicle Operation, and, of course, Exercise/Skill Development.

Sports games (like Tony Hawk and Madden NFL) emphasize playing and, often, formulating strategies to successfully defeat (or have the best performance time against) opponent teams through competition.

Construction Management/Strategy games (such as Sim City and Age of Empires) require the player to build and direct a community of people or a military force to accomplish an objective (such as developing a community or capturing territory). Players are required to account for a wide range of real world factors and challenges in order to be successful. Sports and Construction Management/ Strategy games teach the players skills that are transferrable to their real lives.

Vehicle Operation games are just what the name implies. Players operate vehicles like planes or race cars from the driver's seat. There is very little in the way of violence.

Finally, Exercise/Skill Development games (like Dance Revolution, Wii Sport, and Guitar Hero) can produce health benefits and social bonding while they help the player develop skills. The only violence in these games is to your body or your pride.

In the Shooter and Action Adventure Role Playing formats, the player guides and directs the actions of an individual character. The character is a direct extension of the player, so the principle activity of the game makes a big difference in how it subtly influences the player (and their values). It is games requiring the teen player to engage in violence or immoral behavior that present the greatest dilemma for parents. A character completing fantastic skateboarding tricks has a different influence on your kid than one whose character must destroy, steal, assault, torture, and kill (regardless of the purported noble purpose). As you might imagine, the effects of these games are much more exaggerated on game systems that allow the player to use actual, realistic actions to perform the character's actions (target shooting games, Wii, Kinect, etc.).

The interactive nature of the games results in players actively socializing and shaping their own behavior. What they bring to the game is likely to be reinforced in either a desirable or undesirable direction. This affects what kind of problem or benefit your teen will get from the game.

**Problems.** What are the potential negative effects of video game playing? Video game playing is associated with greater aggressiveness and callousness in kids who have impulse and aggression problems.

(This means the trait and the game activity go together. It doesn't mean that video games have been shown to cause aggression.) The content of many of the most popular video games and the social rules of play among gamers often encourage kids to curse and use profane language. They are confronted with and expected to use violence as a primary and glorified means of dealing with most situations. In these games, kids are exposed to extreme levels of violence and callousness toward others. The characters often promote the objectification of women and sexuality through overexposure and exaggeration.

Kids can be trained by the demands of the game to be more distractible. Familiar story lines, presented over and over through repeated play, establish metaphors and scripts that can be translated into their everyday lives. Social relationships of all game types and at all levels are characterized by competitiveness rather than cooperation. They are also simplistic and scripted (like reality TV shows). Leadership is marked by denigration, insults, and bullying. Traditional male stereotypes are pervasive, including the glorification of the lone hero and self-aggrandizing forms of courage, sacrifice, and dominance.

**Benefits.** With that being said, video games also have a number of benefits. They're fun. The gaming environments are astonishing in their realism and beauty. They are really difficult to master and require extensive practice to become skilled, an accomplishment that earns admiration by peers. Gaming can be a great means of dealing with stress, given the ability to become immersed in the activity. Games provide an alternative means of bonding and socializing with peers, particularly for kids who are more socially isolated.

Video game play has been shown to improve the player's eye-hand coordination and visual-motor skills. It also improves a player's resistance to distraction and promotes the ability to detect information on the outside edges of perception. Gamers learn how to integrate multiple sources of information in the formulation of responses and action plans. They get practice in quick and effective decision-making (otherwise you die—digitally, of course).

Some form of strategic thinking is a fundamental require-ment for most video games. Kids learn a lot about successful (and catastrophic) planning. If they pay attention, they also learn how criminal activity and aggressive and violent styles of problem-solving will lead to death, incarceration, and social exclusion.

**Know the games.** It is generally not a good idea to trust your kids to monitor themselves when it comes to issues of morals and exposure to extreme sexual or violent content. As discussed above, video games are socializing your kid in the same way that exposure to any experience that communicates values and tolerance for certain beliefs and behaviors does. Don't let a video game into your house before you have reviewed it. There are a number of general video game review sites online, as well as sites specifically geared toward providing reviews for parents. Links to these sites can be found on the References page of this book's website.

**Signs of trouble.** Video gaming is a fun, entertaining diver-sion. Kids can play video games without it poisoning their minds or disrupting their lives—*but* gaming also can become a problem, ranging from mild to serious. The first, lowest level of trouble is reflected in your teen's lack of self-monitoring around game playing. Are they staying up too late, which is making it difficult for them to get up in the morning? Is their game playing interfering with other important activities (like chores, exercise, studying, and time spent in direct contact with real humans)? This would warrant a discussion with a clarification of the consequences should they not be able to balance game playing with their other responsibilities.

The second level of trouble is indicated by your teen's reactions while playing the game. Are they screaming at and ranting about the game? Are they gloating ("I've crushed you!) and exaggerating other's inferiority ("You are a worthless piece of crap!") when they succeed—as opposed to just whooping it up and being pleased? Are they cursing and otherwise emotionally venting instead of maintaining some degree of self-restraint when frustrated or angry? Are they taking out their frustration about the game on others, during or after game play?

Kids who are showing these kinds of behavior can be inadvertently training themselves to have difficulty maintaining their equilibrium when experiencing frustration and failure. It will be important to require teens having these problems to practice self-restraint and frustration management. Immediate suspension of game playing when these behaviors appear can help teens become more aware of when they are demonstrating these behaviors, while simultaneously discouraging them from continuing to behave this way.

The third level of trouble is reflected in a refusal to log off or arguments about logging off and moving on to other things. Immediately ground them from the game for an extended period of time if they do not stop game playing within five minutes of being told to stop.

The fourth level of trouble reflects what video game researchers have become concerned about: violence and lack of compassion by gamers for other players or people in their lives. Is your teen aggressive and confrontational in everyday life? Do they curse and berate others during game play, rather than just saying occasional curse words in frustration? Do they generally show a callousness or disrespect for others, especially females or people perceived as weak?

Are your teen's arguments with you marked by intensity and getting "in your face?" Have they broken things (especially game machine parts) when frustrated or mad about game play? If your teen is demonstrating any of these symptoms, eliminate all video game playing in your home. (You might also want to ban all songs with violent or demeaning lyrics, just for good measure.) Seriously consider consulting with a mental health professional to review your kid's behavior and get some suggestions about how to move forward in helping them learn to function in civilized society.

**Addiction.** A final general issue regarding video gaming is the concept of addiction. An addiction is indicated when your kid is engaging in any activity or behavior in a compulsive fashion to the neglect or detriment of other important life activities, like relationships, employment, and school as well as self-care such as hygiene and sleep. If your kid is showing these behaviors, it is time to consult.

Now that you have some ideas about the general issues with video games you will need some ideas about how and when to set limits.

# VIDEO GAMING

## Part 2:
### Setting Limits

S o you have a kid who is a gamer. You have educated yourself about general issues related to video games. Now the trick is how to keep them from becoming an obese, reclusive, socially inept high school drop-out with anger control problems.

This chapter discusses:

- The importance of watching your teen play the game

- Reviewing your concerns with your kid

- Setting limits and eliminating the problem

As with any other adolescent activity, it is important to establish video game-playing guidelines and identify the consequences for violating your expectations.

### WHAT'S A PARENT TO DO?

First, get some data about your kid's game playing. You will use this information to set up guidelines around time spent gaming.

**Learn about the games.** As reviewed in the previous chapter, you should know something about the games your teen is playing. If you want to know more, do an online search for the name of the video game(s). You'll find a wealth of information about the games.

**Playing the odds.** Teenage gamers typically spend an average of fourteen hours a week playing video games. Teens who play MMORPG ("massively multiplayer online role playing games" like World of Warcraft) average twenty-five hours of play a week. (Imagine what your kid could accomplish if they dedicated two to three hours a day to some productive activity?) Keep track of how much time your kid spends gaming every week. Compare that to how many hours a week they spend in productive, healthy activities like studying and moderate physical exercise.

**Peanut gallery.** Spend some time watching your kid play the video game. See what is actually happening. You may be horrified, especially with how players talk to each other during MMORPGs. Or you may be reassured. If you want to have a little fun, start offering suggestions while you are watching. "Watch it! Watch it! It's gonna jump you!" "Check the bookcase. There might be something there." Sound really sincere, as if you think you are actually helping. It's funny to see their reactions. (Then, when they yell at you to leave them alone, you can punish them for being disrespectful. See? Parenting can be fun.)

**What's too much?** The key is balance. Your kid's day should be composed of work, leisure, and personal growth activities (including relationships). In school, kids receive approximately five hours of instructional time. They have approximately eight hours between the time school ends and bedtime (assuming they are in bed by 10:30 or so). What are they doing with that time? How much is spent playing video games? How much is spent in physical activity? What is the ratio of productive to unproductive time?

Once you have a sense of how much time they spend gaming and how they actually conduct themselves during and after playing, you are ready to set some ground rules. Here are some suggestions.

**Time to talk.** Begin by having a talk with your kid about your concerns with video game play. This doesn't mean that you should only talk to them if you are worried. If they are using video games in reasonable ways and have a reasonable attitude, use this opportunity to complement them on their priorities. Either way, be sure to let them talk. This should be a discussion, even if you are going to end up putting some limits on their gaming. The information you gathered during the data-collection phase will come in handy here. ("I noticed that you cussed like a sailor, denigrated your team-mates, and threw a fit when you lost." "You haven't moved from that chair all week except to get something to eat." "I was really happy to see that you are only playing after you take care of your other responsibilities.")

**Informed consumers.** Kids need to be aware of the influence the media has on them, especially when it is self-selected. (A site that provides some interesting information on the strategies game developers use to keep kids hooked on gaming can be found on the References page of this book's website.) Having a talk about gaming can provide a useful exercise in making your kid aware of marketing influences. If they argue that video games are harmless, require them to provide actual, logical support (see the Argumentative Teens chapter and Negotiating chapter for ways to help them practice these skills). Emotional arguments like "But I really like it!" and "You're just being mean." and empty counter-arguments ("Those researchers are just wrong!" and "You don't know what you're talking about.") are not acceptable ways to defend their position. Make them get proof. Require the proof to be legitimate—which means nothing from the "Parents are stupid if they won't let you play video games" website. It is about time they use the internet for something constructive. Also, you will be putting them in the position of proving gaming isn't harming them by making sure they are not showing any of the harmful side effects.

**Transparency.** As with all electronic activities, you should have complete, immediate access at all times. If they complain, shut it off.

**Public spaces.** Where are the computers and game systems that can access the internet in your house? Internet use should take place in public spaces. Public locations create a natural constraint on taking things too far (whether it is the language they use, the sites they visit, or the people they are chatting with). Ignore this recommendation at your kid's peril. Don't make more work for yourself by not catching trouble (porn, predatory activity, unregulated peer influences on behavior, etc.) soon enough.

**Get involved.** For some parents, playing along with their kid is actually appealing. Gaming together can be a bonding experience while providing you with an opportunity to monitor how gaming may be influencing your kid. It can also be fun. But keep in mind that this is a modeling moment. If you start cursing, yelling at people, and mocking and degrading your opponents during play—or if you are ticked off for the rest of the day after a humiliating defeat—then you should probably not consider gaming as quality time with your kid.

**Limit exposure.** Video games are entertainment, not a lifestyle. Negative consequences begin to appear when kids play more than the average kid. Set a limit on game play. You can do this directly by establishing a maximum game time policy (for example, two hours a day or a total of fourteen hours a week if played in blocks of time). You might also consider having your teens earn video game play time by engaging in activities that you consider more healthy or desirable.

If you are not too concerned about how video game play is affecting your kid (see the Signs of trouble section) you can also set limits indirectly. Require your kid to engage in healthy, productive activities (studying, exercising, reading, spending time in the fresh air, doing chores, etc.) and specify that these activities must be completed before teens are allowed to play video games. Set bed times and, especially, wake-up times (see the Summer Planning Guide chapter). Many games and all game systems have built-in controls that allow you to limit game play or restrict access. You will find a pamphlet from the Entertainment Software Rating Board that provides instructions for setting parental controls on various games or game systems on the References page of this book's website.

**Game suspension.** Any infraction of your video game policy should result in grounding your kid from the game or system. Every time they scream, curse, or are verbally inappropriate during or around game play should result in an immediate loss of game playing privileges. Start with one day and add a day for each subsequent infraction (one day for the first infraction, two days the second time it happens, three days for the third time, etc.). If your kid takes out their frustration over gaming on others, suspend them from game play until they demonstrate reasonable, considerate behavior towards others for a set number of days (for example, they might be grounded until they have demonstrated seven straight days of relatively pleasant and agreeable behavior).

**Eliminate the problem.** Any attempt by your kid to avoid, ignore, or get around punishment regarding video game play should be taken as a sign that video games have become an evil influence that undermines their very character and may have even become an addiction. In either case, the solution is detox and abstinence—ground them from the game for a period of months. If you have repeated trouble, ditch the game, video game system, or access to internet video game play. You can give your teen's game system to a local charitable organization, erase their character from the online game, and remove the game from the computer. As with the need for any extreme intervention, you might also benefit from consultation with a mental health professional to see if persistent attempts to play video games, despite the consequences, are a sign of something more complicated. And last but not least ...

**Check back regularly.** It isn't enough to set everything up right. You will need to keep an eye on things. It is easy to lose track of how much time your kid is gaming, especially if they are not being much trouble. You might be thinking their behavior problems are just a part of adolescence. Be sure to keep tabs on video game influences throughout their teens.

# ABOUT THE AUTHOR

**D**r. James G. Wellborn is a clinical psychologist in private practice focusing on adolescents and families. A published author of scholarly works on motivation, coping in childhood and adolescence and academic engagement, he has been a consultant to school districts in developing system-wide programs to address motivation and academic engagement for at-risk youth in both New York and Tennessee.

Dr. Wellborn has appeared on local talk shows, in the print media and on radio as an expert in child development and parenting. He has written a monthly column for a local parenting magazine and currently writes a weekly column on parenting teens for www. BrentwoodHomePage.com. An invited speaker to local groups, agencies and churches on parenting and teenage issues, he has also conducted workshops for parents, teachers and school counselors on adolescent development, motivating teens, mental health issues and intervention strategies.

Dr. Wellborn is the father of two children and lives with his wife in Nashville, Tennessee. For more information, visit his website at www.drjameswellborn.com.

# ACKNOWLEDGMENTS

There are a few folks who have been particularly instrumental in the creation of this book. Without them, this book would not have been.

The publishing world is in turmoil. The old system is in flux. The internet and digital media has opened up the possibility for almost any yokel to publish a book (even one on parenting). There is one little thing though. Bringing a book to publication is complicated and confusing and overwhelming! What's a writer to do? Get a book shepherd. I had the great good fortune to discover Ellen Reid (www.indiebookexpert.com), a professional who helps you start with ideas and end up with a book. Ellen's knowledge, experience, enthusiasm and connections in the publishing world enabled her to gather a talented team of independent consultants to complete every step of the publication process. Laren Bright (www.larenbright.com) pulled the manuscript together and helped me create the right titles and all the additional copy that goes around the actual content of the book. Patricia Bacall (www.bacallcreative.com) is the brilliant creative designer behind all things visual and artistic. Pamela Guerricri (www.proofedtoperfection.com) hunted down and corrected every punctuation, grammatical mistake and repetitive phrase. Chris Fryer (http://fryerphoto.blogspot.com/) took photo after photo in an effort to capture the real me (but without retouching ANYTHING because, as a professional photojournalist, he breaks out in hives just thinking about an image not being COMPLETELY natural and unscripted). Unfortunately for me, he got what he wanted.

This book evolved out of the weekly column I wrote for Brentwood Home Page (www.brentwoodhomepage.com), the local, online news source for Brentwood, Tennessee and the surrounding area.

Founding editors Susan Leathers and Kelly Gilfillan have been generous, enthusiastic supporters while also showing patience with my trouble letting a column go and my rather unique writing style (including a somewhat questionable sense of humor).

Brentwood United Methodist Church has been a source of support, camaraderie and spiritual inspiration for me. My association began through the wonderful folks in the Parents of Teens Sunday School class who for many years now have regularly invited me to lead conversations on a whole host of topics regarding teens, adolescent development and parenting. These conversations helped me refine and organize many of the ideas found in this book. Then, the church honored me with an invitation to relocate my private practice into their church counseling center. This is when I came to know Kaye Harvey, the Pastor of Congregational Care and Mission/ Outreach. Kaye has been a staunch supporter, refreshing spirit, friend and the kind of smart, deeply spiritual Christian I aspire to be. I could not be more content in this beautiful church home for my secular psychotherapy practice. BUMC has a large, dynamic and vibrant youth ministry led by Travis Garner. Travis has been a valued colleague who is also great company. There are many different ventures we have undertaken together including a year-long, weekly workshop series for parents. This provided the first opportunity for me to work out how to make parenting ideas intelligible and useful outside my therapy office. I feel blessed to have found a professional home with these wonderful examples of Christ's love, compassion, (forbearance!) and healing grace.

Any value or help provided by the parenting ideas in this book is derived from my work with the many kids and parents who have trusted me to be a part of their family during times of emotional distress, miscommunication, strained relationships, trauma and conflict. Together we worked out ways to weather the storms of adolescent passion, heal (or soothe) the effects of psychic and emotional wounds and bring (or keep) these wonderful, maddening adolescents on track. This book represents the collective wisdom of strategies used by these modern parents.

I had the best time growing up. This isn't the place to recount all that I learned from my own parents. But, the most directly relevant contributions my parents made to the completion of this book are that my mom thinks I can do anything (despite consistently proving her wrong) and my dad drove me crazy across my young adult years by always working "You could write a book about that" into the conversation. No, Dad, I couldn't. But I CAN write a book about THIS.

My kids were a constant reminder that parenting is fun, scary, maddening and there are some things you just can't get your kid to do even if you are a highly trained mental health professional.

Finally, this book (along with all the other worthwhile accomplishments of my life) happened because Kim is with me and for me. She is my confidence, my final editor, and my link to normal, conscientious, well-mannered people. This book would certainly not have happened without her. I try very hard to keep her from regretting marrying me because I cannot imagine a life without her.

# REFERENCES

References and resources for each of the chapters are located in the References section of the book page at www.drjameswellborn.com.

# INDEX

CPSIA information can be obtained at www.ICGtesting.com
Printed in the USA
LVOW07s1516180315

431078LV00019B/944/P